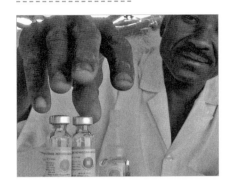

ACCESS

How do good health technologies get to poor people in poor countries?

Laura J. Frost & Michael R. Reich

Published by the Harvard Center for Population and Development Studies

Cambridge, Massachusetts

Distributed by Harvard University Press

To Our Families

Library of Congress Cataloging-in-Publication Data

Frost, Laura J., 1969-

Access : how do good health technologies get to poor people in poor countries? / Laura J. Frost & Michael R. Reich.

p. ; cm. -- (Harvard series on population and international health)

Includes bibliographical references and index.

ISBN 978-0-674-03215-6 (pbk.)

1. Health services accessibility--Developing countries. 2. Poor--Medical care-- Developing countries. 3. Medical technology--Developing countries. 4. Medical innovations--Developing countries. I. Reich, Michael, 1950- II. Harvard Center for Population and Development Studies. III. Title. IV. Series.

[DNLM: 1. Health Services Accessibility. 2. Developing Countries. 3. Poverty. 4. World Health. WA 395 F939a 2008]

RA441.5.F72 2008

362.109172′4--dc22

2008041245

Published by:
Harvard Center for Population and Development Studies
9 Bow Street
Cambridge, Massachusetts 02138
USA
cpds@hsph.harvard.edu

Published in the Harvard Series on Population and International Health

Cover Photo by Ümit Kartoglu/World Health Organization; Indaman, Niger, 2007. Used with permission.
Cover and Interior design by Carol Maglitta one[visual]mind

CONTENTS

FOREWORD

WE LIVE IN AN EXTRAORDINARY TIME IN THE HISTORY OF PUBLIC HEALTH: never before has the world had such powerful technologies to fight disease and improve lives. Yet medical breakthroughs mean little if they fail to reach those in greatest need. Today, millions of people in the poorest countries do not have access to effective vaccines, medicines, and other life-saving tools.

Ensuring global access to health technologies is a complex challenge. Yet, as this important book demonstrates, there is a growing body of evidence that this challenge can be met. Bold leadership, careful planning matched with innovative thinking, and long-term commitment are required to succeed in this endeavor.

We are beginning to see successes on an unprecedented scale. Just five years ago, access to HIV drugs in Africa was considered a fantasy; today, initiatives like the Global Fund to Fight AIDS, Tuberculosis, and Malaria and the President's Emergency Plan for AIDS Relief are delivering treatment to millions of people who are most in need. At the same time, the GAVI Alliance has brought together governments and vaccine manufacturers to increase global immunization rates to all-time highs.

Our urgent task is to build on this recent progress. While a significant proportion of the grantmaking of the Bill & Melinda Gates Foundation focuses on discovering and developing new health tools, we are equally committed to helping ensure that existing and new tools are rapidly delivered to the people who need them. This book and the case studies and frameworks contained within it have helped the Foundation to shape its response to the challenges of improving access to health solutions. We believe the analyses and narratives herein will help others around the world who seek to do the same.

I am hopeful that in the coming years, the speed of improvements in global health will continue. With dedication and ingenuity, we can create a world in which all people have access to the tools they need to live healthy, productive lives.

Tadataka Yamada, M.D.
President, Global Health Program
Bill & Melinda Gates Foundation

PREFACE

THIS BOOK EMERGED FROM A SIMPLE REALIZATION: Just because a good health technology exists does not mean that it will be delivered, used, or achieve its potential to bring good health, especially for poor people in poor countries. Over the past several years, this realization has gained increasing acceptance around the world. Acceptance has grown with many organizations in global health—including the Bill & Melinda Gates Foundation, which has invested huge sums of money to support the development of new technologies for global health. In early 2005, the Gates Foundation was criticized in *The Lancet* for focusing too much on technology development. The author alleged that the Foundation held to "a narrowly conceived understanding of health as the product of technical interventions divorced from economic, social, and political contexts."[1] Ironically, at just the same moment, the Foundation had asked us to help it address these precise issues. What could the Foundation do to improve the chances that the over 50 products under development with Gates support would achieve their potential in health improvement? They specifically asked us to explore the economic, social, and political contexts in detailed case studies. This book is the result.

For some time, the Gates Foundation has been aware that developing technology alone is not sufficient to improve health conditions in poor countries. This recognition is reflected in the sponsorship announcement on U.S. National Public Radio for programs supported by the Gates Foundation: *"making sure life-saving advances in health reach those who need them most."* Bill Gates made a similar point in his speech before the World Health Assembly on May 16, 2005, when he said, "The world has to devote more thinking and funding to delivering interventions—not just discovering them."[2] And subsequently the Foundation reorganized itself into three divisions—discovery, development, and delivery—to emphasize the critical importance of bringing technologies to the people who need them.

We began this project in March 2005 with the goal of seeking to better understand and more effectively plan for success in the introduction of new technologies to help fight the diseases of the global poor. Throughout the project we have interacted with the team inside the Gates Foundation assigned with this task. We agreed to create a framework for thinking about the challenges of introducing good health technologies in poor countries along with a series of case studies illustrating a range of different kinds of technologies. We intentionally avoided the approach of certain consulting companies that present their analysis and results in a thick deck of fancy PowerPoint slides. The Gates Foundation asked us to develop a series of narratives, rich in contextual and historical detail and based on solid academic research, to convey the multiple complexities in creating access for health technologies in poor countries. We were not looking for simple answers. We sought out broad lessons that could help guide the foundation, its grantees, and others around the world concerned with the gap in access. We called the cases our "access stories," from which would emerge cross-cutting themes and lessons.

The two senior members of the research team were Michael R. Reich at the Harvard Center for Population and Development Studies, where he was serving as director until July 2005, when he moved to the Instituto Nacional de Salud Pública in Mexico for a year's sabbatical, and Laura J. Frost at the Center for Health and Wellbeing at Princeton University, where she was researching and teaching until July 2006, when she moved to the Democratic Republic of Congo for two years. In the first year of the project, the research team also included Ilavenil Ramiah, after she completed her post-doctoral studies at Harvard and until she accepted a senior post at UNAIDS in Geneva. Within the Gates Foundation, our main contact was Dan Kress, along with Hannah Kettler; throughout the process they guided and supported us with sound advice, constructive criticism, and warm humor. We also appreciate the enthusiastic support we received from Tachi Yamada after he arrived as the new president of global health at the Foundation in 2006.

We would like to thank the experts who reviewed the book and provided detailed comments. The following people provided comments on individual chapters: Joseph Cook, Sybil Eng, Dirk Engels, Scott Gordon, Doug Holtzman, Dai Hozumi, Karin Jacquin, Heidi Larson, Carla Lee, Kyle Peterson, Laura Reichenbach, Allan Schapira, Craig Shapiro, Veronika Wirtz, Katherine Wolf, and Patrick Zuber. Several people reviewed and commented on the entire manuscript: Richard Cash, Michael Goroff, Joel Lamstein, Adetokunbo Lucas, and George Zeidenstein. We are especially grateful to the many people we interviewed about the cases for generously giving us their time and sharing their stories. We also appreciate the gracious support we received during the review process and the decision to publish our book, from Barry Bloom at the Harvard School of Public Health and Lisa Berkman at the Harvard Center for Population and Development studies.

The book benefited from superb support we received from research assistants and editors. Beth Anne Pratt, Jennifer Nanni, and Taeko Frost provided research support for Laura on the case studies. James Hammersley contributed to an early draft of chapter 3 on praziquantel. Sarah Madsen Hardy copyedited each chapter during the first half of 2007 and again in early 2008, and Jessica Perkins read and commented on the full manuscript during the summer of 2007. Meghan Reidy assisted in collecting the photographs and arranging for permissions. Sarah Coit Timmins assisted us greatly with bibliographic research and formatting. Carol Maglitta provided superb graphic design for the tables, figures, cover, and text of the book, and guided us through the production process.

We wrote each chapter in a slightly different manner, while achieving a full coauthorship of the entire volume by the end of the process. Laura took the lead on drafting chapters 2 and 9, and Michael wrote the first draft for chapter 1. Laura drafted chapters 4 through 7 (the cases on hepatitis B vaccine, malaria rapid diagnostic tests, Norplant, and vaccine vial monitors), with Michael providing comments and revisions. Michael drafted chapter 3 on praziquantel (with Alan Fenwick and Howard Thompson at the Schistosomiasis Control Initiative), and Laura provided comments and revisions. Laura drafted chapter 8 on the female condom, with Beth Anne Pratt as coauthor, and Michael provided comments and revisions. All chapters were drafted in 2006 and then went through multiple versions and seemingly endless discussion and alteration, as drafts bounced back and forth between Michael and Laura, as we sought a common style of narrative and a common framework of analysis. Our discussions about access continued as we moved around the continents, crossing national boundaries, dragging drafts to read, communicating by cell phones, land lines, skype, email, texts, and sometimes even face to face, working hard to produce the book's final draft.

This book expresses our profound belief that access to good health technologies can be addressed and resolved for poor people in poor countries and can produce tangible benefits for them. The two of us have worked on access issues with various public, private, and partnership organizations over the past two decades. This book represents our collaborative effort to show how progress can be achieved—and how to make it happen more rapidly than is now happening.

Finally, we wish to thank our families for supporting us throughout this project and for allowing this book to pervade our lives over the past several years.

Laura J. Frost
Kinshasa, DRC

Michael R. Reich
Brookline, Mass.

May 2008

Endnotes

[1] Anne-Emanuelle Birn, "Gates's Grandest Challenge: Transcending Technology as Public Health Ideology," *The Lancet* 366 (2005): 514–519.

[2] Bill Gates, "Remarks of Mr. Bill Gates, Co-founder of the Bill & Melinda Gates Foundation, at the World Health Assembly," Fifty-eighth World Health Assembly, Geneva, Switzerland, 16 May 2005, http://www.who.int/mediacentre/events/2005/wha58/gates/en/index.html (retrieved January 2, 2008).

CHAPTER 1

THE ISSUE OF ACCESS

MANY PEOPLE IN DEVELOPING COUNTRIES DO NOT HAVE ACCESS TO HEALTH TECHNOLOGIES, even basic ones. These technologies include life-saving medicines, such as antiretrovirals for HIV/AIDS, as well as life-enhancing medicines, such as antiasthma medications that help stop asthma attacks and improve breathing. Many parents do not have access to vaccines that can prevent debilitating diseases for their children. Moreover, access is limited for a wide range of other existing health products such as diagnostics for infectious and chronic diseases, preventive technologies like insecticide-treated bednets, and various kinds of contraceptives, from condoms to pills and injectables. In 1995, the World Health Organization estimated that around 1.7 billion people—approximately one third of the world's population—did not have regular access to essential medicines and vaccines; and the WHO's estimates since then have continued in the same range.[1] Indeed, the WHO's estimate of one third without access has remained at about the same level since the mid-1980s.[2]

A major obstacle to access is cost. This economic limitation is what many people—policy analysts as well as the general public—think about first. This focus on cost makes sense, especially when looking at access for the poorest people in the world. They often lack the money to purchase medicines and other health technologies. And their poverty is exacerbated by the high prices they often confront, particularly for new technologies—new medicines, new devices, new diagnostics. Severe resource constraints also affect governments in poor countries that seek to purchase health technologies for use in public facilities. These governments confront chronic shortages in public budgets that limit their ability to purchase technologies that could help improve health conditions. In 2002, for example, per capita health expenditure for an entire year ranged from $26 in South Asia and $32 in sub-Saharan Africa to an average of $218 in Latin America and the Caribbean and $3,039 in high-income countries.[3] In short, health technologies are often unaffordable for both governments and individuals in resource-poor settings.

But cost is far from the only barrier to access. Other obstacles abound. These barriers to access include the limited capacity of public health systems, a lack of political commitment to health improvement, persistent corruption in public and private health facilities, international trade and patent disputes, cultural attitudes toward both disease and treatment, and difficulties in distributing, prescribing, delivering, and using products. And this list is representative rather than exhaustive.

Many bottlenecks thus block access to health technologies in developing countries. Sometimes the barriers seem to overwhelm all efforts to expand access to beneficial health technologies. A growing literature examines the challenges that confront efforts to address particular barriers (such as pricing or patents or end-user demand). As part of this project, we conducted a literature review on specific barriers to access and produced an annotated bibliography of 44 selected recent articles.[4] But few studies have comprehensively explored the many social, economic, political, and cultural processes that shape access to health technologies in developing countries—including how such technologies are perceived differently by key players.

Despite progress with placing access to medicines on the global policy agenda, enormous problems persist in the access gap for all sorts of health technologies—not just medicines. While the most contentious debates have focused on drugs and vaccines, similar problems exist for other kinds of health technologies. The problems with access to diagnostics, for example, have remained relatively unexplored in policy debates. And the focus on certain types of access barriers (especially pricing and patents) has tended to obscure other important barriers to access, such as distribution, delivery, and adoption problems. Too often, the assumption has been that once a medicine is included in a list of essential medicines, the problems of access are solved. This perspective overlooks the problems of distribution, delivery, and demand. For instance, even after praziquantel (the medicine for treatment of schistosomiasis) declined in price during the 1990s, serious problems of access persisted, especially in the poorest countries of the world (where the disease existed). When patents for praziquantel expired, more producers entered the global market, but these changes alone did not produce access. In chapter 3, we explore what happened with praziquantel, why problems in access persisted, and what has recently changed to improve the situation.

This book explores the challenges and approaches to improving access to health technologies for poor people in poor countries. Our goals are to develop and illustrate a way to think systematically about the barriers to access and to identify strategies that can help improve access. Ultimately, we are looking for specific measures that can be implemented with real-world consequences. Other researchers have tackled these issues with similar goals. Aday and Andersen, for example, developed a framework in the 1970s to study access to medical care in the United States.[5] Their framework also addressed the role of health systems and population factors in shaping access. Our approach, however, is broader and also incorporates global factors. Another example is a group at the London School of Hygiene and Tropical Medicine who published a series of papers on "expanding access to priority health interventions" as the basis for analyzing the constraints to scaling up.[6] Our general concerns and some of our ideas overlap. But our approach has some differences. We have an explicit focus on health technologies (while they focus on "interventions") and we follow the flow of technologies through different phases of access (while they are concerned with "levels" and "constraints"). Finally, we illustrate our analysis of access through a series of narratives about specific health technologies.

This book emerged from the policy debate about access that has taken place over the past two decades. We have been engaged with various organizations in the access debate—international agencies, public-private partnerships, private voluntary organizations, private corporations, foundations, universities, national governments, and direct service groups. Many attempts to improve access have been tried, but few of these efforts have been systematically and comprehensively documented and analyzed. This book seeks to explain what has worked and what has not in these experiences by focusing on specific products: medicines, vaccines, diagnostics, medical devices, contraceptive products, and other kinds of preventive technologies. We focus on technologies that hold the potential for making significant health improvements in developing countries. We are concerned with tangible products that can be bought and sold rather than procedures.[7] For instance, while we examine vaccines such as the one to prevent hepatitis B, we do not assess procedures such as new surgical techniques for trichiasis.

We look in depth at a series of case studies in order to grasp the nature of the problems and the solutions—and how both were perceived by the actors involved. We describe our cases in detail and in context. Each case is an access story about a single health technology, some distinctly more successful than others, with six cases presented in six narrative chapters. Our goal is to tell these stories in ways that will lead to more general conclusions about what works and what does not—always a tricky goal in analysis based on specific cases, as we explain below in our discussion of methods. Our hope is that this narrative approach will add to the understanding of how access to health technologies in poor countries can be improved.

Access Is on the Global Health Agenda

The issue of access recently reached the top of the global development policy agenda, going beyond its previous position within the global health policy community. The Millennium Development Goals include *access* as Target 17 under Goal 8—to develop a global partnership for development—as follows: "In co-operation with pharmaceutical companies, provide access to affordable essential drugs in developing countries."[8] Access to medicines is on the agenda of political leaders in both rich and poor countries. The United Kingdom's Department for International Development, for example, has created a new program to promote access to medicines in poor countries, with emphasis on a "multi-stakeholder approach" to improving transparency and accountability in the medicines supply chain.[9] Non-governmental organizations, such as Oxfam and Médecins Sans Frontières, have developed major advocacy efforts on access issues. Even the U.S. government, under Republican George W. Bush, has spent billions of dollars to improve access to antiretroviral medicines in the world's poorest countries hit by the HIV/AIDS pandemic.

This focus on access to medicines for government policy extends back over three decades of actions by the World Health Organization.[10] In 1975, the WHO's director-general, Halfdan Mahler, issued a report to the annual meeting of the World Health Assembly that identified national medicines policies as a top priority for developing countries. At that time, WHO defined essential drugs as "those considered to be of the utmost importance and hence basic, indispensable, and necessary for the health needs of the population. They should be available at all times, in the proper dosage forms, to all segments of society."[11] The report called for drug policies that would meet health needs and economic priorities and stressed the essential drugs approach as an effective means to improve health conditions in poor countries. The document built on a history of concern at the WHO with various aspects of pharmaceuticals, expressed even in the first World Health Assembly in 1948.[12] But the report in 1975 marked a clear step toward creating a new campaign on pharmaceuticals, one focusing on the concept of essential drugs, with the goal of influencing government policy in poor countries.

The first model Essential Drugs List was published in 1977 and included 224 drugs and vaccines.[13] Most of the products on the list were known to be therapeutically effective and were no longer protected by patent rights. That step, according to the program manager of essential drugs in the early 1980s, marked the start of a "peaceful revolution in international public health."[14] The organization was seeking to change the rules over who had access to certain technologies as part of its efforts to improve global health. These efforts to change the rules—turning WHO into an advocate for greater access—had important implications for the relationship between public health and technology within the broader debate over development.

In the late 1970s, the WHO integrated the concept of essential medicines into broader ideas about health care in poor countries. The WHO's goal of "Health for All by the Year 2000" included the regular supply of certain essential drugs as a key indicator to evaluate progress toward this inspirational target of health for all. The Declaration of Alma Ata in 1978 expanded on this idea by identifying the provision of essential drugs as a basic element of primary health care.[15] Then, in 1978 and 1979, the WHO took formal steps to establish an Action Program on Essential Drugs and Vaccines, which began operation in February 1981.

Over time, WHO's activities on essential drugs have continuously expanded their scope.[16] The initial emphasis on the *selection* of appropriate drugs changed in the late 1970s to stress the *use* of essential drugs, reflected in a title change of the WHO's basic document. Following the establishment of the Action Program, the scope expanded again to encompass nearly all aspects of national drug *policies*, including selection of drugs, supply of drugs, assurance of quality, manpower training, legislation and regulatory control, and financial resources. The program sought to shape national policies on drug policy and to persuade governments to adopt the essential drugs concept. By the mid-1980s, more than 80 countries had officially adopted this concept.[17]

The international public health community continued to address the drug access problem in the 1980s and 1990s, as reflected in the Bamako Initiative's support for community-based approaches to drug financing in poor countries.[18] In late November 1985, the WHO convened the Conference of Experts on the Rational Use of Drugs, which brought together specialists from differing perspectives, including industry, consumer groups, academics, and national policy makers. Participants disagreed over a number of topics related to "rational use," including the idea of a WHO marketing code for medicines and the market implications of an essential drugs list. But the meeting did produce consensus on some core issues, as articulated by the WHO director-general. Those issues included the importance of drug information, national drug regulatory programs, ethical advertising for medicines, appropriate prescribing, and better training for prescribers. WHO Director-General Mahler reviewed the responsibilities of different groups in making drug use more rational and consistent with a principle of social equity. He also stressed that WHO had an "*inter*national as opposed to *supranational* role," meaning that "policies can be defined in WHO but cannot be imposed by WHO."[19] Ultimately, decisions on drug policy had to occur at the national level through political processes.

In the late 1990s, access became an issue of global policy concern when activist groups pressured specific companies to make their AIDS medicines more available in poor countries. The advent of new antiretroviral treatment for HIV/AIDS dramatically depressed mortality rates in rich countries with early access to these medicines. With the availability of new antiretrovirals, the age-adjusted death rate for AIDS declined by 48% in the United States from 1996 to 1997, with similar decreases in Western Europe and Australia.[20] This dramatic decline in mortality showed in a very tangible way that access to medicines in some cases is directly related to questions of life and death—and sometimes on a global scale. Importantly, 95% of individuals worldwide who were infected with HIV at that time lived in poor countries, with almost no access to these life-prolonging treatments because of programmatic and institutional problems as well as cost barriers.[21] At the end of 1998, 67% of the people in the world with HIV/AIDS lived in sub-Saharan Africa, where over 80% of the world's AIDS deaths were recorded.

This global movement in the campaign over access to AIDS medicines grew to include AIDS activists, people living with HIV/AIDS, generic pharmaceutical companies, international non-governmental organizations, and international agencies. They succeeded in placing the issue of access to AIDS medicines high on the international health agenda and, even more importantly, onto the policy agenda of the United Nations and the G-8 countries.[22] The policy impacts included the establishment of company-specific drug donation programs, the Doha Declaration on the TRIPS Agreement, the broader industrywide Accelerating Access Initiative with multiple UN agencies, and the creation of the Global Fund to Fight AIDS, TB, and Malaria. All of these efforts contributed to greater access to medicines for AIDS and other illnesses.

The stark difference between the fates of people living with HIV/AIDS in rich versus poor countries—due to differences in access to medicines—fueled a global mobilization around the idea of a right to essential and new drugs. This growing international movement enhanced opposition to the idea that intellectual property rights should trump other policy considerations. Within a relatively short time, the boards of major multinational pharmaceutical companies were discussing how to improve access to some of their best-selling products for some of the poorest people in the world's poorest countries, driven by increasing public pressure and targeted protests against the companies. This reflected a sea change in thinking about access. Recently, the debate has included explicit reference to access to medicines as a human right.[23]

The global struggle for access to AIDS medicines expanded the question of access from one that focused primarily on the availability and affordability of essential drugs to one that confronted broad and comprehensive trade and development concerns. The issues that generated the greatest debate were pricing policies, intellectual property rights, and the global trade regime—as well as the impact that decisions on these topics would have on the future development of new medicines for neglected diseases and diseases that primarily affect poor people in poor countries.

What Do We Mean by Access?

Stated simply, access refers to people's ability to obtain and appropriately use good quality health technologies when they are needed. Access is not only a technical issue involving the logistics of transporting a technology from the manufacturer to the end-user. Access also involves social values, economic interests, and political processes. Access requires a product as well as services and is linked to how health systems perform in practice. We think of access not as a single event but as a process involving many activities and actors over time. Access is not a yes-or-no dichotomous condition, but rather a continuous condition of different degrees; more like a rheostat than an on-off switch. Our cases illustrate these complexities and these degrees of access.

The definition of access contains a substantial normative dimension. What is the right level of product quality? When is product use deemed "appropriate"? How is "need" defined? Access to a health technology depends on providing the "right" product at the "right" place with the "right" protocol at the "right" time. But how that is accomplished varies depending on public policies and social values.[24] One common way of defining what is right for access is through a cost-effectiveness perspective (getting the "biggest bang for the buck," based on utilitarian principles) in which a government seeks to maximize health for a particular population under certain resource constraints. A different normative perspective on how to provide access would be a market-based approach that makes products available for sale to people who can pay the prevailing prices (set by producers and others). A third approach, based on egalitarian values, would preferentially provide financially subsidized access to effective health technologies for those groups that are worst off within a population. Another approach would be to provide free access to live-saving health technologies for those individuals who are worst off in terms of health, following a rule-of-rescue principle.[25] Most countries combine different ethical values in their national policies and approaches to access.

Access can also mean that a patient receives too many drugs. An article on the "irrationality of pharmaceuticals in the developing world," for instance, presents the case of a child with diarrhea who was seen by three different physicians and ended up with a total of 12 medicines, some with the same chemical in different boxes and some labeled in a foreign language.[26] The child received seven different antimicrobial medicines, including a prescription from a professor of pediatrics for an antibiotic combination, a constipative and rehydration fluid, an antimotility drug, and vitamins. The article's title describes the problems as "deranged distribution, perverse prescription, unprotected use."

The power of health technologies derives in part from the many symbolic meanings associated with these products. Medicines, for example, are often perceived (and presented) as offering magical cures to deeply troubling problems of the body and spirit. One textbook on pharmaceutical marketing identified 27 "latent functions" of pharmaceutical preparations, ranging from a "symbol of the power of modern technology" to "political tool" to "expression of physician's control."[27] Customers, in turn, are willing to sacrifice much in order to obtain not only the explicit physical functions but also the implicit latent functions of health technologies.

We conceive of access as a means to address the ill health of poor people in poor countries; we are not concerned with access as an end in itself. Ill health is a complicated problem, both caused by poverty and a cause of poverty. In developing countries, poverty exposes people to a broad range of health risks that richer people can avoid. At the same time, social research in China (and elsewhere) has shown that ill health of one member can drive a family deep into poverty.[28] Simply providing drugs, vaccines, or other health technologies does not solve the complex challenges posed by the nexus of ill health and persistent poverty. But the absence of these technologies "can constitute an insuperable barrier to the achievement of health goals."[29] Improving access is one component—and often a necessary component—of an integrated approach to addressing disease and poverty.

Access to a drug, vaccine, diagnostic, or other health product does not automatically translate into improved health, especially in poor countries. Too often, access means merely that patients are obtaining poor quality drugs that may cost money but have no impact on their health status. Patients and consumers of health technologies often receive little information from the dispenser about how to use a product appropriately. In many parts of the developing world, medicines are dispensed in bits of paper, with no instructions and no information. This practice can deleteriously affect product quality and use and health outcomes. For these reasons, we include quality and use in our definition of access.

Connecting access to technologies with improved health of populations is thus complex. Through our cases, we explore how different activities and actors combine to create access to health technologies in developing countries. In doing so, the case studies illustrate examples where successful technology access does and does not positively influence health outcomes.

Why Is Access So Difficult?

One underlying reason why access is difficult to achieve is that most instances of inadequate access are not single-failure problems. Access problems result from a combination of market failures, government failures, and non-governmental agency failures. Addressing the multiple failures requires many steps directed at global, national, and local level actors and is dependent on various kinds of expertise. The solutions often involve economic, political, and perceptual strategies. Rarely can access problems be solved simply by providing more money.

Similarly, intellectual property rights can constitute a formidable barrier to access for new products, yet removing patent barriers does not immediately or necessarily create access (even when prices decline with the entry of new firms and the rise of effective competition). In our cases, we examine an example where the product patents expired without an immediate surge in access (praziquantel in chapter 3); we also examine a case where the patent issues were negotiated away and many problems still remained (Norplant in chapter 6). The focus on patents may be appropriate for many new products, but it is not the only problem that obstructs access, as we illustrate in several of our cases.

Access is also very difficult because it depends on particular forms of human behavior. A single technology can be used in quite different ways, sometimes in ways not at all anticipated by the product developers. In Zimbabwe, for example, the rings on female condoms became a source of "bangles" for women to use as fashion accessories (see the female condom case study in chapter 8).[30] Changing individual behavior so that people use the technology as intended by the developers can be deeply challenging. For some technologies, the apparently simple use of a product can raise complex issues of stigma (for example, the sigma associated with HIV diagnostic testing). The use of some technologies must be negotiated as part of intimate sexual behavior (for example, the use of both male and female condoms). Other technologies require changes in behavioral patterns, creating problems of adherence (for example, the correct continuing use of medication for chronic diseases, such as schizophrenia and diabetes, as well as medicines for HIV/AIDS and tuberculosis). In short, getting people to use health technologies "appropriately" is not easy.

Finally, access is difficult because many problems are product specific. The problems differ by technology, by health problem, by country, even by ethnic group or community. Our goal in this book is to illustrate these complex interwoven problems for a series of technologies and show how they can be analyzed and addressed. This exercise, we believe, will help identify approaches for technology developers and promoters to be more successful in their missions.

Organization of the Book

We have organized this book in three sections. First, we present some general ideas on access. Next, we tell a series of access stories based on original research. Finally, we discuss the general lessons learned from the cases.

The first section includes the current chapter and chapter 2, where we present our analytical framework of the access process for health technologies. Our approach draws on existing studies of access in the literature, with special attention to architecture, availability, affordability, and adoption. Chapter 2 explains these four dimensions of access, examining specific activities that occur at the global, national, and local levels. The framework illustrates how the activities related to access interact and how the diverse actors interact at the different levels.

The next section presents six in-depth case studies (chapters 3 through 8) that tell the access stories of various health technologies in developing countries. Guided by the framework of chapter 2, we examine the development and dissemination of six health technologies with analysis of the key actors, barriers and facilitating factors, and strategies for improving access.

The report's final chapter, chapter 9, discusses the lessons learned from the case studies. We explore the themes that cut across the cases, including factors that promote successful access and factors that block access. We conclude the report with a number of specific suggestions that can facilitate the processes of introducing and scaling up new health technologies and thereby lead to expanded access. A glossary in the back of the book provides definitions of access terms used in our analysis, as well as public health concepts and diseases and health conditions referenced in the case studies.

Our Methods

Our research for this book involved the analysis of published and unpublished documents as well as in-depth interviews with key participants involved in the development and delivery of each technology. We attempted to speak with as many different types of people as possible and to analyze a diversity of written material in order to understand access issues from different perspectives.

Four criteria guided our selection of case studies. First, we chose cases that span different types of health technologies: a medicine (praziquantel in chapter 3), a vaccine (hepatitis B vaccine in chapter 4), a diagnostic (malaria rapid diagnostic tests in chapter 5), a contraceptive (Norplant in chapter 6), a device (vaccine vial monitors in chapter 7), and a dual protection technology (female condoms in chapter 8). Second, we chose case studies that reflect a range of health problems, including schistosomiasis, sexually transmitted infections (including HIV), malaria, hepatitis B, and unintended pregnancy.

Third, we selected cases that span different phases of access in order to identify facilitating factors, barriers, and strategies specific to each phase. For instance, cases such as the female condom (chapter 8) focus primarily on the introduction phase of access. Other cases, such as praziquantel (chapter 3), study the scaling-up phase of access. The case studies chosen for this book, however, do not examine the final access phase, where individual countries seek to sustain the use of a technology for long-term prevention, control, or eradication of the related disease. We do not include this final phase in part for reasons of space and in part because it would have required a separate national-level analysis that is beyond the scope of our research. We provide a more detailed explanation of the different phases of access in chapter 2.

Finally, we selected cases that allow us to study examples that have been successful as well as those that have encountered obstacles and faltered. In many of the cases, it is too early to say whether an access process has "failed" as these are not completed stories of history but ongoing efforts to expand access. In addition, for many cases, the provision of access has been uneven—successful in certain countries and problematic in others. In examining a diversity of access outcomes, we seek to identify the processes that help produce success.

While our research has investigated access issues at the national and regional and community levels, we have not undertaken in-depth case studies of an individual technology within a series of country contexts. Instead, the analytical focus for the case studies is the *processes* that influence access to health technologies. We hope that this comprehensive perspective can help expand access and thereby help improve the health conditions of poor populations in poor countries.

Endnotes

[1] World Health Organization, *The World Medicines Situation* (Geneva: WHO, 2004), 61.

[2] World Health Organization, *The World Drug Situation* (Geneva: WHO, 1988), 53.

[3] Pable Gottret and George Schieber, *Health Financing Revisited: A Practitioner's Guide* (Washington, DC: The World Bank, 2006), 36.

[4] Beth Anne Pratt, Ilavenil Ramiah, Laura Frost, and Michael R. Reich, "Annotated Bibliography on Access Issues" (Working Paper for Access Project, September 1, 2006).

[5] Lu Ann Aday and Ronald Andersen, "A Framework for the Study of Access to Medical Care," *Health Services Research* 9 (1974): 208–220.

[6] Kara Hanson, M. Kent Ranson, Valeria Oliveira-Cruz, and Anne Mills, "Expanding Access to Priority Health Interventions: A Framework for Understanding the Constraints to Scaling-Up," *Journal of International Development* 15 (2003): 1–14.

[7] A similar approach is used by: Michael J. Free, "Achieving Appropriate Design and Widespread Use of Health Technologies in the Developing World," *International Journal of Gynecology and Obstetrics* 85 (2004): S3–S13.

[8] United Nations, *Road Map Towards the Implementation of the United Nations Millennium Declaration, Report of the Secretary General* (New York: United Nations General Assembly, September 6, 2001, A/56/326), 58.

[9] Department for International Development, *Increasing Access to Essential Medicines in the Developing World: UK Government Policy and Plans* (London: DfID, June 2004); and Editorial, "MeTA: A Welcome Force for Access to Medicines," *The Lancet* 371 (2008): 1724.

[10] This section is based on material from: Michael R. Reich, "Essential Drugs: Economics and Politics in International Health," *Health Policy* 8 (1987): 39–57.

[11] Halfdan Mahler, *Report to the 28th World Health Assembly*, Official Records of the World Health Organization, No. 226, Annex 13 (Geneva: WHO, 1975), 96–110; and "National Drug Policies," *WHO Chronicle* 29 (1975): 337–349.

[12] Resolutions of the World Health Assembly from 1948 to 1975 related to various aspects of drug policy appear in: WHO, "The Role of WHO in the Transfer and Dissemination of Information on Drug Quality, Safety and Efficacy," in *The Rational Use of Drugs: Report of the Conference of Experts, Nairobi, 25–29 November 1985* (Geneva: WHO, 1987), 109–141.

[13] World Health Organization, *The Selection of Essential Drugs*, WHO Technical Report Series No. 615 (Geneva: WHO, 1977).

[14] Ernst Lauridsen, "But Some Are More Essential Than Others!" *World Health,* July 1984, 3–5.

[15] World Health Organization, *Declaration of Alma Ata: Report on the International Conference on Primary Health Care (Alma Ata, USSR)* (Geneva: WHO, 1978).

[16] Reich, 43.

[17] "The First Four Years—So Far, So Good!" *Essential Drugs Monitor* 1 (1985): 2.

[18] Alec Irwin and Eva Ombaka, *Background Paper of the Millennium Project Task Force on Major Diseases and Access to Medicine, Subgroup on Access to Essential Medicines* (New York: UN Millennium Project, 2003), 4.

[19] World Health Organization, "Director-General's Summing Up of the Issues," in *The Rational Use of Drugs: Report of the Conference of Experts, Nairobi, 25–29 November 1985* (Geneva: WHO, 1987), 6.

[20] Anthony S. Fauci, "The AIDS Epidemic: Considerations for the 21st Century," *New England Journal of Medicine* 341 (1999): 1046–1050.

[21] UNAIDS and World Health Organization, *AIDS Epidemic Update: December 1998* (Geneva: UNAIDS and WHO, 1998).

[22] Michael R. Reich and Priya Bery, "Expanding Global Access to ARVs: The Challenges of Prices and Patents," in *The AIDS Pandemic: Impact on Science and Society*, eds. Kenneth H. Mayer & H. F. Pizer (New York: Academic Press, 2005), 324–350.

[23] Hans V. Hogerzeil, "Essential Medicines and Human Rights: What Can They Learn from Each Other?" *Bulletin of the World Health Organization* 84 (2006): 371–375.

[24] Marc J. Roberts and Michael R. Reich, "Ethical Analysis in Public Health," *The Lancet* 359 (2002): 1055–1059.

[25] John McKie and Jeff Richardson, "The Rule of Rescue," *Social Science and Medicine* 56 (2003): 2407–2419.

[26] Stephen J. Fabrican and Norbert Hirschhorn, "Deranged Distribution, Perverse Prescription, Unprotected Use: The Irrationality of Pharmaceuticals in the Developing World," *Health Policy and Planning* 2 (1987): 206–207.

[27] Mickey C. Smith, *Principles of Pharmaceutical Marketing* (Philadelphia: Lea and Febiger, 1983), 112.

[28] William C. Hsiao and Y. Liu, "Economic Reform and Health: Lessons from China," *New England Journal of Medicine* 335 (1996): 400–406.

[29] Irwin and Ombaka, 5.

[30] Steve Vickers, "Zimbabweans Make Condom Bangles," *BBC News,* February 10, 2005, http://news.bbc.co.uk/2/hi/africa/4250789.stm (retrieved January 22, 2007).

CHAPTER 2

THE ACCESS FRAMEWORK

IN THIS CHAPTER, WE PRESENT AN ANALYTICAL FRAMEWORK FOR UNDERSTAND-
ING THE MULTIPLE PROCESSES that limit and facilitate access and the particular
actors who influence the production of access. The chapter explains how we apply
the analytical framework in telling the six stories of access for health technologies
that follow. We also describe how the framework can be used to analyze access to
new health technologies.

As we noted in chapter 1, our focus throughout this book is on tangible technologies that can help improve health conditions in developing countries. We
examine examples of medicines and vaccines, but also diagnostics, contraceptives,
and devices. For our technologies of interest, access requires various activities—
funding, institutions, interventions, and thinking—from public and private
actors at global, national, and local levels. The framework we present in this chapter conceptualizes access for health technologies in developing countries in terms
of these diverse actors at multiple levels. In this sense, the framework draws on
and extends work that we have done previously on the role of public-private partnerships in public health.[1]

Key Elements of the Framework

As shown in Figure 2.1, our analytical framework includes many processes
involved in access to health technologies. Our framework is based on four A's:
architecture, the organizational structure and relationships for access; availability,
which emphasizes the supply components of access; affordability, the cost issues
for various players; and adoption, which includes demand factors and acceptance.
Our framework builds on and adapts the approach developed by the Global Alliance for TB Drug Development called "the AAA strategy."[2] We have changed
some terms and added some ideas in ways that we believe improve both the clarity
and comprehensiveness of the analysis. Our framework adds an organizational
dimension (architecture) to a supply component (availability), a cost component
(affordability), and a demand component (adoption).

Our framework conceives of these four A's as activity streams that occur simultaneously. The framework provides more complexity to the traditional, linear
"value chain" concept that many analysts use for product development and access
(see Figure 2.2 for the pharmaceutical value chain). We argue that getting the four
activity streams right can produce successful access for health technologies. The
first activity stream concerns decisions about organizational structure, which we
call *architecture*, that are required for coordinating the other three activity streams
to produce access. The second activity stream involves the *availability* of health

Figure 2.1 | The access framework

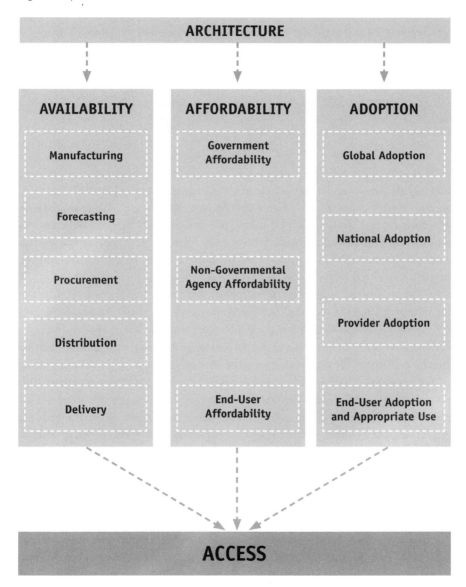

Figure 2.2 | The pharmaceutical value chain

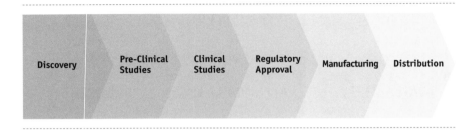

technologies. This stream includes activities at multiple levels to ensure a reliable and regular supply of the technology, with attention to supply logistics. The third activity stream concerns the *affordability* of technologies for developing country governments and individual end-users. The final activity stream addresses the *adoption* of health technologies. This stream involves activities at the global, national, district, and community levels to ensure acceptance and demand for the health technology, with a focus on demand generation.

A deeper understanding of the facilitators, barriers, and key actors involved in achieving architecture, availability, affordability, and adoption is necessary for better access planning. Our framework addresses this challenge by mapping the activities required to produce access from the global level to the end-user. As shown in Figure 2.1, we break down the process of access into *access activities*, which are defined by specific events, and which must occur for access to achieve its potential health benefits (see Table 2.1 for definitions of specific access activities). In the framework, we conceptualize access as beginning in the product development stage and concluding when end-users (providers, patients, or consumers) are appropriately using the technology. Importantly, we have extended our view of access beyond just reaching the end-user because we recognize that *how people actually use technology* plays a major role in the ultimate effects produced. Thus, our concept of access extends into the area of use and includes ideas about both appropriate and inappropriate use of technology.

In our framework, each activity is associated with a specific *actor or set of actors* who carry out the activity. Actors involved in access activities include: international organizations, such as the WHO; private-sector organizations at the global level, such as multinational pharmaceutical companies; and private- and public-sector donor organizations at the global level, such as the Bill & Melinda Gates

Table 2.1 | Definitions of access activities

ACCESS ACTIVITIES	DESCRIPTION
ARCHITECTURE: Organizational structures and relationships established with the purpose of coordinating and steering the availability, affordability, and adoption activities.	
AVAILABILITY involves the logistics of making, ordering, shipping, storing, distributing, and delivering a new health technology to ensure it reaches the hands (or mouth) of the end-user.	
Manufacturing	The processing of raw materials into finished products for use or sale.
Forecasting	The assessment of how much of a product is likely to be purchased and used, and at what price.
Procurement	The process of purchasing health technologies from private or public suppliers and includes all decisions related to the specific quantities obtained, prices paid, and the quality of health technologies received.
Distribution	The process of moving technologies through public or private channels, or a public-private mix.
Delivery	The point in the supply chain at which the technology is physically transferred to its intended end-user by private or public channels.
AFFORDABILITY involves ensuring that health technologies and related services are not too costly for the people who need them.	
Government and NGO affordability	Affordability of the technology by national governments' procurement units in developing countries and by NGOs.
End-user affordability	Affordability of the technology by individual patients and consumers.
ADOPTION involves gaining acceptance and creating demand for a new health technology from global organizations, government actors, providers and dispensers, and individual patients.	
Global adoption	Acceptance of the technology from international agencies such as WHO, UNICEF, UNAIDS, and UNFPA, and from technical experts.
National adoption	Acceptance of the technology by policy makers in developing countries' government ministries, involving political commitment, regulatory approval, and adoption of treatment protocols.
Provider adoption	Acceptance of the technology by the provider and appropriate prescribing.
End-user adoption and appropriate use	Acceptance of the technology by the patient or consumer, which includes appropriate use of the technology.

Foundation and bilateral aid agencies. Within countries, the actors include: private distributors of technologies; national public-sector actors such as the ministry of health or a national regulatory authority; public-sector regional, district, and community agencies such as health care providers in public clinics; community-based distributors of health technologies; and end-users including patients and consumers.

We have organized the framework by access activities because this allows the identification of specific factors that influence the success or failure of these activities.[3] Factors that limit activities are known as constraints or *barriers*. Factors are *facilitators* when they assist the successful movement of a health technology through the architecture, availability, affordability, and adoption activities to the end-user. In the next section, we identify some of the barriers and facilitators that influence the transitions from one activity to the next in improving access. The factors we identify are drawn from existing information in the literature about barriers to technology access in developing countries. Examples are health system capability, political commitment, disease and technology characteristics, and patient adherence. These barriers and facilitators are complex and have many social, cultural, economic, political, technical, and legal dimensions.

Our focus on barriers and facilitators that influence specific activities in the access process highlights the strategic choices for addressing these factors. Once identified, factors can be assessed according to the degree they are fixed or modifiable. *Access strategies* can then be designed to overcome barriers and enhance facilitators. In the next section, we describe each activity stream and identify associated access activities, actors, barriers, and facilitators.

The Four Activity Streams

Activity Stream 1: Architecture

Providing access requires work by many different individuals and their organizations. We refer to the network of organizations involved in access for a particular health technology as the *architecture* that is required to steer and connect the activities in the other three access streams (availability, affordability, and adoption).

The first step in the architecture stream involves the decision to introduce a new health technology. This decision-making involves the standard regulatory assessments of safety and efficacy but also a comparative assessment of existing technologies and potential benefits. This assessment typically occurs at the national level but can also occur at a multinational or regional level, as happens in Europe (in the European Agency for the Evaluation of Medicines). In some countries, the comparative assessment can involve a formal cost-effectiveness analysis of the technology (as required for new medicines in Australia and New Zealand). This assessment could also consider the context of health system capabilities and user needs in geographic areas where the technology is needed. A framework developed for assessment of contraceptive introduction describes four possible outcomes of the decision-making process: (1) introduce the new technology; (2) improve utilization of the current technology (if any exist); (3) do not introduce the technology; (4) discontinue the currently available technology (if any exist).[4] If a decision is made to introduce the new technology, more in-depth analysis (conducted by the technology owner, advocate, or regulator) may be necessary for planning how to introduce it in particular contexts. Applied research such as introductory trials and the assessment of service delivery and user perspectives may be necessary before proceeding with product introduction.

An important question is who makes the decision to introduce a new technology. This actor needs to move to the next step of bringing together all the organizations—public and private, from developing and developed countries—that are necessary for ensuring technology access. Bringing these diverse groups together to cooperate is rarely a straightforward or simple endeavor. The organizational architecture can take various forms. One study of global health partnerships by McKinsey & Company identified five different structural models: simple affiliation, lead partner, general contractor, secretariat, and joint venture company (independent entity).[5] In the six case studies in this volume, we assess the key partners in each process of global health technology access. We assess how these partners established an organizational architecture through which they produce access and how these structures differ, depending on the specific product and circumstances, in form and responsibilities. We assess which individuals and organizations took on leadership roles and look for lessons learned in the creation and implementation of different structures. For standard commercial products, the manufacturer does not usually create this kind of formal partnership architecture for technology introduction and scaling up. For the technologies we discuss in this book, however, the conventional market approach does not work (especially to reach poor people in poor countries), so creating architecture that brings together different partners is an essential component of successful access.

In his study of strategic alliances, Austin identifies seven organizational challenges ("the seven C's of strategic collaboration").[6] These are clarity of purpose;

congruency of mission, strategy, and values; creation of value; connection with purpose and people; communication between partners; continual learning; and commitment to the partnership. The literature on public-private partnerships in global health has shown how important these factors are for the success of global health partnerships. For example, in the Mectizan Donation Program, Merck and the Task Force for Child Survival and Development created value, commitment, and shared purpose through the use of common objects, people, and ideas (which we called "boundary objects" in an earlier essay).[7] These commonalities (which they constructed and then maintained) allowed the partners to create a successful collaboration—to span diverse social worlds and pursue the shared objective of treating onchocerciasis (river blindness) in poor countries with donations of ivermectin.

Other factors associated with the success of health partnerships include establishing a clear governance structure among partners, maintaining transparency in decision-making and program accountability, having the capability to coordinate needed activities, establishing performance metrics for assessing program success, and involving developing country governments to ensure national ownership and sustainability. The example of the Global Alliance for the Elimination of Leprosy (GAEL) shows the importance of partner agreement on success metrics and program strategies. Rinaldi describes how the perceived success of the leprosy campaign resulted in a WHO declaration in 2003 that the "global target of leprosy elimination" had been reached.[8] Others, however, objected to WHO and GAEL's choice of indicators for leprosy elimination and continue to believe that leprosy remains an important global health problem. WHO's reiteration of "prevalence" and "elimination" as key strategies for antileprosy campaigns eventually led to a rift in the coalition against leprosy that culminated in the 2001 expulsion of the primary federation of antileprosy associations from the global alliance. Subsequently, GAEL has been encouraged by evaluators to shift its focus away from elimination strategies towards those of control and to concern itself less with prevalence than with prevention of transmission, reduction of new cases, and postleprosy support strategies.

In the six case studies in this book, we investigate the factors associated with the success or failure of creating and implementing partnerships for health technology access. We hope that this information will lead to better understanding of how to design and manage the architecture for access and how to develop, implement, and evaluate effective partnerships at the global, national, and local levels (although we do not discuss the local level in detail in this book).

Activity Stream 2: Availability

Availability involves the logistics of making, ordering, shipping, storing, distributing, and delivering a health technology to ensure it reaches the end-user. The key availability activities shown in Figure 2.1 are manufacturing, forecasting, procurement, distribution, and delivery. These activities take place at global, national, district, and community levels by both public and private actors.

Manufacturing in general involves the processing of raw materials into finished products for use or sale. For pharmaceuticals, *manufacturing* typically involves two major steps. First is primary manufacturing, the production of active ingredients, which often occurs in developed countries. Next is secondary manufacturing, which entails formulation of the final product. This is usually a less complicated technical process than the production of the active ingredient. However, formulation can be complicated for certain types of pharmaceutical products, such as vaccines, many biological agents (including genetically engineered medicines), and time-release medicines. The complexity of manufacturing depends on the specific product involved. Problems with obtaining the active ingredient of a pharmaceutical product can lead to supply shortfalls for a technology. For example, the production of artemisinin-combination therapies (ACTs) for malaria treatment has been plagued by a global shortage of raw artemisinin, a plant-derived compound. The plant can only be found in a few geographic areas and requires a lengthy cultivation time. To address this supply bottleneck, efforts are underway to develop synthetic alternatives and introduce plant cultivation in new geographic regions.

Who produces the technology depends on the patent arrangements. Production can be carried out by the product patent holder, by the process patent holder (in countries that don't recognize product patents), by a producer that is licensed by the patent holder, or by generic producers if the technology is no longer on patent (or is not patented in the country). A manufacturer's decision about whether to produce a technology is influenced by the patent arrangements, national policy and legal frameworks, and the manufacturer's perception of the market, including estimates of market size and profitability, and who actually selects and buys the product.[9] The case studies in this volume explore different kinds of manufacturers of health technologies for developing countries and the key factors that influence their decisions to enter these markets.

Once a manufacturer decides to produce a health technology for developing countries, the next step is demand *forecasting*. This assessment examines how much of the product is likely to be purchased and used, and at what price. Demand forecasting enables manufacturers to plan and invest in production capacity to ensure sufficient supply to meet expected demand.[10] Accurate forecasting is essential to ensure reliable supply and bolster confidence in the technology and the producer. When recipients do not believe that the requested quantity of a product can be produced and made available, they may reduce the size of their orders, creating shortages and hindering access to the technology. Furthermore, manufacturers are often reluctant to invest in the production of health technologies without reliable demand forecasts.[11] A Global Health Forecasting Working Group, convened by the Washington-based Center for Global Development in 2006, provides recommendations to the global health community for improving forecasting. The proposals include the establishment of an "infomediary" that would allow product demand to be mobilized and information shared among manufacturers and global health partners in a coordinated way.[12]

Procurement is the process of purchasing health technologies from private or public suppliers and includes all decisions related to the specific product quantities obtained, prices paid, and the quality of products received.[13] For many technologies, developing country governments procure directly from multinational or local suppliers, often through official tender procedures. Constraints that occur in procurement include difficulties in locating and selecting suppliers, budget constraints, and irregular payments. International procurement agencies, such as the International Dispensary Association (IDA), address procurement barriers and assist governments in purchasing health technologies. International procurement agencies (mostly nonprofit organizations) use bulk purchasing and minimal cost-plus mark-up to make technologies more affordable to governments; they also help with locating and selecting suppliers and in assuring quality control. A few international organizations have been established to assist developing country governments with the procurement of specific technologies (often for particular diseases). The Global Drug Facility, for example, was set up in 2001 to ensure uninterrupted access to TB drugs through bulk purchasing, technical assistance to national TB programs, and grants to countries that qualify for support.[14]

The *distribution cycle* for technologies begins when products are dispatched by the manufacturer or supplier. Distributor processes include port clearing, receipt and inspection, inventory control, storage, transport to health facilities, and consumption reporting.[15] Public or private entities can be used for carrying out these tasks. In a typical distribution system, purchases are received by one or more primary stores, then sent to intermediate stores, and end up at individual health facility stores. Storage and distribution costs are significant; they can be a large portion of a technology's cost to the end-user. Many factors influence health technology distribution. A study of the drug supply chain in Nigeria found that a shortage of vehicles was a key factor affecting distribution. Other important constraints were administrative failures, such as the lack of a functioning drug management information system and a system to monitor and evaluate staff performance.[16]

Delivery of health technologies to the end-user occurs in a wide variety of public and private settings, including the pharmacies of public hospitals and health centers, private pharmacies, formal and informal shops, and in communities during mass campaigns. In Egypt, delivery of oral rehydration salts (ORS) took place through the public sector, involving five delivery centers and 37 sub-branches as well as through "depot-holders" (community leaders, traditional birth attendants, and health workers trained in ORS use) who gave out ORS packets in rural villages.[17] Delivery was also conducted through private pharmacies where ORS had to compete with more profitable antidiarrheal drugs. As a financial incentive to promote ORS, pharmacies were given free measuring cups that they could sell with ORS packets, thereby raising their profit margins. For most health technologies, effective delivery requires giving the end-user clear instructions and advice about product use. The quality of delivery is affected by many factors, such as training, supervision, and available product information as well as the structure of incentives. Heavy patient load can also affect delivery, as can the low social status of some deliverers in certain societies.[18]

Delivery is a complex access activity, even for seemingly simple products. For example, Babu et al. examined a mass drug administration program of low-cost, single dose diethylcarbamazine (DEC) and albendazole to eliminate lymphatic filariasis in Orissa state, India.[19] Their study found that in spite of statewide mobilization and seemingly fewer program hurdles due to the single-dose-per-year treatment regimen, both drug coverage and drug compliance remained relatively low, with less than 70% coverage in three out of four surveyed districts and only 41% treatment compliance overall. The authors attribute poor coverage and compliance in part to issues related to end-user discomfort and distrust of the campaign. Problems included lack of involvement of primary health care staff, poor training of health workers and lack of strategies to manage unpleasant side effects, misinformation about side effects and safety perpetuated by local newspapers, uncoordinated or absent community participation and mobilization activities, and public mistrust of the campaign's motivations. In the words of focus group participants, "we are not willing to swallow" and "suspicion is there."[20] Similar problems of distrust had a major negative impact on the polio vaccination campaign in northern Nigeria, with consequences that spread to many other countries.

Activity Stream 3: Affordability

The affordability stream involves ensuring that health technologies and related services can be purchased at a reasonable price by the people who need them. Whether or not a technology is considered affordable depends on the technology's price, cost of services (such as user fees) related to accessing the technology, and the availability of funds for purchasing (which depends on the purchaser's available resources and perceptions of expected benefits and costs, including side effects, and other factors such as social acceptance). The primary purchasers of health technologies in developing countries are governments and individual consumers, although social security organizations are increasingly important in middle-income countries. In the world's poorest countries, most medicines are purchased by households using their own funds or by governments with public budgets.[21] Household funds and government budgets are very limited in most developing countries, pointing to the importance of low prices for health technologies. Much of the literature on access to medicines has focused on high prices as a key barrier to widespread access and has shown that affordability is a prerequisite for ensuring access. This is true not only for medicines, but also for other health technologies in developing countries.

As we mention in the adoption and availability sections of this chapter, affordability influences many access activities shown in Figure 2.1, including government procurement, delivery to the end-user, national adoption, and end-user adoption. For example, in their study of the affordability of miltefosine for the treatment of visceral leishmaniasis in India, Sundar and Murray find a linkage between affordability and appropriate use of the product.[22] The cost of miltefosine (initially US$200 for a 28-day course treatment, but down to US$145 in 2005) prevents access to this treatment for most patients (90% of whom live in rural Bihar state, India's poorest state, where the average per capita income was $94 a year in 2005). The high cost, coupled with a loosely regulated system of over-the-counter dispensing, has led impoverished patients to self-medicate, purchasing just enough of the drug to feel better and resume work. This has led to concerns about the potential for rapidly developing drug resistance. In their study of artemisinin-based combination treatments (ACTs) for malaria, Laximinarayan et al. explore how strategies to increase product affordability (in this case, subsidization) can also have unintended consequences for appropriate use.[23] They examine how subsidies could encourage over-use and hasten the emergence of parasite resistance to what is currently the most effective frontline therapy for malaria. Using mathematical modeling, the authors find that any subsidy of ACTs—whether full or partial—would dramatically increase the number of deaths averted, even if parasite resistance increases slightly as a consequence. The authors recommend that global actors move quickly to implement subsidization programs, while at the same time integrating resistance surveillance strategies into their programs.

While the literature has most often pointed to high cost as a primary deterrent to access, low cost can sometimes be an obstacle. One study found that a technology's low price had unexpected effects.[24] In this example, the low cost of magnesium sulphate (for treatment of pre-eclampsia and eclampsia, important causes of maternal and infant morbidity and mortality) slowed registration of the product because producers expected small profits, which limited the economic incentive for producers to register it. The drug's low price, combined with its relatively small market, also meant that companies did not actively market or promote it to central purchasers. These examples show both the importance of product price and the complexity of its influence.

What factors influence a technology's price? A technology's price consists of the manufacturer's selling price plus all the add-on costs, such as import tariffs, wholesale and retail mark-ups, and sales and value-added taxes. The manufacturer's selling price is based on costs of research, development, production, and marketing, plus profits. A technology's price can differ considerably across countries and between the public and private sectors within a country.[25] This is due to different corporate strategies, policy circumstances, tariffs, exchange rates, and negotiating conditions.[26] A key factor in setting prices is the national and international patent system, a focus of much of the existing literature on access to medicines.

The influence of prices and patents on health technology access came to the forefront of international attention in the debate over access to antiretroviral drugs (ARVs) for treating HIV/AIDS. Due to efforts by activist organizations, producers, UN agencies, and groups such as the William J. Clinton Foundation, the prices for triple-drug AIDS therapy dropped 98% between 1999 and 2003, from US$12,000 a year to less than US$200 a year.[27] While pricing controversies for most health technologies are usually less dramatic than has been the case for ARVs, global and national organizations are using a variety of strategies to influence health technology prices in developing countries. Many of the case studies in this volume examine what has worked and what has not in reducing prices.

Activity Stream 4: Adoption

Adoption involves gaining acceptance and creating demand for a new health technology from actors at several levels: global organizations, government actors in developing countries, providers and dispensers, and individual consumers and patients. Some partnerships for product development have not addressed adoption issues until the technology is licensed and ready for delivery. We argue in this book that adoption concerns are key to the success of access efforts, and that more consideration of adoption factors—particularly the end-user's perspective—is necessary and should begin early in the product development phase.

Global adoption involves the production of acceptance for the technology from expert groups, donors, international agencies such as WHO, UNICEF, UNAIDS, UNFPA, and other agencies, depending on the specific technology. Previous studies have emphasized the importance of "expert consensus" about the use of technologies, interventions, and strategies to fight disease within both international technical agencies and the broader international public health community.[28] We view the production of acceptance as an active process of social construction, not a passive process of waiting for various experts to agree on key elements related to the use of a health technology.

Failure to reach expert consensus about the need for or use of a technology can be a significant barrier to promoting access. For example, one bottleneck in ensuring wider availability of multi-drug resistant tuberculosis (MDR-TB) drugs was the lack of scientific consensus about how to manage MDR-TB in resource-poor settings. To address this problem, WHO asked a group of experts with clinical, program, and laboratory expertise to develop basic guidelines for the implementation of pilot projects.[29] These pilot projects then generated evidence to guide policy formulation for the management of MDR-TB.[30] For other technologies, reaching consensus within international technical agencies may involve official decisions about a technology and the related disease or health condition. For example, a resolution on the global elimination of blinding trachoma by the 51st World Health Assembly in May 1998 raised the profile of trachoma and helped promote new efforts to make azithromycin available in trachoma-endemic countries. Existing literature offers little information about the specific barriers and facilitators associated with the global adoption of health technologies. In the case studies, we examine these factors in depth and assess strategies used to overcome bottlenecks at the global level. We also assess the importance of global consensus, the key participants in the consensus process, and the particular issues that are contested.

Adoption at the national level involves acceptance of the new health technology by policy makers in various government ministries in developing countries. At least three arenas of activity are relevant here. First, political commitment has been shown repeatedly to be a key factor for the success of health technology access. For example, the African Comprehensive HIV/AIDS Partnerships (ACHAP) project in Botswana has shown that the highest levels of political leadership in Botswana, particularly the president's commitment to addressing AIDS, paved the way for establishing the ACHAP partnership and enabled the government to make effective use of ACHAP to implement the national ARV program.[31] Second, registration of the technology is often required by national regulatory authorities and has in some cases been a reason for delay of product introduction. Registration involves standard procedures to examine the quality, safety, and efficacy of health technologies, and provider and patient information. The process depends in large part on a nation's regulatory authority policies and market incentives but also on various market imperfections that can slow down the process of regulatory approval. For example, a study examining why magnesium sulphate (for treatment of pre-eclampsia and eclampsia, as noted above) is not widely available in Zimbabwe found that drug companies lacked economic incentives to advocate for registration because of the drug's low cost and low potential volume of use.[32] Registration fees, information and bureaucratic barriers, problems of corruption, and the costs of preparing submissions for registration can also block widespread use of a technology.

The third arena that is important for national level adoption is acceptance of the technology by policy makers within health ministries, especially in countries with a large public healthcare sector whether or not the government is an important provider (either through the ministry or social security). Acceptance can involve development of treatment protocols, allocation of funding in the health budget for the use of a new technology, and in some cases the willingness to take control of program interventions associated with the new technology. Health ministries can produce national treatment protocols, which are systematically developed statements that assist health workers in deciding on diagnosis and therapy for clinical problems.[33] This process, however, can be laborious and contentious, particularly when new technologies are replacing existing methods of treatment. A study that assessed the process of changing national malaria treatment policies found a number of bottlenecks, including lack of available and affordable supply of new malaria drugs, uncertainty about the ideal timing of policy change, emotional attachment to previous technologies, lack of standardized data, ineffective translation of research into national policy, and lack of communication among stakeholders.[34] Whether treatment protocols affect health workers' practice depends on several factors, including who develops them and their credibility, involvement of health workers in development of the protocols, complexity and format of the guidelines, and how they are disseminated.[35]

Gaining acceptance and creating demand for a new technology among providers is a key component of the adoption process, particularly for drugs and vaccines administered by health professionals and for technologies (such as diagnostics) where the provider is the end-user. Providers often decide which treatment, vaccine, or diagnostic to administer to a patient based on available information, peer practices, product price, insurance reimbursements, and company incentives. In a study of oral rehydration therapy, Ruxin argues that the medical establishment in the United States did not readily accept the low cost therapy in part because of financial reasons: Hospitals received much higher insurance reimbursement for treating a dehydrated child with intravenous therapy than for using oral rehydration therapy.[36] Inappropriate prescribing practices can result from inadequate training, lack of objective information, heavy patient load, and pressure to use certain technologies from patients, peers, and producers.[37] Lack of supply, persistent habits, loyalties to existing technologies, and provider/patient dynamics are also factors that can block provider adoption of new technologies. Another study of oral rehydration therapy, this one in Northeast Brazil, found that physicians opposed home-made and home-administered oral rehydration therapy because they viewed the simple technology (that does not require a provider for administration) as a threat to their social status and power in the community.[38] Provider decisions about health technologies are thus affected by many different factors and are critical to actual usage in practice. There is increasing recognition of the importance of efforts to change provider behavior through incentive programs, social marketing, and mechanisms like formularies and treatment protocols.[39] A combination of these approaches can help change provider understanding, acceptance, and prescribing practices.

For health technologies where the end-user is the patient or consumer, *acceptance of the technology by the individual* is key to successful access. Patient or consumer adoption can involve what is often called "health-seeking behavior." This includes decisions about going to see a health provider, attending a community-based health campaign, or purchasing a health product (such as condoms or bednets) in a store. It also involves individual perceptions and acceptance of the new technology, whether it is a health product like oral rehydration salts or contraceptives, or a new drug or vaccine. A large literature in the social sciences examines the diffusion of new tech-nologies and how end-users adopt technologies at different rates. Two classic publi-cations are the study by Everett Rogers (in 1962) on the diffusion of innovations,[40] and the analysis by Zvi Griliches (in 1957) on the introduction of hybrid corn.[41] These two studies emphasize the processes of adoption by end-users, a key compo-nent of our larger framework on access.

As discussed above under affordability, cost is a key factor that influences health-seeking behavior and the adoption of new health technologies. A recent study on childhood febrile illness in Tanzania, however, found that economic fac-tors were not the most important in explaining why mothers waited to seek treat-ment at a government facility for their children.[42] The study found that the most important factors were cultural knowledge about disease symptoms, previous experience with childhood febrile illness, perceptions about illness severity and the efficacy of medications, and the micropolitics of communication about illness diagnosis and therapy management between health care providers and mothers. The study concluded that efforts to make new treatments widely available must pay more attention to contextual factors and sociocultural dynamics (such as mothers' daily concerns, their access to social support, their understanding of malaria symptoms, and health care provider communication). Perceptions of dis-ease and treatment thus have enormous influence on consumers' decisions about what to do for health problems such as febrile illness.

A study of factors influencing acceptance and refusal of vaccination placed the complex issues influencing end-user adoption within a broader theoretical model. In this model, both health condition and health technology variables are mbedded in dynamic interactions among individual, culture, social structure, and political-economic conditions.[43] For health condition variables, important factors were the perception of disease severity, perception of self and other's vul-nerability to the disease, perceived causes of the disease, and perceived availability and efficacy of preventive measures and treatments. For technologies, important factors were the perceived purpose of the technology, perceived efficacy, perceived risks and benefits (e.g., risk of adverse effects), perceived costs, desired character-istics, and delivery logistics. This approach gives a major emphasis to the role of perception for both the health condition and the health technology. Understand-ing how these perceptions are produced and managed is a major challenge in the access process.

Experience with the introduction of antiretroviral therapy similarly demon-strates the importance of both health condition and technology factors. Patient demand for ARVs in some countries was initially much lower than expected. This unanticipated low level of demand was related to the disease (in terms of widespread reluctance of people to be tested for HIV due to denial and stigma) and also to the technology (in terms of people's low level of knowledge about ARVs).[44] Not only are both technology and health condition variables important but often they are interrelated. For instance, if an end-user perceives a disease as not very serious, a technology's side effects may become a greater concern.[45] Our case study on the contraceptive Norplant examines the linkages between technology (contraceptives) and health condition (pregnancy) variables. In all of our case studies, we examine the role of technology and disease variables in the entire access process and assess how to address these variables in the product development phase.

The end point of adoption is *how the patient or consumer uses the technology.* An important question is whether this can be considered "appropriate use." The final use of technology is related to prescribing factors (correct technology, appropriate indication, appropriate end-user, and appropriate dosage, administration, and duration of use) and delivery factors (such as information provided to end-users about the technology) as well as end-user factors related to adherence. Factors that influence adherence include provider explanations, limited dosages (number and time), acceptable side effects, written or symbolic instructions accompanying the technology, and individual beliefs and attitudes.[46] The cost of the technology also affects how people use the product. Finally, consumer preference influences patient or consumer use of even the most cost-effective and beneficial health technologies. In a study of mosquito net use at the household level in five African countries, Baume finds that consumer preference helps explain the gap between net ownership and use.[47] Nets, consumers said, were hot, difficult to hang, and could be easily substituted with coils or aerosol sprays. In addition, newer nets (those less than two years old) were more likely to be used than older ones, purchased nets more likely than donated ones, and treated nets more likely than untreated ones.

How individuals use a health technology depends on the experiences and values that shape their attitudes toward disease, medication, treatment regimens, and side effects. In addition, even if a technology has an affordable price or is free of charge, there may be indirect costs of use and adherence in resource-poor settings. One study of adherence to antiretroviral therapy (ART) argues that patients internalize these factors and use them to provide meaning to their AIDS experience.[48] For example, one person may not seek treatment for undesirable side effects of ART because of lack of money to travel to a health clinic, while another person may knowingly miss a dose when asymptomatic to pretend AIDS is not an issue. Castro contends that in order to understand failure to adhere to drug regimens, researchers should adopt a biosocial approach, combining quantitative and qualitative methodologies to assess the interactions among the clinical manifestations of the disease, the technological aspects of ART regimens, and the social, economic, and cultural contexts of medication use in the developing world.[49] Attention to these biosocial factors, Castro suggests, opens up new avenues of possibility for AIDS care programs to facilitate ART adherence by balancing technological innovation with comprehensive social and economic interventions.

Variations of the Framework

The activities and actors in our analytical framework vary by health technology and country context. For example, public-sector efforts to expand access to technologies in some countries may require private distributors while others may rely only on public distributors. Also, the location for obtaining a health technology differs depending on the specific product. For example, patients may receive their medicines in hospital or community pharmacies, while they purchase insecticide-treated bednets in shops. Furthermore, specific activities and actors will differ depending on who the end-user is. While the end-user for drugs, vaccines, and other health products is the patient or consumer, the end-user for many diagnostic tests is the health professional in public or private clinics.

The framework also differs according to the phase of access. We conceive of the access process in four main phases (see Figure 2.3). The first phase is *product development*, when, for example, developers make decisions about a technology's design that may have implications for end-user adoption and use. This is followed by an *introduction* phase, often involving pilot programs or demonstration projects, in which the health technology is initially provided in a context where it did not previously exist. In this phase, approaches to access are developed and tested, drawing out lessons learned and refining approaches. The introduction phase usually occurs after clinical testing has been completed and regulatory approval obtained. Next is *scaling up*, or increasing the number of people with access to the technology, with the ultimate goal of providing access to all who need it. This is often referred to as "quantitative" scaling up.[50] The scaling-up phase, however, can involve additional elements including "organizational" scaling up (increasing organizational strength to improve effectiveness, efficiency, and sustainability of activities), "functional" scaling up (expanding the number and type of activities to its operational range), and "political" scaling up (moving beyond service delivery toward activities that address underlying power structures and causes of poverty).[51] The fourth and final phase involves *sustaining access to the health technology over time* as long as it is needed. This phase is often marked by product and program fatigue that can impede ongoing access to the technology. As mentioned in the previous chapter, in this book we do not examine this final access phase in depth.

While there is significant overlap in terms of actors and activities in these four phases, they can differ significantly. More importantly, the barriers and facilitators will vary in the phases and will require different strategies for ensuring successful access. Each case study in this volume focuses on one or more phases of access and draws out the phase-specific barriers, facilitators, and strategies for ensuring access.

Using the Framework

The framework presented in this chapter can be used both as an explanatory and a prescriptive tool. In its explanatory application, analysts can use the framework to identify the activities, actors, and barriers to access in past efforts at expanding product access. Planners can also use the tool to map their past experiences with introducing a new health technology, extract lessons learned, and refine strategies for scaling up. As a prescriptive tool, analysts can use the framework to propose key activities that need to be achieved and actors for carrying them out, predict potential barriers and identify opportunities, and develop strategies for guiding the technology to the end-user.

Our framework has several limitations worth noting. First, it is not a "one size fits all" approach. The access story for each health technology differs by product and context. A second limitation is that the framework is not the only way to organize or think about access to health technologies. For some, this framework may be too complicated to be useful; for others, it may not include enough detail about the different activities or actors. We have tried to find a balance between detail and simplicity and to identify categories that speak to practical action but also draw upon theoretical concepts. We believe that the comprehensive approach we have taken in designing this framework is useful to explain past successes and failures in access. We feel the ideas can also assist product developers who have demonstrated that their product can improve the health of poor people in developing countries but then are confronted with a set of new problems. The framework can help in identifying critical bottlenecks and in proposing strategies for overcoming those problems.

We turn now to our case studies that tell the access stories of six different products and follow the flow of products through different access phases and

Figure 2.3 | The access phases

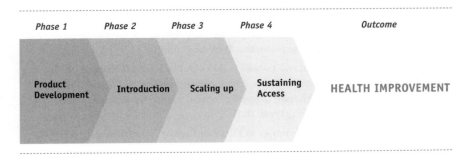

Phase 1	Phase 2	Phase 3	Phase 4	Outcome
Product Development	Introduction	Scaling up	Sustaining Access	HEALTH IMPROVEMENT

activities. Our approach in these case studies draws from anthropological research that has traced the "life-cycles" or "biographies" of drugs from production to the end-user.[52] In our case studies, we examine a wider set of health technologies and follow their flow through access activities, identifying key actors, barriers, and facilitators, as well as what worked and what did not in producing access. We hoisispe that through careful assessment of past experience, we can improve access to good health technologies for poor people in poor countries in the future.

Endnotes

[1] Michael R. Reich, ed., *Public-Private Partnerships for Public Health* (Cambridge, MA: Harvard Center for Population and Development Studies, distributed by Harvard University Press, 2002).

[2] The Global Alliance for TB Drug Development refers to the supply component as "access." In our framework, we conceive of the overall process as "access" and the supply component as "availability." For a more complete description of the AAA strategy, visit http://www.tballiance.org.

[3] This approach is similar to that used in a framework designed for the Commission on Macroeconomics and Health (CMH) for categorizing "constraints" to scaling up priority health interventions within developing countries. Our framework is more comprehensive in that it conceptualizes barriers (constraints) but also facilitators, and does so at the global level as well as within developing countries. See: Kara Hanson, M. Kent Ranson, Valeria Oliveira-Cruz, and Anne Mills, "Expanding Access to Priority Health Interventions: A Framework for Understanding the Constraints to Scaling-Up," *Journal of International Development* 15 (2003): 1–14.

[4] Joanne Spicehandler and Ruth Simmons, *Contraceptive Introduction Reconsidered: A Review and Conceptual Framework* (Geneva: UNDP/UNFPA/WHO/World Bank Special Programme of Research, Development and Research Training in Human Reproduction, 1994, WHO/HRP/ITT/94.1).

[5] McKinsey & Company/Bill & Melinda Gates Foundation, *Developing Successful Global Health Alliances*. Retrieved January 24, 2007, from Eldis, Institute of Development Studies, Sussex, http://www.eldis.org/static/DOC11504.htm.

[6] James E. Austin, *The Collaboration Challenge: How Nonprofits and Businesses Succeed through Strategic Alliances* (San Francisco: Jossey-Bass Publishers, 2000).

[7] Laura Frost, Michael R. Reich, and Tomoko Fujisaki, "A Partnership for Ivermectin: Social Worlds and Boundary Objects," in *Public-Private Partnerships for Public Health*, ed. Michael R. Reich (Cambridge, MA: Harvard Center for Population and Development Studies, distributed by Harvard University Press, 2002).

[8] Andrea Rinaldi, "The Global Campaign to Eliminate Leprosy," *PLoS Medicine* 2(12)/e341 (2005): 1222–1225.

[9] Michael J. Free, "Achieving Appropriate Design and Widespread Use of Health Technologies in the Developing World," *International Journal of Gynecology and Obstetrics* 85 suppl. 1 (2004): S3–S13.

[10] Center for Global Development Global Health Forecasting Working Group, *A Risky Business: Saving Money and Improving Better Demand Forecasts* (Washington, DC: Center for Global Development, 2007).

[11] Neelam Sekhri, "Forecasting for Global Health: New Money, New Products and New Markets" (Background Paper for the Forecasting Working Group, Washington, DC: Center for Global Development, 2006).

[12] Center for Global Development.

[13] Management Sciences for Health, *Managing Drug Supply: The Selection, Procurement, Distribution, and Use of Pharmaceuticals* (W. Hartford, CT: Kumarian Press, 1997).

[14] Jacob Kumaresan, Ian Smith, Virginia Arnold, and Peter Evans, "The Global TB Drug Facility: Innovative Global Procurement," *The International Journal of Tuberculosis and Lung Disease* 8 (2004): 130–138.

[15] Management Sciences for Health.

[16] Kazeem B. Yusuff and Fola Tayo, "Drug Supply Strategies, Constraints and Prospects in Nigeria," *African Journal of Medicine and Medical Sciences* 33, no. 4 (2004): 389–94.

[17] Ruth Levine, *Millions Saved: Proven Successes in Global Health* (Washington, DC: Center for Global Development, 2004).

[18] Management Sciences for Health.

[19] B. V. Babu and S. K. Kar, "Coverage, Compliance and Some Operational Issues of Mass Drug Administration During the Programme to Eliminate Lymphatic Filariasis in Orissa, India," *Tropical Medicine and International Health* 9 (2004): 702–709.

[20] Babu and Kar, 706.

[21] World Health Organization, *Health Reform and Drug Financing: Selected Topics* (Geneva: WHO, 1998, WHO/DAP/98.3).

22 Shyam Sundar and Henry W. Murray, "Availability of Miltefosine for the Treatment of Kala-Azar in India," *Bulletin of the World Health Organization* 83 (2005): 394–395.

23 Ramanan Laxminarayan, Mead Over, and David L. Smith, "Will a Global Subsidy of New Antimalarials Delay the Emergence of Resistance and Save Lives?" *Health Affairs* 25 (2006): 325–336.

24 E. Sevene, S. Lewin, A. Mariano, G. Woelk, A. D. Oxman, S. Matinhure, J. Cliff, B. Fernandes, and K. Daniels, "System and Market Failures: The Unavailability of Magnesium Sulphate for the Treatment of Eclampsia and Pre-Eclampsia in Mozambique and Zimbabwe," *British Medical Journal* 331 (2005): 765–769.

25 Margaret Ewen and Dalia Dey, "Medicines: Too Costly and Too Scarce," Health Action International, http://www.haiweb.org/medicineprices (retrieved January 24, 2007).

26 Michael R. Reich and Priya Bery, "Expanding Global Access to ARVs: The Challenges of Prices and Patents," in *The AIDS Pandemic: Impact on Science and Society*, eds. Kenneth H. Mayer and H. F. Pizer (San Diego, CA: Elsevier Academic Press, 2005).

27 Reich and Bery.

28 Levine.

29 Rajesh Gupta, Alexander Irwin, Mario C. Raviglione, and Jim Yong Kim, "Scaling-Up Treatment for HIV/AIDS: Lessons Learned from Multidrug-Resistant Tuberculosis," *Lancet* 363 (2004): 320–324.

30 Thuridur Arnadottir and Rajesh Gupta, eds., *Guidelines for Establishing DOTS-Plus Pilot Projects for the Management of Multidrug-Resistant Tuberculosis* (Geneva: WHO, 2001).

31 Ilavenil Ramiah and Michael R. Reich, "Public-Private Partnerships and Antiretroviral Drugs for HIV/AIDS: Lessons from Botswana," *Health Affairs* 24 (2005): 545–551.

32 Sevene et al.

33 Management Sciences for Health; and R. O. Laing, Hans V. Hogerzeil, and Dennis Ross-Degnan, "Ten Recommendations to Improve Use of Medicines in Developing Countries," *Health Policy and Planning* 16 (2001): 13–20.

34 Holly Ann Williams, David Durrheim, and Rima Shretta, "The Process of Changing National Malaria Treatment Policy: Lessons from Country-Level Studies," *Health Policy and Planning* 19, no. 6 (2004): 356–70.

35 Laing et al.

36 Joshua Nalibow Roxin, "The History of Oral Rehydration Therapy," *Medical History* 38 (1994): 363–397.

37 Management Sciences for Health.

38 Marilyn K. Nations and L. A. Rebhun, "Mystification of a Simple Solution: Oral Rehydration Therapy in Northeast Brazil," *Social Science and Medicine* 27 (1988): 501–522.

39 Marc J. Roberts, William Hsiao, Peter Berman, and Michael R. Reich, *Getting Health Reform Right: A Guide to Improving Performance and Equity* (New York: Oxford University Press, 2004): 281–307.

[40] Everett M. Rogers, *Diffusion of Innovations* (New York: Free Press of Glencoe, 1962).

[41] Zvi Griliches, "Hybrid Corn: An Exploration in the Economics of Technological Change," *Econometrics* 25 (1957): 501–522.

[42] Vinay R. Kamat, "'I Thought It Was Only Ordinary Fever!' Cultural Knowledge and the Micropolitics of Therapy Seeking for Childhood Febrile Illness in Tanzania," *Social Science & Medicine* 62 (2006): 2945–2959.

[43] Linda M. Kaljee, Rob Pack, Al Pach, Andrew Nyamete, and Bonita F. Stanton, "Sociobehavioural Research Methods for the Introduction of Vaccines in the Diseases of the Most Impoverished Programme," *Journal of Health, Population, and Nutrition* 22, no. 3 (2004): 293–303.

[44] Ramiah & Reich.

[45] Kaljee et al.

[46] Management Sciences for Health.

[47] Carol Baume, "Understanding Mosquito Net Use at the Household Level: Are Household Mosquito Nets Being Used? If So, Who Uses Them?" *Global HealthLink* 138 (2006): 8, 20.

[48] Arachu Castro, "Adherence to Antiretroviral Therapy: Merging the Clinical and Social Course of AIDS," *PLoS Medicine* 2, no 12 (2005): e338.

[49] Paul Farmer, *Infections and Inequalities: The Modern Plagues* (Berkeley: University of California, 1999).

[50] Peter Uvin, "Fighting Hunger at the Grassroots: Paths to Scaling Up," *World Development* 23 (1995): 927–939.

[51] Uvin.

[52] Sjaak Van der Geest, Susan Reynolds Whyte, and Anita Hardon, "The Anthropology of Pharmaceuticals: A Biographical Approach," *Annual Review of Anthropology* 25 (1996): 153–179; Susan Reynolds Whyte, Sjaak Van der Geest, and Anita Hardon, *Social Lives of Medicines* (Cambridge: Cambridge University Press, 2002); and Susan Reynolds Whyte, Michael A.Whyte, Lotte Meinert, and Betty Kyaddondo, "Treating AIDS: Dilemmas of Unequal Access in Uganda," in *Global Pharmaceuticals: Ethics, Markets, Practices,* eds. Adriana Petryna, Andrew Lakoff, and Arthur Kleinman (Durham: Duke University Press, 2006), 240–262.

CHAPTER 3

PRAZIQUANTEL:

Access to Medicines

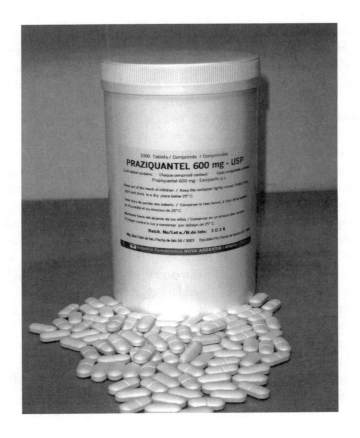

With Alan Fenwick and Harold Thompson

THIS CHAPTER EXAMINES THE PROCESSES IN EXPANDING ACCESS TO PRAZIQUANTEL, the drug of choice for treatment of schistosomiasis. This infectious disease is caused by parasitic worms (schistosomes) that live in the blood vessels of the human host. There are three major species that infect humans, two of which are found in Africa—*S. haematobium* and *S. mansoni*. Schistosomiasis is the second most prevalent parasitic disease after malaria, and according to the World Health Organization, an estimated 200 million people are infected, including 180 million in sub-Saharan Africa. Nearly 40 million people either have serious morbidity or will develop serious morbidity unless treated. About 1 million per year die from bleeding, bladder cancer, or liver and kidney infections. Schistosomiasis causes mild to serious health problems such as malnutrition, anemia, growth retardation, cognitive impairment, and chronic health problems and can contribute to increased susceptibility to other infections such as HIV/AIDS and tuberculosis. In short, schistosomiasis is a major cause of ill health in Africa.

The schistosome life cycle depends on both a human host and a snail host, with transmission occurring in fresh water lakes, rivers, and irrigation schemes. The adult male and female schistosomes, which are about one centimeter in length, live together in human blood vessels, and female worms can produce up to 300 eggs each per day. In heavy infections of *S. hemaetobium*, particularly in children, urine can be bright red with fresh blood. In the other species of schistosome (*S. mansoni*), the eggs and blood are found in the stool. The eggs that leave the human host in the urine or feces depend on reaching fresh water so that they can hatch. Emerging from the egg is a small larva that seeks out and infects a fresh water intermediate host snail. The larvae multiply in the snail, and four weeks later, thousands of the next stage larvae emerge from the snail into the water and swim around looking for a human host so that the cycle can continue.

Over time, schistosomiasis produces chronic health problems, as the bladder wall and the intestinal wall become thickened and fibrotic from the accumulation of eggs. Cancer of the bladder and colon can develop. In the liver, the build up of millions of eggs leads to fibrosis and blocking of the liver, blood pressure increases, the abdomen swells, and finally the pressure leads to a (usually fatal) episode of bleeding from burst blood vessels. People at risk for schistosomiasis are often the poorest of the poor, especially children and women in rural villages, as well as particular occupational groups (such as farmers, fishermen, and others with regular exposure to water). People in poor rural communities often depend on schistosoma-infested waters for household water, leisure activities, and crop irrigation, and become exposed to schistosomiasis through daily activities that require contact with water. They often lack access to potable water and sanitation that would limit their exposure or re-exposure to infection.

This chapter focuses on access to a specific medicine (praziquantel) and the efforts of a particular organization (the Schistosomiasis Control Initiative) to expand access with important contributions from the World Health Organization. We are especially interested in ways to expand and sustain access to praziquantel through use of the market and other mechanisms. In only a few years, the Schistosomiasis Control Initiative (SCI) significantly increased access to praziquantel in Africa through a series of strategies that we examine: procurement, collaboration, information, registration, local formulation, and donation. We are particularly interested in the implications of these strategies for continued access to praziquantel (PZQ). Future access to praziquantel will depend on many factors, including the evolving market for the product, the actions of key players, the availability of international aid funding, and the perceptions of national ministries of health regarding both the disease and its treatment.

The case of praziquantel demonstrates that even very inexpensive medicines do not easily achieve their full potential effects in treatment and improving human welfare due to persistent obstacles to access. While affordability was a major problem in the past and remains an important obstacle to access, the current barriers are mostly related to adoption (low consumer demand and low government demand) and availability (lack of information about suppliers and price). The SCI greatly expanded access in a short time through massive funding from the Bill & Melinda Gates Foundation starting in 2002. But major challenges to sustained access remain in 2007 as SCI confronts a transition in its financing and activities.

Product Development (Phase 1)

Praziquantel was developed first for the veterinary market and then for the human market through interfirm collaboration between two German pharmaceutical companies, Bayer and E. Merck. The compound's curative efficacy against various platyhelminths pathogenic to man was confirmed in testing during the 1970s.[1] A single dose of PZQ (40 mg/kg body weight) was shown to effectively treat all schistosome species infecting humans (the three major ones being *S. haematobium*, *S. mansoni*, and *S. japonicum*).

PZQ was patented in Germany in December 1973 and in the United States in 1977.[2] For the human market, Bayer approached the WHO in the late 1970s to request collaboration in multicenter clinical trials to demonstrate PZQ's safety and efficacy. The resulting collaboration in organizing the clinical trials achieved scientific success. From the time that PZQ was first patented in 1973 until one decade later, more than 400 articles were published on the preclinical and clinical aspects of the new product.[3] By 1982, PZQ had been used for safe and effective treatment in 25,000 patients on three continents.[4] The therapeutic validity of the initial trials of PZQ thus was confirmed through many experiments, broad clinical experience, and large-scale field control programs.[5]

WHO's assistance in helping to organize the clinical trials of PZQ was critical in this phase of drug development. The case thus represents an important instance of public-private collaboration in drug development for a tropical disease. By the mid-1990s, Bayer and E. Merck had registered the patent for PZQ in 38 countries.[6] The public-private collaboration, however, did not effectively address issues of access to the product in poor countries:

While the collaboration between Bayer and WHO was quite successful in conducting clinical trials for praziquantel, the relationship apparently did not include a written agreement on issues of pricing or distribution methods once the product was fully developed and registered. Some observers mentioned the existence of a 'good faith agreement' between individuals involved in the two organizations. Our research, however, was unable to identify any documents that would support the existence of an agreement between the two organizations or individuals on critical questions of how praziquantel would be made available.[7]

This experience provides important lessons about public-private partnerships—that access issues need to be addressed as an integral part of product development efforts and that agreements on access need to be explicit, written, and transparent through an access plan.

Introduction of Praziquantel (Phase 2)

Praziquantel became available in Europe after 1978 and became generally available on the international market in the 1980s.[8] It became recognized by experts and by the WHO as the drug of choice for all forms of schistosomiasis in humans because of its high efficacy, low toxicity, and ease of single oral administration.[9] Oxamniquine, for example, was effective against *S. mansoni* but not against other schistosomes, and its use consequently declined. The decline was hastened by development of resistance in Brazil, and the fact that oxamniquine was not as effective against *S. mansoni* in Africa as against *S. mansoni* in Brazil. By 1985, about 200 million people were estimated to be infected globally by schistosomiasis, while approximately

1 million had been treated with PZQ.[10] Studies of these experiences demonstrated that PZQ could effectively reduce the morbidity associated with schistosomiasis and reduce the excretion of schistosome eggs from infected individuals.[11] The studies also showed, however, that even mass treatment of a community did not easily interrupt the transmission of schistosomiasis because of the high risk of reinfection in endemic areas and factors such as PZQ's lack of efficacy against schistosomulae and immature schistosome worms in the human body. Regular treatment of school children and high-risk populations was thus needed to reduce the intensity of infection, reduce the risk of serious morbidity, and thereby produce major public health benefits.[12]

But access to PZQ was limited during the 1980s and 1990s in most schistosomiasis-endemic countries. The key barrier was the drug's affordability. When PZQ was originally marketed by Bayer in the 1980s, it was made available to developing countries at a discounted price of approximately $1 per 600 mg tablet (below the market price of $6.50 per tablet in Germany), equivalent to $4 to treat a 60 kg individual at the recommended dose of 40 mg/kg. Even at the discounted price, however, no African government could afford to embark on a schistosomiasis control program without external funding. External funding was provided by donors for some African countries (such as Mali, by the German aid agency GTZ) so that these countries could establish a national program using PZQ. But when this external funding ceased, so did the treatment programs; these early programs were totally unsustainable.

Subsequently several countries used international financing to establish successful national control programs for schistosomiasis. The best known examples are Egypt, China, and the Philippines, all using PZQ. Brazil also initiated a national program, but it relied on oxamniquine for many years (for treatment of *S. mansoni*) and only switched to PZQ in recent years. These countries depended on various sources of international financing. Egypt, for example, relied on loans from the World Bank and the African Development Bank to purchase PZQ, and a grant from the U.S. Agency for International Development (USAID) for research associated with the control program. China and the Philippines relied on World Bank loans to fund the programs.

The case of Egypt illustrates how PZQ treatment strategies (and consumption volumes) change as a control program evolves. In 1993, Egypt had total annual consumption of about 10 million tablets of PZQ, with sales of about 2 million tablets in the private market and 8 million purchased by the government.[13] This figure increased from 1996 on, as mass chemotherapy replaced diagnosis and treatment. Eventually PZQ use reached about 25 million tablets per year to treat 10 million people annually. As a result, by 2004 the reported national prevalence of schistosomiasis had declined to less than 5%. By 2005, the annual consumption of PZQ in Egypt had dropped back to approximately 5 million tablets as treatment focused on school children in the Nile Delta. This example illustrates that use of PZQ will generally be quite high in the first five years of a national control program using mass treatment and then will decline to a lower plateau of sustained treatment. This assumes that the high intensity infection areas are treated first and that the overall program is well managed. Later results from control programs in Burkina Faso, Mali, and Niger (initiated under SCI) suggest a similar pattern in these countries.[14]

An assessment of the global market for PZQ in the early 1990s showed major gaps between supply, demand, and need for this product.[15] The estimate of global supply in 1993 was 89 million tablets. This figure was based on a survey of active-ingredient production by the major firms then involved in PZQ production: Bayer and E. Merck in Germany and Shin Poong in South Korea. During the 1980s, the international market structure for PZQ production (raw material) had changed dramatically. Bayer and E. Merck started with 100% in 1981, but their market share dropped to 80% in 1985 with the emergence of Shin Poong's manufacturing facility. Shin Poong's production and market share continued to grow, reaching 55% in 1993, while the German firms declined to a combined 27% and Chinese companies rose to nearly 18%.

These trends in the production of PZQ's active ingredient continued through the 1990s and beyond, with diminished production by Bayer and E. Merck and growing production by several Chinese companies. In 2004, five firms were identified as the major producers of active ingredient. Table 3.1 shows the estimated annual production by company for that year.

The global *demand* for PZQ, however, has historically been limited by a lack of national adoption by schistosomiasis-endemic countries and a low priority in global adoption for the disease by international agencies and non-governmental organizations (the "donors"). Donors make their decisions about funding priorities based on analysis, opportunities, and geopolitical factors, as well as trends and fads in international assistance. These decisions have great influence on the health policy strategic plans of countries that depend on foreign assistance to operate their health sectors. In some cases, donors have influenced national perceptions about the desirability of implementing a national schistosomiasis control program; in many cases, the availability of donor funding has been the critical factor

Table 3.1 | Producers of PZQ active ingredient, 2005

COMPANY	LOCATION	ANNUAL PRODUCTION[a]
Shanghai OSD Co., Ltd.	China	70 metric tons (112 million tablets)
Nanjing Pharmaceuticals Factory Co., Ltd.	China	50 metric tons (80 million tablets)
Shin Poong	Korea	50 metric tons (est.) (80 million tablets)
E. Merck	Germany	10 metric tons (16 million tablets)
Hang Zhou Minsheng Pharmaceutical, Ltd.	China	20 metric tons (32 million tablets)
Other manufacturers	China	Not available
TOTAL	Global	200 metric tons (320 million tablets)

Note. From "A Major Gap: The Supply of Praziquantel," by World Health Organization, 2006, Geneva: Author. Adapted with permission.

[a] Estimated annual production, 2005; lack of data underestimates total production.

determining the feasibility of implementing a national schistosomiasis control program, which has then affected the demand for PZQ in the global market. In short, donor funding has frequently determined the level of demand and the level of access to PZQ in Africa.

The global *need* for PZQ presents a very different picture. In the 1980s, the WHO produced a global atlas of schistosomiasis and estimated national need for PZQ based on available data for schistosomiasis prevalence, population estimations, and assuming a strategy of selective treatment for all infected persons (at 40 mg/kg body weight).[16] According to this calculation, there was a global need of 424 million tablets, compared to an estimated global supply of 89 million tablets in 1993. Supply at this time thus provided roughly 20% of the estimated global need.[17] It is worth noting that the estimates of both supply and need were based on extrapolation from patchy and limited data, making the figures rather uncertain. Nonetheless, these calculations demonstrated an extremely low level of access to PZQ in the 1980s and 1990s—far below the quantity required to treat people infected with schistosomiasis.

Information is very limited on the actual availability of PZQ in African countries before 2002, when SCI began its operations. But it appears that several countries in sub-Saharan Africa purchased a small quantity of PZQ each year, probably up to 200,000 tablets per country in the endemic countries in West Africa and around 300,000 tablets per endemic country in East Africa. These supplies were typically purchased through the government's central medical stores and distributed to both private and government pharmacies. The drugs were used when patients came to a private clinician or government health center with symptoms (i.e., through a passive, patient-driven distribution system). If prescribed privately or at the health center, patients frequently ended up paying a relatively high price (between $2 and $10 per treatment, or two to ten times the initial procurement price of the pills). This practice continued through 2006. This higher price at the point of treatment reflected the costs of procurement, storage, and distribution, as well as the operating costs of the health center, plus the profits of the various distributors, middlemen, and prescribers involved in the delivery process.

Scaling Up through the Schistosomiasis Control Initiative (Phase 3)

In June 2002, the Schistosomiasis Control Initiative was established with $27.8 million funding from the Bill & Melinda Gates Foundation. The SCI marked a major turn-around in global attention to schistosomiasis control, which had been neglected in international development aid, global health policy, and national health policies since its last major surge in attention in the 1980s. As explained in the SCI's final proposal to the Gates Foundation in March 2002, the goal of SCI was to "promote the development of sustainable schistosomiasis control programs in sub-Saharan Africa."[18] At about the same time, advocates for schistosomiasis control within the World Health Organization were pushing for greater global attention. They achieved two important milestones in global adoption with the passage of a resolution by the World Health Assembly in May 2001[19] and the establishment of a broad and inclusive new entity called the Partners for Parasite Control. SCI would assist selected countries in implementing the WHO's May 2001 resolution with the target of providing regular treatment for "at least 75% of all school-aged children at risk of illness from schistosomiasis and soil transmitted helminths by 2010." This would help increase demand for treatment throughout Africa. The new initiative would seek to demonstrate "proof of principle"—to the Gates Foundation and the broader international health community as well as national governments—to show that "schistosomiasis and concurrent worm infections can be controlled, at what cost, and with what impact on health."[20]

With its funding from the Gates Foundation, the SCI (based at Imperial College in London with Alan Fenwick as director) became a major product champion, along with WHO's parasite control experts, for PZQ and the treatment of schisto-somiasis in Africa. These two product champions collaborated and supported each other in their efforts to promote greater financial resources and policy attention to PZQ access for the treatment of schistosomiasis. The idea for the SCI emerged from Fenwick's personal experiences and his conviction that PZQ treatment could make a significant difference in the lives of millions of people affected by schisto-somiasis. Fenwick had worked on research and control programs against schistoso-miasis in Tanzania, Sudan, and Egypt, and had lived and worked in Africa for 35 years. He served on the WHO expert panel for schistosomiasis and had many publications on snail control, drug evaluation, chemotherapy, epidemiology, and zoonosis of schistosomiasis. He firmly believed that countries could be persuaded to initiate national control programs and that PZQ treatment could reach 40 to 80 million Africans in a four-year period, serving as an example for the rest of Africa. As stated in the proposal for a planning grant in 2000 (submitted by Fenwick and Reich), "Today there is no reason why anyone should suffer serious disease due to schistosomiasis."[21]

Due to funding limitations, SCI decided to focus on a relatively small number of countries and selected six (Burkina Faso, Mali, Niger, Tanzania, Uganda, and Zambia) from twelve that applied for support for national control programs. In 2004, SCI ran its first international tender for PZQ; the initiative purchased 32.7 million tablets in 2004, 30.2 million in 2005, and 12.5 million in 2006. SCI also received a donation of 13.7 million tablets in 2005, with additional donations in 2006 and 2007 (from MedPharm in Alexandria, Virginia). SCI thus became the single largest purchaser of PZQ ever on the global market, absorbing an estimated 90% of global trade of this drug in 2004 and 2005. SCI directed these supplies primarily to the six target countries. SCI planned to continue making purchases through the life of the project (initially five years from 2002 but then extended for several years more by the Gates Foundation) and expected that the donations through MedPharm would continue as well (Table 3.2).

In 2004, several African countries not receiving SCI support began to develop their own schistosomiasis control programs, and SCI donated small quantities of PZQ to non-governmental organizations (NGOs) and government agencies working in those countries. Recipients included the World Food Program and ICS (a Dutch-Kenyan NGO working in Kenya), along with government pro-grams in Cameroon, Guinea, Kenya, Malawi, and Mozambique. The SCI hoped that its assistance to the six main country control programs would stimulate demand for PZQ in other African countries and that this demand would then be

Table 3.2 | PZQ delivered by SCI, 2003–2007 (Actual), purchases and donations

MILLIONS OF PRAZIQUANTEL TABLETS DELIVERED/CALENDAR YEAR

Country	2003	2004	2005	2006	2007	Total
Burkina Faso	-	6.15	4.48	2.5	7.0	20.13
Mali	-	4	13	3	8.85	28.85
Niger	-	4.68	9.26	2	7.5	23.44
Tanzania (incl. Zanzibar)	-	4.85	13.7	8	10.2	36.75
Uganda	3.5	9	2	3.66	7.5	25.66
Zambia	-	1.5	4	3.3	4.2	13
Total	3.5	30.18	46.44	22.46	45.25	147.83
Donated[a]	-	-	13.7	10	10	33.7
Purchased	3.5	30.18	32.74	12.46	35.25	114.73

Note. Tablets were procured from the following companies: Shin Poong, MedPharm, Pharmchem, IDA, TPI, and Shelys. From Schistosomiasis Control Initiative, London, 2008. Used with permission.

[a] The donated tablets came from MedPharm.

funded (and sustained) by other donors, such as the World Bank, the African Development Bank, the EU, and USAID. SCI's efforts have generated some additional funds, but whether the financing will be sustained remains to be seen.

A major factor that assisted in the Gates Foundation's decision to support SCI was the falling price of PZQ. Starting in the late 1990s and through the early 2000s, the price of PZQ dropped sharply from its initial concessionary price of $1 per 600-mg tablet. The decline in prices resulted from a combination of factors: technical innovation in production processes, competition from new suppliers in South Korea and China, and the expiration of the original product patents held by Bayer and E. Merck and of the later process patents held by Shin Poong (which expired in 1994). Chinese companies had copied the production process for the active ingredient and were thus poised to respond to increased demand for PZQ due to the increased funding for control through SCI. In August 2004, SCI identified eight potential suppliers of PZQ, with prices ranging from $0.174 to $0.072 per tablet (Table 3.3). At this much lower price, the product became more affordable to both individuals and governments in Africa.

SCI found that the quality and price of PZQ tablets are determined in large part by the quality and price of the active ingredient, as well as by the size of the specific order and the scale of a purchaser's commitment to future procurement over coming

Table 3.3 | Potential PZQ suppliers, August 2004

POTENTIAL PZQ SUPPLIER	PRICE (USD) AT AUGUST 2004 (CIF)	WHO-RECOGNIZED	SUPPLIER OF ACTIVE INGREDIENT
GSK	0.096	Yes	Yixing City Ying Yu Medicine Chemicals Co., Ltd
IDA	0.087	Yes	Shanghai OSD (and others)
MedPharm (CIPLA)	0.001[a]	Yes	Hang Zhou Minsheng Pharmaceutical, Ltd.
Panacea Biotech	0.174	Yes	Shin Poong
Pharmchem	0.074	No	Nanjing Pharmaceuticals Factory Co., Ltd.
Shin Poong	0.072	Yes	Shin Poong
TPI (prices at Nov 04)	0.078	No	Shanghai OSD
Shelys (prices at Nov 04)	0.078	No	Shanghai OSD

Note. From Schistosomiasis Control Initiative, London, 2005. Adapted with permission.

[a] MedPharm's very low price in this tender is because it agreed to donate 13.7 million tablets in 2004. It also bid on CIPLA's behalf at the price of about US$0.075 per tablet.

years. Two companies, Shin Poong (Korea) and Shanghai OSD (China), met international quality standards for their products, so they could provide the active ingredient for PZQ to WHO, UN agencies, and various manufacturers.

SCI also sought to change perceptions of both the disease and the treatment by both global and national actors, and thereby promote adoption. In collaboration with WHO and supported by the advocacy efforts of the WHO-initiated Partners for Parasite Control, SCI actively approached ministries of health in Africa (through personal visits, publications, and training programs) to make them more aware of the low price of PZQ and the high morbidity due to schistosomiasis—and therefore the cost-effectiveness of treatment using PZQ. These outreach efforts (combined with the incentive of financial support) helped persuade a good number of African countries to become interested in schistosomiasis control and to compete for SCI support, and thereby adopt PZQ treatment as a national priority.

SCI's Strategies to Expand Access

SCI developed and implemented six strategies to increase access to PZQ in Africa in their scaling-up efforts. These were the following:

- *Procurement*: Use external financing (from the Bill & Melinda Gates Foundation) to procure PZQ for six national schistosomiasis control programs and shape the market for PZQ in Africa
- *Collaboration*: Collaborate with international agencies to stimulate national demand for schistosomiasis control and for PZQ
- *Information*: Improve information flows about PZQ, its safety, efficacy, and low price
- *Registration*: Stimulate the registration of PZQ in endemic countries to create conditions for competitive tenders
- *Local formulation*: Stimulate the formulation of PZQ in Africa by manufacturers with Good Manufacturing Practice (GMP) approval
- *Donation*: Receive donations of PZQ and use them to support national control programs

These six strategies were designed to help correct market failures that adversely affected the PZQ market in Africa. The overall goal was to create a well functioning market, with multiple producers competing in a serious way for government tenders issued by national procurement agencies. This model would assure good quality, low prices, and continuing supply to government control programs. Below we review each strategy, its implementation, and limitations.

Procurement

SCI used procurement as a means to promote PZQ access for national control programs and also to stimulate competition for the product in Africa, thereby seeking to address some aspects of imperfect competition (a classic market failure). SCI used its purchasing power (from the Gates Foundation grant) to encourage several manufacturers and tablet formulators to develop their production capability and expand their presence in the African market. SCI continued making large purchases through 2006 and has funds to continue through 2008. SCI decided not to award its original tender in 2004 to a single supplier but to apportion it among the four bidders who prequalified with SCI for the tender (to encourage involvement by more manufacturers): Shin Poong, a for-profit private pharmaceutical company in South Korea; IDA, a nonprofit pharmaceutical procurement agency based in Holland; MedPharm, a pharmaceutical supplier and generic contract manufacturer with a donation program based in the United States; and Pharmchem/Flamingo, a pharmaceutical formulator in India. Two other companies in Tanzania, TPI and Shelys, were included in SCI's procurement after the original tender in order to encourage African formulation of PZQ.

These two Tanzanian companies (discussed below) were found to meet U.S. Pharmacopoeia standards (after tablet sample analysis conducted by SCI on all batches purchased from all sources), and their price quotation was competitive with the other suppliers. SCI thus used its procurement opportunities to shape the market for PZQ in Africa and encourage competition among different kinds of companies as ways to reduce prices and create affordability.

Shin Poong entered the PZQ market in the 1980s, when it developed a new synthesis process that significantly reduced the production cost of the active ingredient. This technical innovation contributed to declines in the price of PZQ tablets by over 90% during the period 1990 to 2004. In the late 1990s, Shin Poong began to market its PZQ tablets in Africa through direct sales in countries and contacts with WHO, SCI, and the World Bank. Shin Poong's sales in Africa initially were small but have kept growing, making the company the leading supplier of PZQ to Uganda, Tanzania, and Zambia (through SCI) by 2006.

The International Dispensary Association, known as IDA, is a leading nonprofit procurement agency based in Holland. IDA developed a successful business of selling competitively priced generic pharmaceutical products for developing countries while guaranteeing international quality standards through extensive in-house quality control. IDA initially manufactured some drugs in wholly owned facilities but by 2006 had abandoned direct manufacture and instead purchased drugs from suppliers worldwide (especially from China and India), thereby providing lower priced but high quality products. IDA seeks the cheapest and best quality product at the time (therefore using a number of manufacturers), and then packs under the IDA label. Furthermore, IDA has worked closely with procurement agencies in developing countries to gain their confidence in IDA products and ensure that IDA products are registered in the destination countries. SCI purchased PZQ from IDA in 2003 and 2004, along with albendazole (for treatment of various common worm infections transmitted through soil) (see Table 3.3).

The third major supplier for SCI was MedPharm, a U.S.-based pharmaceutical company. In 2004, SCI and WHO were approached by MedPharm to consider whether SCI's objectives and activities were suitable for the company's drug donation program. While running a wholesale pharmaceutical business, MedPharm also promotes and supports deworming programs in the developing world through a drug donation initiative. In the donation program, MedPharm buys drugs from European and Indian formulators using donated funds from a Canadian NGO (called Escarpment Biosphere Foundation) through the Canadian Humanitarian Trust. In February 2004, MedPharm donated 680,000 PZQ and 1 million albendazole tablets to SCI for use in Zanzibar and Zambia. In June 2004, MedPharm pledged to donate a further 13.7 million PZQ tablets, which were delivered by the end of 2004, then added a further 12 million tablets in 2005. MedPharm suggested it could repeat the donation annually for the life of the original SCI project (through 2007). This pledge was met in 2004 and 2005. MedPharm then pledged to meet most of the needs of Tanzania in 2007 through its donated product.

Collaboration

To promote increased attention to schistosomiasis control in national health policies in African countries, SCI has collaborated with international agencies and other organizations. Three key international players are the World Health Organization, the World Food Program, and the World Bank. These activities have promoted both global and national adoption of PZQ use.

The World Health Organization has played a major role in setting global policy on schistosomiasis control and has been a central collaborator for SCI and global advocate for PZQ treatment. In May 2001, WHO set a global priority for the control of schistosomiasis and soil transmitted helminths (STH) by passing resolution 54.19 at the World Health Assembly. As noted above, this resolution states that all member states where these infections are endemic should provide regular treatment for schistosomiasis and intestinal helminths to 75% of all school-aged children by the year 2010. This statement of global adoption helped pave the way for SCI activities at the national level and helped stimulate national interest in control programs and PZQ. To create a positive collaboration, SCI included an ex-officio representative of WHO on its board of directors and a representative of the Special Programme for Research and Training in Tropical Diseases (TDR) on the expert advisory committee for the Schistosomiasis Research Program.

SCI also collaborated with the World Food Program (WFP) to stimulate demand for PZQ through its school feeding program. In the early 2000s, the WFP fed about 5 million children in countries in sub-Saharan Africa. With funding from the Canadian International Development Agency (CIDA), the WFP began efforts to deworm children widely and, where applicable, to treat children within the WFP school feeding program using albendazole against intestinal helminths and PZQ in schistosomiasis-endemic areas. The annual deworming was expected to increase the benefit of the food to the children rather than feed the worms that the children were harboring. The WFP also began looking for continued funding to support the deworming program since it did not have guaranteed funds to purchase PZQ or albendazole. SCI provided small quantities of these medicines to the WFP for use in countries not selected for SCI-supported programs.

SCI also worked with the World Bank's education program to stimulate schistosomiasis control programs in Africa. As part of its education reform efforts, the World Bank, with UNICEF and WHO, created the FRESH strategy (Focusing Resources on Effective School Health), which included deworming and other health interventions inside schools. The Bank offered to assist countries engaged in education reform with a school health component. As a result, the Bank committed over $1 billion to school health in 20 countries. Only a few countries, however, used the FRESH funds for school health (as of summer 2006). SCI and WHO have continued seeking ways to promote more effective use of this financing source for deworming through the education sector.

Information

A third major strategy adopted by SCI was to improve information flows about PZQ. For more than a decade prior to 2003, there was a serious lack of information about PZQ in Africa, which held back sales and consumption in many countries. First, PZQ manufacturers were not aware of sales opportunities in African countries because they did not have an established market presence there. Second, national governments in Africa were not aware of potential suppliers and the lower prices for PZQ then available.

Part of this information problem resulted from national drug procurement agencies in African countries that had cumbersome mechanisms for tendering, making it difficult to learn about new suppliers or their competitive prices and acceptable standards. In addition, national decision-makers about tenders were often committees that were content to accept monopoly prices from single prequalified sources rather than run a bona fide and open tendering process. By addressing these information gaps that affect both sellers and buyers, SCI has improved the market functioning for PZQ and improved the chances of effective competition in the tendering process.

Registration

A fourth strategy was to encourage the registration of PZQ products in different national markets in Africa. If a product is not registered, then it cannot be considered for government procurement or private sector purchase. Even the major supplier Shin Poong, for example, had not registered its PZQ products in many possible national markets in Africa. SCI worked with Shin Poong (Korea), Med-Pharm (USA), and Flamingo (India) to help each company with the registration process for PZQ products in several African countries. Subsequently CIPLA (India) solicited SCI assistance in registering PZQ, and CIPLA in 2006 started a joint venture drug production facility in Uganda which may formulate PZQ. The result has been to increase competition for PZQ in national markets and thereby contribute to lower purchase prices for governments.

For example, in Burkina Faso, the national procurement agency (CAMEG) wanted to buy PZQ tablets for the national schistosomiasis control program. Histori-cally, they had secured prices at approximately US$ 0.14 per tablet. By registering Shin Poong and Pharmchem/Flamingo in Burkina Faso, SCI increased the number of recognized suppliers from one, IDA (CIPLA), to three. (The Pharmchem/Fla-mingo partnership subsequently dissolved.) As a result, in 2004, CAMEG purchased PZQ at US$ 0.09 CIF (including the costs of insurance and freight) per tablet, sub-stantially below the price originally offered by IDA when it was the sole seller in that country. It is expected that continuing market competition will maintain the lower prices for PZQ available in Burkina Faso after 2006. SCI also supported a direct order of PZQ by the Pharmacie Populaire du Mali, resulting in the purchase of 2 million tablets at US$.08 each (compared to a previous price paid of $0.12).

Local Formulation

SCI has also supported African companies that formulate praziquantel. Over the past decade, several African companies have formulated PZQ for sale (mostly to their own governments). Those companies include Cosmos (Kenya), EIPICO (Egypt), Shelys (Tanzania), and an ill-fated Shin Poong joint venture in Sudan. However, none of these companies has successfully marketed its product outside of its own country. EIPICO supplied almost 70 million tablets to the domestic Egyp-tian market (formulated with active ingredient from Shin Poong), but demand in Egypt has declined since 2002 after prevalence there dropped to below 5%. Several established manufacturers of PZQ's active ingredient (including Shanghai OSD and Shin Poong) have indicated their willingness to supply active ingredient to a WHO-approved GMP African company to formulate tablets. Shanghai OSD has already supplied active ingredient for testing by the UK Government Chemist and to African manufacturers to validate their formulation process. These develop-ments suggest that African pharmaceutical companies could produce PZQ at a quality and price acceptable to donors, international agencies, and national gov-ernments (depending in part on the size and duration of the orders).

Action Medeor, a leading German NGO, is also seeking to stimulate drug formulation in Africa. Action Medeor has developed a new business model (similar to
the IDA model) in which drugs formulated in Africa can be purchased for international distribution. Like IDA, Action Medeor would quality-assure the drugs
and test each batch. One of Action Medeor's first suppliers would be based in
Tanzania. Another group with similar objectives and working methods to IDA is
La Centrale Humanitaire Médico-Pharmaceutique (France). This not-for-profit
agency provides both drug and equipment procurement services and technical
support through consultancies.

Recent changes in the Tanzanian market for PZQ illustrate the opportunities
and challenges in seeking to promote local formulation in Africa. In 2001, the
Tanzanian Food and Drug Authority declared that all companies wishing to sell
medicines to the Tanzanian government must be approved by WHO for Good
Manufacturing Practice (GMP). The deadline for compliance was June 2005.
WHO GMP approval is an internationally recognized endorsement for the standard of manufacturing practices and the quality of drugs. This decision was taken
to address problems of substandard quality, poorly formulated drugs in the Tanzanian market. These substandard medicines included both donated products and
locally manufactured products.

Tanzania has seven domestic pharmaceutical companies that are largely dependent on government contracts, and several Tanzanian companies responded to the
new government policy by investing considerable private funds in their plants to
meet both Tanzanian GMP standards and international GMP standards. Over
the two years from 2002 to 2004, $15 million was invested in the Tanzanian
pharmaceutical industry. The majority of these funds came from private sources,
including the CDC Capital Partners of the UK, a risk capital investor in emerging
markets. At least three companies achieved GMP certification by January 2005. It
is expected that these GMP-certified companies would explore opportunities to
export their drugs to other markets in Africa. Two Tanzanian pharmaceutical
firms supplied PZQ to SCI at competitive prices in 2005.

The Tanzanian Pharmaceutical Industries Limited (TPI) is a privatized pharmaceutical company whose management has worked to turn around a failing
nationalized business and return it to profitability. The company's management
invested considerable private funds to achieve GMP standards by replacing obso-
lete facilities with a new plant and machinery. TPI was selected by Action Medeor
as a potential supplier for its proposed procurement venture to internationally distribute drugs formulated in Africa. TPI is also the chosen supplier for the proposed

venture of the Thai AIDS advocate, Krisana Kraisintu. Kraisintu expanded the availability of ARVs to Thailand and now works with TPI to formulate ARVs in Tanzania to the same international standards achieved in Thailand.[22] She demonstrated that ARVs could be formulated in Thailand to international quality and price standards. Her success was confirmed when Médecins Sans Frontières International started purchasing and distributing TPI's products. TPI previously formulated PZQ, but recently outsourced PZQ contracts to another Tanzanian pharmaceutical company, Shelys.

Shelys is the largest pharmaceutical company in East Africa. The company has ambitious expansion plans and by 2006 had completed a new facility close to Dar es Salaam. Prior to 2002, Shelys formulated PZQ for a small domestic market (100,000 tablets per year). Samples of tablets formulated by Shelys have been analyzed and found acceptable at U.S. Pharmacopoeia and European Pharmacopoeia standards. Shelys facilities were reported to be WHO GMP compliant by June 2005.

In 2006, both Shelys and TPI were formulating PZQ with active ingredient supplied by a Chinese firm, Shanghai OSD, and were confident that their tablets would meet international standards. The ultimate test for both companies will be their ability to satisfy the standards of other African governments in terms of both quality and price. SCI tested the product of both companies at the Laboratory of the UK Government Chemist, and they conformed to US Pharmacopoeia standards in 2005 and 2006. Both TPI and Shelys indicated that they will proceed to register their companies and products in Uganda and other African countries and hope to secure the export licenses needed for entry to foreign markets.

Donation

In contrast to other neglected diseases, schistosomiasis has not been the target of a significant corporate donation program. The originating company for PZQ, Bayer, refused for many years to provide substantial quantities of the drug for donation, although numerous approaches were made by WHO and others. Bayer's response was to provide only relatively small quantities of PZQ for donation in Africa—in contrast to the major donation programs initiated by Merck for ivermectin, Pfizer for azithromycin, GlaxoSmithKline (GSK) for albendazole, and various companies for AIDS-related drugs. While Bayer did not take any major steps toward SCI, MedPharm (as noted above) approached the new organization and offered to donate substantial quantities of PZQ to the organization (providing nearly 14 million tablets in 2005, 10 million in 2006, and 6 million in 2007).

It is uncertain how the drug donations by MedPharm have affected the development of a market for PZQ in Africa or how this donation program could affect market development if donations were continued in the future. A drug donation program, for example, could have the unintended effect of suppressing the development of an African market for PZQ by making free product widely available. The extent of this impact, however, would depend on the size and duration of donations of praziquantel. Another risk is the program's long-term sustainability (similar to questions raised about other single-product donation programs). As of 2006, however, the MedPharm donation was a relatively small proportion of SCI's total delivery of PZQ, suggesting a relatively low risk of negatively affecting the African market for PZQ (although they could be concentrated and significant in particular countries or for specific companies).

Another possibility would be to use donated funds to purchase PZQ formulated in Africa by local companies. This approach would support local production and sales of good quality drugs at competitive prices in schistosomiasis-endemic countries. This approach could also stimulate the development of an African market for PZQ, which could help ensure continued availability of treatment at good quality and affordable prices. In 2008, however, MedPharm was unable to make a donation of praziquantel to SCI.

Challenges of Sustaining Access (Phase 4)

Through the combination of these six strategies, SCI dramatically expanded access to PZQ by growing the global supply of PZQ and increasing global demand for PZQ. As shown in Figure 3.1, SCI delivered a total of 40.29 million treatments in its six countries in Africa, to about 19.28 million individuals, from 2003 through June 2008. About half the treatments were first treatments with praziquantel, and about half second and third treatments. While this accomplishment represents a significant success for SCI, the effort has reached only about 10% of the population estimated to be infected with schistosomiasis and needing treatment with praziquantel. In addition, major challenges remain in providing the recommended repeat treatments with PZQ to assure adequate control of the symptoms and morbidity associated with the disease.

SCI's ability to expand access to PZQ has depended in part on the low price of the active ingredient. Since 2002, the active ingredient price, which largely determined the factory gate price of the tablets, has ranged from a low of $76 per kilo to a high of $103 per kilo. The fluctuation resulted partly from the weakness of the U.S. dollar. At $76 per kilo, the active ingredient in each tablet cost about

Figure 3.1 | **Annual treatments in the six SCI countries, 2003-2008**

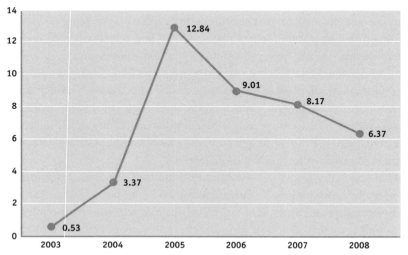

Number of treatments (millions)

Note. This figure shows the number of praziquantel treatments delivered per year by SCI-supported national programs in Uganda, Burkina Faso, Niger, Mali, Tanzania, and Zambia. The data for 2008 are as of June 1 in that year. The data include new treatments plus second and third treatments for some individuals; approximately 40.29 million total treatments were delivered to about 19.28 million individuals—out of an estimated 180 million people in sub-Saharan Africa who need treatment for schistosomiasis. Data from SCI.

US$0.046, compared to US$0.062 at $103 per kilo. For the near future, the increased demand from SCI's purchases could have two possible effects. First, increased demand could push up the price for PZQ if supplies are limited and companies try to profit from the rising demand. Second, the price could be pushed lower, as new companies initiate production and compete for a share of the growing market. So far, the impact of SCI's increased demand has been the latter— driving down the price of PZQ tablets in the global market.

Future consumption of PZQ in Africa will depend on a number of factors. First is the treatment strategy adopted by the national control program. WHO recommends morbidity control as the overall goal, with new treatment programs first targeting high-infection populations. After these communities have been treated, a routine maintenance program aimed at school-aged children can be implemented. To reach this stage will take time—probably up to five years to reach all high-risk populations. However, once this coverage has been achieved, it should be possible for national governments to continue to provide treatment for the newly exposed and at-risk populations. Consumption thus will depend on the treatment strategies adopted by national programs and the evolution of the national programs.

Most importantly, the development of national treatment programs for schistosomiasis in Africa will depend on additional external funding (unless national governments can be persuaded to use their own resources) and on the development of national capacity to implement the programs. SCI is trying to address both of these concerns. SCI has been seeking to secure long-term institutional funding from various external donors (outside the Bill & Melinda Gates Foundation) and also to support capacity-building in national ministries of health for schistosomiasis control programs. An important step in finding additional financing occurred in September 2006, when the U.S. Agency for International Development awarded a $100 million collaborative program to RTI International to implement integrated disease control for seven neglected tropical diseases, including schistosomiasis. SCI was named as one of five partner organizations collaborating with RTI, and Alan Fenwick was appointed project director, a post he held for four months before reverting to his position with SCI. The new program of integrated disease control was initially expected to operate in five African countries (Tanzania, Uganda, Burkina Faso, Mali, and Niger) with plans to expand to other countries and continents.

SCI estimated the consumption of PZQ in Africa during 2004 at approximately 40 million tablets. In 2005, this increased to about 70 million. With recent estimates of 180 million infected in sub-Saharan Africa, the amount of drug needed to treat all these people one time would be approximately 600 million tablets. If mass treatment were employed in high prevalence areas, the needed tablets could be half as much again. Based on these figures and the likelihood of some expansion to other countries with active programs, SCI estimated that around 260 million tablets might be required by 2007 and a similar amount per year for five successive years. This level of treatment would require approximately $20 million per year (at US$0.08 for a 600 mg tablet) for the drug costs alone. It is highly unlikely that African countries would be willing to provide these funds from their own domestic health budgets, which tend to be a patchwork of externally financed projects and donations. To achieve this level of treatment, therefore, donors will need to step forward to support national schistosomiasis control programs and the implementation of large-scale mass treatment. Between 2007 and 2010, treatment programs could continue to require 250 million tablets annually, assuming that SCI and WHO advocacy continues to be successful. After this initial phase of mass treatment, consumption could settle at around 50 million tablets annually, assuming that most high-infection populations are treated first and that programs then shift to recurrent treatment of school children living close to lakes, rivers, and irrigation schemes. These estimates assume successful fundraising by SCI and WHO—and the newly formed Global Network for Neglected Tropical Disease Control (www.gnntdc.org). If sufficient funds are not secured, then consumption of PZQ could collapse—undermining any chance for sustained use of the technology.

All five suppliers of the active ingredient for PZQ have indicated that they would willingly expand production in response to serious orders. The supply of PZQ, therefore, could meet the demand—which depends largely on national government decisions on health priorities and international donor decisions on available funding.

The announcement of a new donation program in 2007 opened up another possible avenue for supporting access to PZQ into the future. WHO officials had spoken for years with Bayer (which sold PZQ for both human and veterinary use), with no progress on persuading the company to make signigicant product donations, and then met with representatives of E. Merck (the manufacturer of PZQ) twice in 2006. As Lorenzo Savioli, director of WHO's Department of Control of Neglected Tropical Diseases, put it to the *Financial Times*, "Bayer tells us to talk to Merck, and Merck says to talk to Bayer."[23] In April 2007, finally, E. Merck agreed to donate some praziquantel through WHO for schistosomiasis control. The initial agreement was for 200 million tablets over 10 years, which will offer about 8 million additional treatments per year for school-aged children—out of an estimated 180 million people in need of treatment in sub-Saharan Africa. WHO officials applauded the new donation and hoped that it would be used to demonstrate further the highly positive health effects of treatment with praziquantel and perhaps lead to further donations.

Conclusions

SCI's concerted efforts to increase access to praziquantel in Africa has shown that it is possible to increase the demand for PZQ and reduce the price of the drug in African countries (and thereby increase both adoption and affordability), that manufacturers can be induced to enter the PZQ market and expand their production of the active ingredient (and thereby expand availability), and that competition can be created among producers of the end product (and thereby expand affordability for both governments and consumers) (see Table 3.4 for a summary of access barriers and strategies). SCI has also demonstrated that a single major buyer can expand access to an essential drug and can help push down prices as long as the buyer has adequate funds for purchases. (SCI thus has what economists call "oligopsony power," in which a small number of purchasers can affect the market price for a product through the sheer volume they buy.)

The major issue now is how to ensure *continued access* to PZQ in Africa after SCI stops its funding of PZQ purchases as supported by the Gates Foundation grant. Sustaining access to PZQ over the long term will depend on heightened adoption—the development of both government and consumer demand for the product. Any decision by governments to use public financial resources to purchase PZQ will depend on their perception that the product is affordable and that the treatment is effective and important for the wellbeing of their populations at risk of schistosomiasis. In late 2006, SCI was examining its options after funding from the Gates Foundation stops; that time was postponed by an additional grant of $4.128 million that the foundation awarded in 2006 (largely to cover budget deficits due to the weak dollar). And in 2006, the Gates Foundation agreed to add a further $10 million to SCI to continue the program and integrate other diseases in selected countries. Some advisors to the SCI believe that other donors can be persuaded to take on the commitment for schistosomiasis treatment in Africa. Others suggest that integration with other infectious disease control programs could provide the answer (presumably still supported by international aid).[24] But few believe that African countries will be willing to pay the costs of schistosomiasis treatment from their own government budgets in the short or the medium term; local funds are typically consumed largely by personnel costs. Sustaining access to PZQ thus will continue to depend on flows of external aid to African governments for some time.

The situation at mid 2008 provided some optimism for continued external support to supply praziquantel in Africa: In 2006 USAID launched a 5-year $100 million multi-country project to support integrated control of Neglected Tropical Diseases (NTDs). In September 2006, the U.S. consulting company RTI was awarded a contract to manage the funds. In FY 2007, $13 million were allocated for implementing integrated control of NTDs and another $13 million came through for FY 2008. It is hoped that for FY2009, up to $25 million will be allocated by the U.S. Congress, providing the first two years have shown adequate progress. SCI received a grant from RTI to implement the project in Burkina Faso and Niger, to assist with implementation in Uganda, and to procure praziquantel for 2007–2008 (and probably through 2011). This USAID project, therefore, will help ensure that some praziquantel will continue to be delivered to Burkina Faso, Ghana, Mali, Niger, Uganda, Sierra Leone and South Sudan, until 2011. Then in February 2008, outgoing President George W. Bush unexpectedly announced that the U.S. will provide $350 million for the control of NTDs and urged other G8 countries and other donors to bring the amount to $1 billion as soon as possible. If this request is met, external funds for PZQ supplies could be maintained for some years to come. Advocacy efforts by the WHO and others have resulted in two additional partners coming forward. The first is Legatum, a private equity company, which has donated $8.9 million for the control of NTDs in Burundi and Rwanda. The second is the Bill & Melinda Gates Foundation, which has initiated meetings aimed at raising the $1 billion needed to control NTDs in Africa.

The development of a consumer-based market for PZQ will depend on adoption at the individual patient level, along with an ability to recognize and seek treatment for schistosomiasis. At present, there is a regular (though small) private-sector market for PZQ, available generally in private pharmacies in the cities and in some government health centers in rural areas throughout sub-Saharan Africa. The price in these outlets is often 10 to 30 times the price obtained by SCI in international tenders. This consumer price typically includes the procurement costs of the national procurement agency, the distribution costs, and the pharmacy's profit. The middle class urban population can meet these costs with little difficulty. But this private pharmacy market is unlikely to be a major factor in national treatment of schistosomiasis because rural populations (where the disease is most prevalent) are believed to be unwilling and unable to pay these market prices. Whether rural residents would be willing to pay for treatment with PZQ (perhaps at a price close to cost) if they knew they were infected with schistosomiasis remains to be seen.

Changing perceptions—including global, national and end-user perceptions—about both the disease and its treatment have contributed to the expanding access to PZQ. In the six countries directly supported by SCI and in the five others partially supported, national and end-user knowledge of the symptoms of schistosomiasis and the appropriate treatment have significantly increased.[25] With over 30 million people having received treatment, many of them at least twice, awareness and demand for further treatment are now significantly higher at both community and government levels. Nonetheless, there is still a long way to go before the target of the WHO resolution will be reached in non-SCI countries or can continue to be reached in the SCI countries.

Table 3.4 | Praziquantel access table

	BARRIER	STRATEGY	SPECIFIC ACTION
ARCHITECTURE	Need for a global champion to promote treatment of schistosomiasis	Identify effective leadership and design partnerships for the technology	The Gates Foundation provided a major grant to establish the Schistosomiasis Control Initiative (SCI) and a grant to WHO to support and expand ongoing activities
ADOPTION	Low priority given to schistosomiasis by international agencies, donors, and governments	Assure adequate quality of the product to persuade end-users to adopt the technology	SCI collaborated with WHO and other international agencies to stimulate demand for schistosomiasis control and for PZQ
	Low government demand	Work with governments to give higher priority to treatment of schistosomiasis	SCI representatives visited African countries to negotiate agreements on schistosomiasis control and on providing PZQ with support from Gates Foundation and other sources
	Low consumer demand	Create information campaigns to raise public awareness of both schistosomiasis and its treatment	SCI supported the production of videos and other materials on schistosomiasis control and treatment to raise awareness in both developed and developing countries
AFFORDABILITY	Lack of affordability by both governments and end-users	Improve external financing for procurement and seek out donations	SCI used Gates Foundation support and sought additional sources of financing for procurement and donations of PZQ for SCI programs in African countries
		Produce price reductions by creating more competition among providers	SCI supported PZQ registration in African countries to create more competition for government procurement
AVAILABILITY	Lack of information about sales opportunities, existing supplies, and price from different suppliers	Improve information flows to both sellers and buyers	SCI worked with providers to assist them in market entry in Africa and worked with buyers in Africa to make them aware of prices and alternative suppliers

----

Endnotes

[1]   D. H. Wegner, "The Profile of the Trematodicidal Compound Praziquantel," *Arzneimittel-Forschung/Drug Research* 34 (1984):1132–1136.

[2]   Jürgen Seubert, Rolf Pohlke, and F. Loebich, "Synthesis and Properties of Praziquantel, a Novel Broad Spectrum Anthelmintic with Excellent Activity against Schistosomes and Cestodes," *Experientia* 33 (1977): 1036–1037.

[3]   Peter Andrews, Herbert Thomas, Rolf Pohlke, and Jürgen Seubert, "Praziquantel," *Medicinal Research Reviews* 3, no. 2 (1983): 147–200.

[4]   Wegner.

[5]   Andrew Davis, "Antischistosomal Drugs and Clinical Practice," in *Human Schistosomiasis*, eds. Peter Jordan, Gerald Webbe, and Robert Sturrock (Cambridge: Cambridge University Press, 1993), 367–404.

[6]   Michael R. Reich and Ramesh Govindaraj, "Dilemmas in Drug Development for Tropical Diseases: Experiences with Praziquantel," *Health Policy* 44 (1998): 1–18.

[7]   Michael R. Reich, ed., *International Strategies for Tropical Disease Treatments: Experiences with Praziquantel* (Geneva: WHO, Action Program on Essential Drugs, 1998, WHO/DAP/CTD/98.5), 19.

[8]   Charles H. King and Adel A. Mahmoud, "Drugs Five Years Later: Praziquantel," *Annals of Internal Medicine* 110, no. 4 (1989): 290–296.

[9]   World Health Organization, *The Control of Schistosomiasis: Report of a WHO Expert Committee*. Technical Report Series, 728 (Geneva: WHO, 1985).

[10]   World Health Organization.

[11]   Michael Doenhoff and Livia Pica-Mattoccia, "Praziquantel for the Treatment of Schistosomiasis: Its Use for Control in Areas with Endemic Disease and Prospects for Drug Resistance," *Expert Review of Anti-Infective Therapy* 4, no. 2 (2006): 1–12.

[12]   Alan Fenwick, et al., "Drugs for the Control of Parasitic Diseases: Current Status and Development in Schistosomiasis," *Trends in Parasitology* 19, no. 11 (2003): 509–515.

[13]   Reich and Govindaraj.

[14]   Amadou Garba, Seydou Touré, Robert Dembelé, Elisa Bosque-Oliva, and Alan Fenwick, "Implementation of National Schistosomiasis Control Programmes in West Africa," *Trends in Parasitology* 22, no. 7 (2006): 322–326.

[15]   Reich and Govindaraj.

[16]   J. A. Utroska, M. G. Chen, H.Dixon, Soon-Young Yoon, Margaretha Helling-Borda, Hans V. Hogerzeil, et al., *An Estimate of the Global Needs for Praziquantel within Schistosomiasis Control Programs* (Geneva: WHO, 1989).

[17]   Reich and Govindaraj.

[18]   Schistosomiasis Control Initiative, *The Control of Schistosomiasis in Africa. Proposal Submitted to the Bill & Melinda Gates Foundation* (London: SCI, Imperial College, March 2002), 3.

[19] World Health Organization, *Schistosomiasis and Soil-Transmitted Helminths: Fifty-Fourth World Health Assembly Resolution WHA54.19* (Geneva: WHO, May 22, 2001).

[20] Schistosomiasis Control Initiative, 3.

[21] Harvard School of Public Health, *Proposal for a Planning Grant: The Schistosomiasis Control Initiative, Submitted to the Bill & Melinda Gates Foundation* (Boston, MA: Harvard School of Public Health, May 2000), 2.

[22] Julie Clayton, "Out of Thailand, into Africa," *Nature* 430 (2004): 136–137.

[23] Andrew Jack, "WHO Calls on German Groups to Donate Drugs," *Financial Times*, October 25, 2006.

[24] David M. Molyneux, Peter J. Hotez, and Alan Fenwick, "Rapid-Impact Interventions: How a Policy of Integrated Control for Africa's Neglected Tropical Diseases Could Benefit the Poor," *PLoS Medicine* 2 (2005): 1064–1070.

[25] Garba et al.; Narcis B. Kabatereine, Fiona M. Fleming, Ursuline Nyandindi, James C. Mwanza, and Lynsey Blair, "The Control of Schistosomiasis and Soil-Transmitted Helminths in East Africa," *Trends in Parasitology* 22, no. 7 (2006): 332–339.

CHAPTER 4

HEPATITIS B VACCINE:

Access to Vaccines

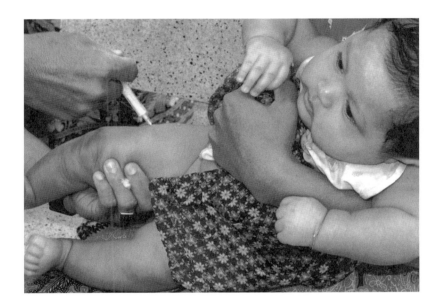

HEPATITIS B IS A SERIOUS LIVER INFECTION CAUSED BY THE HEPATITIS B VIRUS (HBV). HBV is transmitted through blood and infected bodily fluids. The virus can spread through direct blood-to-blood contact, unprotected sex, unsafe injections and blood transfusions, and from a woman infected with HBV to her newborn during the delivery process. Because of similar transmission paths, there is a high degree of HBV and HIV co-infection. An estimated 10% of people living with HIV worldwide also have HBV infection.

When people first contract HBV, they experience a period of acute infection, in which they may either have no symptoms or become seriously ill. While many people recover completely from the acute infection, those who still have the virus in their blood for more than six months are diagnosed with chronic infection. Most of the disease burden associated with HBV is from the chronic condition. Though many chronic sufferers do not feel sick for decades after infection, in later life they can die from cirrhosis (a serious liver condition characterized by irreversible scarring of the liver) and liver cancer (a malignant tumor of the liver, also called hepatocellular carcinoma). Approximately 1.8 billion people (one third of the world's population) have serological evidence of HBV infection. Of these, WHO estimates that 360 million people have chronic infection, and at least 600,000 chronically infected people die annually from liver cancer and cirrhosis.[1] Those people who have hepatitis B but do not have symptoms (because their immune systems do not see the virus as foreign) are known as carriers and can unintentionally infect other people.

Age is a key factor in determining the outcome of HBV infection. Ninety percent of adults with acute infection recover and rid the virus from their blood, so that only 5–10% go on to develop chronic infection. However, of infants who become infected with HBV in the first year of life, 80–90% will develop the chronic condition, and 30–50% of children aged one to four years will do so.[2] Preventing HBV infection among children ages five years and younger is therefore a priority in tackling hepatitis B, and this is now possible through vaccination. Estimates suggest that at least 85–90% of deaths associated with hepatitis B can be prevented using this technology.[3]

The HBV vaccine first became available in 1981, but introduction in developing countries in the 1980s and 1990s was slow and limited. This case study examines the barriers to access for the hepatitis B vaccine during this time period and how key groups in the architecture of hepatitis B vaccine—including both WHO and a product champion known as the International Task Force on Hepatitis B Immunization—effectively undertook a series of actions to solve major problems

of availability, affordability, and adoption in collaboration with a range of partners, including international agencies, private foundations, non-profit organizations, vaccine producers, and developing country governments. The combined
efforts led to a change in the global architecture for hepatitis B vaccine access,
resulting in dramatic increases in the vaccine's use in the 2000s.

Product Development (Phase 1)

While studying hepatitis during and after World War II, the British doctor F. O.
MacCallum identified two types of the disease and named them hepatitis A and
hepatitis B (see Table 4.1 for a description of the different types of viral hepatitis).[4] In the 1950s and 1960s, researchers attempted to find the causal agent for
these two categories of hepatitis. An important breakthrough came in the 1960s,
when Baruch Blumberg discovered a blood test for the surface component of the
hepatitis B virus.[5] This discovery occurred at a time when Blumberg was investi-
gating a different topic—whether people have inherited differences (rather than
just environmental differences) in susceptibility to disease. In the course of collecting and analyzing blood samples from populations around the world, Blumberg and a team of researchers based at the U.S. National Institutes of Health
developed a method for testing the blood of people who had received multiple
blood transfusions. This method allowed them to test the hypothesis that patients
with multiple blood transfusions would develop antibodies against foreign proteins that they had not inherited. Blumberg and his team used this blood test in
their search for genetic differences linked to disease susceptibility. In doing so,
they found an antibody that had never been seen before which reacted with a
protein found in an Australian aborigine's blood sample. They called this protein
the *Australian antigen*. (For definitions of antibodies, proteins, and antigens, see
the Glossary.)

For a time, the researchers were unsure of the significance of the Australian
antigen. In 1966, virologist Alfred Prince of the New York Blood Center suspected that the antigen was associated with the hepatitis B virus and began inves-
tigations that suggested the Australian antigen was linked to the development of
hepatitis B.[6] In the years that followed, other researchers independently confirmed
that the Australian antigen was part of the virus that caused hepatitis B, and the
antigen's name was changed to HBsAg, standing for hepatitis B surface antigen.
Blumberg won a Nobel Prize in Medicine in 1976 for his part in this discovery.
According to historian William Muraskin, this finding had a "revolutionary
impact on medical science" because it allowed researchers to proceed with the

Table 4.1 | Types of viral hepatitis

TYPE OF VIRAL HEPATITIS	TRANSMISSION	PREVENTION
Hepatitis A (HAV)	Contaminated food and water	Safe HAV vaccine
Hepatitis B (HBV)	Infected blood, sexual contact, and needles From an infected mother to her newborn	Safe HBV vaccine
Hepatitis C (HCV)	Infected blood and needles	No vaccine
Hepatitis D (HDV)	Must already have hepatitis B Infected blood, sexual contact, and needles From an infected mother to her newborn	HBV vaccine is appropriate
Hepatitis E (HEV)	Contaminated water	No vaccine

Note. From *ABCs of Viral Hepatitis* by the Hepatitis B Foundation, 2003–2008, available at http://www.hepb.org/hepb/abc.htm. Copyright 2003–2008 by Hepatitis B Foundation. Adapted with permission.

examination of hepatitis B epidemiology and to begin work on a blood test for the hepatitis B virus and the development of a vaccine.[7]

In the late 1960s, Blumberg developed a prototype hepatitis B vaccine with his colleague, Irving Millman, at the Fox Chase Cancer Center (FCCC) in Philadelphia. This discovery forged a new approach to vaccine development. The three previous methods of vaccine development involved (1) using whole viruses or bacteria that had been killed to prevent infection, (2) using weakened strains of pathogenic organisms that produced mild or no symptoms when injected as a vaccine but protected recipients from the more serious wild strains, and (3) using whole viruses that did not cause disease themselves but were closely related to viruses that did.[8] Blumberg and Millman's new method used only subunits of human virus (the HBsAg particles) obtained from the blood of hepatitis B carriers. As Blumberg recalls in his personal account of the vaccine's development,

We took antigen from individuals who had a great deal of it and used it to inoculate others who didn't have any: a "people's vaccine," as we sometimes jokingly called it. Our ability to do this was based on the fact that the virus produced very large quantities of the small, noninfectious particles containing only the surface antigen.[9]

The FCCC patented the method for this prototype hepatitis B vaccine in 1969 but was not equipped to test and produce the vaccine. Blumberg and his colleagues thus sought a pharmaceutical manufacturer to carry out these tasks.[10] New Jersey–based Merck & Co. was interested in the vaccine if the company could have exclusive patent rights.[11] But the funder of Blumberg's research, the National Institutes of Health, insisted that the technology be licensed to more than one company to avoid a monopoly situation. After extensive discussions between Blumberg, his colleagues, and executives at Merck, a solution was found that gave the company exclusive rights to the vaccine in markets outside the United States. The company reached agreement on a license for the technology from the FCCC in 1975.[12] Merck then developed a more sophisticated hepatitis B vaccine based on Blumberg and Millman's original concept. In 1981, Merck's Heptavax became the first hepatitis B vaccine on the market. At introduction, one dose cost $30. In 1982, the Institut Pasteur of France introduced another hepatitis B vaccine known as HevacB. These vaccines are known as plasma vaccines because they both are derived from human blood.

At about the same time in the 1970s, Prince was also pursuing research on a plasma vaccine for hepatitis B. Prince wanted to develop a vaccine that was affordable to developing countries. He worried that Merck and Institut Pasteur used large and expensive centrifuges in the vaccine development process that would make the technology unaffordable for poor nations. In his work, he sought to develop a simple and inexpensive vaccine whose technology could be transferred to the countries that most needed the product.[13] Prince ultimately decided on a flash heat purification method for his vaccine. This much simpler and cheaper procedure increased the potency of the vaccine and reduced the size of doses.[14] In addition, the vaccine required a smaller amount of the most expensive ingredient, the blood of hepatitis B carriers. Prince worked with a company in Korea, the Cheil Sugar Company, to develop this vaccine for commercial use at an affordable price for countries in Africa and Asia. In 1982, Cheil started producing this vaccine.[15]

Since 1981, the production of plasma hepatitis B vaccines has spread to companies in the United States, France, Republic of Korea, China, Vietnam, Myanmar, India, Indonesia, Iran, and Mongolia. But several barriers arose to producing large quantities of the vaccines. The most significant was the need for blood of hepatitis B carriers.[16] Furthermore, some policy makers and end-users worried about the safety of the vaccine because it was derived from human blood.

A technological innovation helped resolve some of the problems with the plasma vaccine. In 1977, William Rutter and his team at the University of California began working on the development of a second generation of hepatitis B vaccines using DNA-recombinant technology. Their new vaccine was synthetically prepared and did not contain any blood products. To make the vaccine, the researchers copied the genetic sequence of a protein contained in the hepatitis virus into a yeast cell, which was then cultured, purified, and prepared into a vaccine. Chiron Corporation, founded by Rutter and colleagues, began working with Merck to commercialize a hepatitis B vaccine using recombinant technology. SmithKline Beecham also began to develop a recombinant hepatitis B vaccine product. The U.S. FDA approved Merck's recombinant vaccine in 1986 (Recombivax HB) and, three years later, approved SmithKline Beecham's product (Engerix-B). To achieve product development, Merck and SmithKline Beecham licensed three important patents belonging to Institut Pasteur, Biogen, and the University of California.[17] They also needed licenses for more than 90 other patents for manufacturing processes such as isolation and purification.[18]

The recombinant vaccines represented a major advance. They induce an immune response but cannot infect recipients with the hepatitis B virus. Other advantages of this new technology are its shorter production cycle (12 instead of 65 weeks), batch-to-batch consistency, and continuous supply of the material. On the other hand, because the recombinant technology was patent-protected, there was a limited number of producers for the resulting vaccines. Product prices at introduction were as high as $40 per dose, above the prices for the plasma vaccines.[19] Despite the high prices, the recombinant vaccines soon pushed the plasma vaccines off the markets in North America and Western Europe. (Merck's Heptavax, for example, was discontinued in 1990.) The plasma vaccines, however, have continued to be produced and used elsewhere, as discussed below.

Today, recombinant hepatitis B vaccines are produced in Belgium, China, Cuba, France, India, Israel, Japan, the Republic of Korea, Switzerland, the United States, and Vietnam (see Table 4.2 for a list of recombinant products that have WHO prequalification). Hepatitis B vaccine is available from these manufacturers in monovalent forms (providing protection against hepatitis B only) and also in multivalent formulations combined with *Haemophilus influenzae* type b (Hib) vaccines, diphtheria-tetanus-pertussis (DTP) vaccines, inactivated polio (IPV) vaccines, and hepatitis A vaccines. Multivalent vaccines are beneficial because they can simplify delivery and can also cost less than two separate vaccines by eliminating expenses for separate vials, packaging, needles, syringes, and cold-chain storage expansion.[20] In a following section, we discuss the factors that enabled the entry of new manufacturers to the hepatitis B vaccine market.

The product development phase for hepatitis B vaccine ended with the existence of plasma and recombinant vaccines, effective in preventing infections if

Table 4.2 | United Nations prequalified hepatitis B vaccines, as of March 2008

PRODUCER	MONOVALENT AND COMBINATION HEPATITIS B VACCINE PRODUCTS
Berna Biotech Korea Corp	• Hepatitis B[a] (recombinant) • DTP-HepB-Hib[c]
Bio Farma, Indonesia	• Hepatitis B[a] filled in Uniject • DTP-HepB[b]
Center for Genetic Engineering and Biotechnnology, Cuba	• Hepatitis B[a] (recombinant)
GlaxoSmithKline, Belgium	• Hepatitis B[a] (recombinant) • DTP-HepB[b] (2 products) • DTP-HepB to be combined with Hib[c] • DTP-HepB + Hib
LG Life Sciences Ltd., Korea	• Hepatitis B[a] (recombinant)
Merck & Co., Inc., USA	• Hepatitis B[a] (recombinant)
Panacea Biotec, India	• Hepatitis B[a] (Enivac B) • DTP (Bio Farma)-HepB (PHB)[b] (1 dose) (1 dose) (Ecovac)
Serum Institute of India	• Hepatitis B[a] (recombinant) • DTP-Hep B[b]
Shantha Biotechnics Private Ltd., India	• Hepatitis B[a] (recombinant) • DTP-HepB[b]

Note. From *United Nations Prequalified Vaccines: WHO List of Vaccines for Purchase by UN Agencies as of March 2008 by WHO, 2008*, Geneva, available at http://www.who.int/immunization_standards/vaccine_quality/pq_suppliers/en/. Copyright 2008 by WHO. Adapted with permission.

[a] Monovalent vaccine

[b] A combination tetravalent vaccine including diphtheria-tetanus-pertussis (DTP) vaccines and hepatitis B (HepB) vaccine

[c] A combination pentavalent vaccine including diphtheria, diphtheria-tetanus-pertussis (DTP) vaccines and hepatitis B (HepB) vaccine plus *Haemophilus influenzae* type b (Hib) vaccine

given either before or shortly after exposure to HBV. These innovations promised major benefits around the world. The challenge was to introduce the hepatitis B vaccine effectively into developing countries.

Introducing Hepatitis B Vaccine in Developing Countries (Phase 2)

Approval of the plasma vaccines in the early 1980s produced only limited uptake in developing countries. The primary reason was the high price that made the vaccine unaffordable to governments. When Merck's plasma vaccine first came on the market in the United States, it cost more than $30 per dose or nearly $100 for the necessary three doses. At this time, the traditional vaccines procured for the WHO Expanded Programme on Immunization (EPI) programs (polio, DTP, measles, and Bacillus Calmette-Guérin) cost less than $1 per child.[21] The high cost of the first hepatitis B vaccines thus blocked their integration into the ongoing EPI programs.

A second reason for limited uptake of the plasma vaccine was related to policy makers' and end-users' concerns about safety because these vaccines came from human blood. These safety concerns led experts in some countries to question the wisdom of launching mass hepatitis B vaccination programs.[22] Questions were raised about connections between hepatitis B vaccine and multiple sclerosis, leading to worried providers and parents in some countries. Although WHO and others examined these safety issues and declared them to be unfounded, the perception of health risks associated with plasma vaccines persisted among some national decision-makers and negatively influenced national adoption.

A third barrier affecting national adoption was a limited understanding of the extent of hepatitis B burden in many countries. Muraskin notes that while many countries in Asia were aware of their hepatitis B problems, African nations often lacked good understanding of or adequate concern about this health problem: "For most Africans, the continent suffered from so many pressing health problems that hepatitis B simply seemed to lack urgency."[23]

The fourth barrier was an availability constraint and involved delivery challenges for the vaccine. Children must receive three doses of hepatitis B vaccine to develop protective antibodies. WHO developed three integration options for countries to incorporate the vaccine into routine childhood immunization schedules (see Table 4.3). Two options involve a dose given as soon as possible after birth (within 24 hours). This dose is important in countries where a high proportion of chronic infections are acquired perinatally. But the difficulty of administering a birth dose, particularly in rural areas where mothers usually give birth at home, posed a major delivery challenge.[24] Furthermore, in some countries, the immunization program was weak and under pressure to deliver the traditional EPI vaccines. Adding another vaccine to the program would stress an already overloaded health system and would require new logistics, training, and management.[25]

These affordability, adoption, and availability problems contributed to limited national and global adoption of the new plasma vaccines. To address these barriers to access, three individuals working on hepatitis B in the developing world—Prince along with Richard Mahoney (director of Program for Appropriate Technology in Health or PATH) and James Maynard (director of Hepatitis

Table 4.3 | Options for adding hepatitis B vaccine to childhood immunization schedules

| | | | | | | HEPATITIS B VACCINE OPTIONS | | |
| | | | | | | NO BIRTH DOSE | WITH BIRTH DOSE | |
AGE	VISIT	OTHER ANTIGENS				I	II	III
Birth	0	BCG[a] [OPV0]1[b]	-	-	-	-	HepB-birth[2]	HepB-birth[2]
6 weeks	1	-	OPV1[b]	DTP1[c]	-	HepB1[3]	HepB2[2]	DTP[c]-HepB1[4]
10 weeks	2	-	OPV2[b]	DTP2[c]	-	HepB2[3]	-	DTP[c]-HepB2[4]
14 weeks	3	-	OPV3[b]	DTP3[c]	-	HepB3[3]	HepB3[2]	DTP[c]-HepB3[4]
9–12 months	4	-	-	-	Measles	-	-	-

Note. From *Introduction of Hepatitis B Vaccine into Childhood Immunization Services: Management Guidelines, Including Information for Health Workers and Parents* by WHO, 2001, Geneva, available at http://www.who.int/vaccines-documents. Copyright 2001 by WHO. Adapted with permission.

[1] Only given in high polio endemic countries

[2] Monovalent vaccine

[3] Monovalent or combination vaccine

[4] Combination vaccine

[a] Bacillus Calmette-Guérin, a vaccine against tuberculosis

[b] Oral polio vaccine, protects against polio

[c] A combination of diphtheria and tetanus toxoids and pertussis vaccine to protect against diphtheria, tetanus, and pertussis infections

Branch, Centers for Disease Control)—established a new entity in April 1986: the International Task Force on Hepatitis B Immunization. The Task Force received initial funding from the Rockefeller Foundation ($50,000) and the James S. McDonnell Foundation (almost $2.5 million for three years) to accomplish two main goals: (1) to identify practical ways for integrating hepatitis B vaccination into mass infant immunization programs, and (2) to ensure the production of hepatitis B vaccines in adequate quantities and at low prices so that developing countries could conduct mass infant immunization.[26] The Task Force sought to achieve these objectives through a series of demonstration projects in Asia and Africa (Indonesia, Thailand, China, Kenya, and Cameroon). The first two demonstration projects were in Indonesia and Thailand, with Mahoney directing the Task Force and PATH serving as the in-country implementing partner.

The Task Force first sought to lower the cost of the plasma vaccine.[27] Prince was already working with the Korean firm, Cheil Sugar Company, to develop his prototype vaccine. The Task Force negotiated an agreement with Cheil to establish a $1 per dose price for a minimum of 5 million doses.[28] Achieving this commitment from Cheil was a major breakthrough for the Task Force in pushing product prices down. It did not, however, provide them with an affordable price for their first pilot project in Indonesia, since that project required less than 5 million doses. The Indonesian government, therefore, decided to foster competitive pricing through a sealed international bid and tender, as recommended by the Task Force. Many companies participated in the bid, with the lowest one ($0.95 per dose) coming from another Korean company, Korea Green Cross Corporation, for its plasma vaccine.

With this price, the Task Force, along with PATH and the Indonesian government, could proceed with its first demonstration project in Indonesia. But government officials initially resisted moving forward with the project for many reasons:

The basic Expanded Programme for Immunization (EPI) vaccines were not being given to most children; there was not enough money to educate the public on health matters; there were not enough syringes for current vaccinations—they were either being used over and over again or illegally diverted to the private market; the cold chain required for vaccines was inadequate and the limited resources that existed were needed for polio and measles; high infant mortality due to diarrheal diseases, tetanus, or upper respiratory tract infections was more important; malaria was spreading.[29]

Finally, and with the backing of Indonesian President Suharto who had lost a close colleague to liver cancer, the Task Force and PATH convinced government officials to implement the pilot project. An important component of this project was the fine-tuning of delivery methods for the birth dose, part of which was the piloting of hepatitis B vaccine prefilled syringes (heat stable for one month outside the cold chain).[30] The demonstration project was successful and, as a result, the Indonesian government decided to begin universal hepatitis B immunization in 1991. Meanwhile, the Task Force continued model programs elsewhere and helped several countries develop international tenders. The price of the plasma vaccine continued to drop, reaching $0.65 per dose offered to the Philippines in 1991.[31]

Official policy development on hepatitis B vaccine at the global level began in the early 1990s. In 1991, WHO and the Task Force convened an international meeting in Cameroon on hepatitis B. The meeting concluded that hepatitis B ranked among the world's most pressing health problems, that vaccination could be feasibly integrated into EPI without harming the program, and that a global fund should be established to purchase and deliver the vaccine.[32] Later that year, the Global Advisory Group of the EPI endorsed these views and set the following timetable: Hepatitis B vaccine should be integrated into national immunization programs in countries with hepatitis B carrier prevalence of 8% or greater by 1995 and in all countries by 1997. The World Health Assembly endorsed this recommendation in 1992, and two years later it called for an 80% decrease by 2001 in the incidence of new hepatitis B virus carriers in children.[33] The Global Advisory Group also recommended that the new Children's Vaccine Initiative work to create a global vaccine fund for hepatitis B vaccine and other vaccines.[34]

The Task Force, by pushing adoption of the hepatitis B vaccine at both national and global levels, achieved several important tasks that promoted greater access. First, the Task Force pushed the product price of the plasma vaccine to $1 per dose through the Indonesian bid and tender agreement. Second, the group helped create consensus on hepatitis B vaccine integration into the EPI through the Cameroon meeting with WHO. Furthermore, the Task Force and PATH showed practical ways of delivering the vaccine in developing countries (particularly the birth dose) through the demonstration projects. The demonstration projects also helped counteract the negative perceptions of safety in the countries in which they were implemented and at the global level as well.

Despite these important achievements and despite a growing global focus on the hepatitis B vaccine, by 1997 it became clear that WHO's targets would not be met. In 1991, when the EPI made its recommendation, approximately 20 countries (mostly in North America, Europe, and Asia) were routinely using the vaccine.[35] By 1995, only 35 of 90 countries with prevalence rates greater than or equal to 8% had begun hepatitis B vaccination programs.[36]

By the end of the 1990s, the central challenge for hepatitis B vaccine advocates was the lack of affordability for governments in developing countries. The Task Force demonstrated this problem in Kenya. EPI staff wanted to integrate the vaccine into their program but could not afford the price of $1 per dose.[37] Though product prices had decreased significantly, they were still not low enough for many developing country governments. Vaccine advocates needed to find other ways to create further price decreases.

Scaling Up Hepatitis B Vaccine (Phase 3)

In the early years of the 2000s, access to hepatitis B vaccine increased significantly in the developing world. The entry of new manufacturers into the market in the mid-1990s created more competition and drove down prices. Also the creation of the Global Alliance for Vaccines and Immunizations (now known as the GAVI Alliance) in 1999 spurred a growth in access, especially as the new organization gave priority to underutilized vaccines such as hepatitis B vaccine.

These two developments occurred in the context of a changing international vaccine market. Since the 1970s, global vaccine production shifted from the public to the private sector. Production objectives, therefore, became increasingly based on market considerations rather than public health needs. This trend accelerated in the 1990s, with pharmaceutical company mergers leading to less flexibility in vaccine production. In the late 1990s, developing countries experienced vaccine shortages when industrialized countries began to introduce more expensive vaccines based on new technology (such as recombinant vaccines), and the production of older vaccines declined. Previously the same vaccines had been used in both rich and poor countries. But now vaccine producers began phasing out production of the older, less expensive vaccines that were being used mainly in developing countries. Between 1998 and 2001, 10 out of 14 producers partially or completely stopped manufacturing traditional vaccines. By 2002, the UNICEF Supply Division (UNICEF's global procurement operation) was buying 65% of its traditional vaccines (apart from oral polio vaccine) from only two manufacturers.[38]

These structural changes in the global vaccine market had important consequences for both availability and affordability. The traditional vaccines became less available while their prices increased. UNICEF responded by developing a "vaccine security strategy" that involved: (1) giving manufacturers sufficient guarantees through purchasing agreements, (2) looking for funding to cover vaccine requirements, and (3) engaging in long-term forecasting to allow companies sufficient time to increase production if necessary.[39] With this new strategy, UNICEF's role shifted from vaccine buyer to strategic partner with producers. This changing context of global vaccine production had critical implications for hepatitis B vaccine access.

Entry of New Manufacturers into the Market
Merck played a major role in the global market for hepatitis B vaccine. The company launched the first plasma hepatitis B vaccine in 1981. Five years later, Merck introduced the first recombinant hepatitis B vaccine. But a host of new companies soon joined the field.

In the late 1980s, new manufacturers from a range of countries (including China, Japan, and Korea) entered the market with their own hepatitis B vaccine products. At the same time, the International Task Force for Hepatitis B

Immunization was negotiating lower prices for plasma vaccine from two Korean manufacturers (Cheil and Green Cross, as noted above). In the following decade, several Indian manufacturers entered the hepatitis B vaccine market. Increasingly, these developing country firms were making the recombinant rather than the plasma vaccine. At the same time, established vaccine producers shifted from traditional vaccine production to newer technologies and more costly vaccines.

The entry of these new producers created more price competition. Prices for the recombinant vaccine reached as low as $0.54 per dose in 1999.[40] With the new competition, companies sought new markets for their products. Some applied for WHO prequalification so they could sell their vaccines to developing countries through UNICEF's Supply Division.

The higher profits of the new recombinant technology provided a major incentive for producers to enter the hepatitis B market. The expiry of patents also encouraged the entry of new firms; for example, Biogen's patent on recombinant technology for hepatitis B vaccine expired in many countries by the mid-1990s.[41] Additional factors explain the entry of new manufacturers as well. Mahoney provides a useful analysis of these factors in regard to Korean companies.[42] Having worked with the Task Force to supply plasma vaccine, Korean producers saw that an international market for the vaccine existed. Three vaccine producers (Cheil, Green Cross, and LG Chem) then began developing the recombinant vaccine. Green Cross achieved this by acquiring patented technology from Rhein Biotech of Germany. This involved the biotechnology company taking a controlling interest in Green Cross. LG Chem learned how to make the vaccine through a joint venture with the Chiron Corporation. Cheil tried to develop its own technology but was ultimately unsuccessful.

Mahoney lists several facilitating factors that led to the entry of the Korean manufacturers into the international market and subsequent WHO prequalification of their products.[43] The Korean Food and Drug Administration had recently improved its operations. Staff from WHO had required these improvements as a condition for prequalifying Korean producers, and the Korean government complied.[44] The establishment and operation of clinical testing sites (with national public and private support) allowed Korean producers to provide high-quality data to national regulatory authorities in developing countries. This is important because regulatory agencies in developing countries have increased their requests for high-quality information from producers instead of simply registering a vaccine because it is licensed in the country of manufacture.

The entrance of Indian firms into the hepatitis B vaccine market in the 1990s also helped promote price competition. New players entered the domestic market in India because of profit margins, high demand, and the possibility of bulk purchases through India's national immunization program.[45] Some of these companies expanded globally and sought WHO prequalification.

In sum, starting in the late 1980s and through the next decade, a number of new manufacturers entered the hepatitis B vaccine market from several developing countries, propelled by market factors and assisted by actions of the Task Force and WHO. The resulting competition helped push down prices dramatically. By 2006, the UNICEF Supply Division price for recombinant, monovalent hepatitis B vaccine reached $0.25 per dose. Further support for the international market for this vaccine came through the actions of a new entity—the GAVI Alliance.

The GAVI Alliance

Restructuring the global architecture to promote hepatitis B vaccine provided a major impetus for increased adoption, both global and national. As mentioned previously, the Global Advisory Group of the EPI argued in 1991 for the creation of a global vaccine fund to finance childhood vaccines, including the hepatitis B vaccine, in developing countries. The group recommended that the Children's Vaccine Initiative (CVI) take on this task. The CVI was established in 1990 by five agencies—UNICEF, WHO, the United Nations Development Program, the World Bank, and the Rockefeller Foundation—with the goal of developing new and improved vaccines and was placed within WHO. One main objective was to bring the public and private sectors closer together to achieve cooperation on vaccine development.[46] Toward the end of the 1990s, it became clear that these efforts to develop new vaccines were failing. The CVI then turned its focus to the introduction of existing underutilized vaccines in developing countries, such as those for hepatitis B, yellow fever, and *Haemophilus influenzae* type b (Hib).

CVI's new goal, however, also proved elusive. Private industry supported CVI's new focus because it felt that public-private cooperation on the development of new vaccines was premature until problems of access to current vaccines were tackled.[47] The public sector's argument that industry had neglected to develop new vaccines for diseases of the poor was not persuasive when existing vaccines, such as hepatitis B, were little used in developing countries.[48] The CVI, however, lacked the financial and political power to make the private sector a full partner in these activities. Experts in both the public and private sectors argued that no single organization (i.e., WHO) could carry out this work to expand access to existing vaccines and that a committed partnership of international agencies was needed. In 1999, WHO, UNICEF, the World Bank, the Bill & Melinda Gates Foundation's Children's Vaccine Program, the Rockefeller Foundation, the International Federation of Pharmaceutical Manufacturers & Associations, and some national governments established the GAVI Alliance. Importantly, the private sector was given an equal place next to the UN agencies in the new initiative.[49] Specifically, private industry received two seats on the 16-member board of directors, one each for developed and developing country industry representatives.

The GAVI Alliance saw itself less as an organization and more as a "movement aimed at ensuring that the universal childhood immunization agenda set up in the 1980s is reenergized, expanded, and brought up-to-date."[50] Tore Godal, a Norwegian immunologist and leader in global health, became executive secretary of the new initiative, and the board of directors took responsibility for GAVI's governance. The founding agencies were concerned that immunization rates had leveled off in some countries and declined in others.[51] Their goal in establishing the GAVI Alliance was to fulfill the right of every child to be protected against vaccine-preventable diseases of public health concern. The GAVI Alliance and the GAVI Fund (previously called the Vaccine Fund) began with an initial Bill & Melinda Gates Foundation grant of $750 million over five years. For these years, the Gates funding comprised half of GAVI's resources, with grants also provided by the United States, Norway, the Netherlands, and the United Kingdom. In early 2005, the Gates Foundation provided a second grant of $750 million for another 10 years. The goal is to reduce Gates funding to less than 20% of GAVI's total resources within that time.[52]

The GAVI Alliance uses a business model based on two principles. First, the GAVI Fund is used to finance the procurement of new and underused vaccines for developing countries. The GAVI Alliance prioritizes vaccines for hepatitis B, as well as for *Haemophilus influenzae* type b, pneumococcal, rotavirus, yellow fever, and measles (second dose). Along with procurement of these vaccines, the GAVI Fund emphasizes the use of combination vaccines and vaccine vial monitors (see chapter 7) to reduce wastage, as well as "auto-disable" injection equipment to prevent unsafe injections.

Second, the GAVI Alliance provides performance-based financial incentives for improving immunization infrastructure and capacity to governments of countries with low immunization rates. GAVI soon discovered that its focus on strengthening "immunization systems" was too narrowly conceived and that broader health-system failures often constrained a country's ability to immunize more children.[53] At the same time, many global health experts argued that initiatives such as GAVI should address sectorwide issues, rather than focusing only on single health issues. In response, GAVI adapted its model to provide support for broader health-system improvements (for example, raising the frequency of supervisory visits).[54]

GAVI also targets its support to the poorest countries in the world. As of March 2008, 72 countries were eligible (countries with an annual Gross National Income per capita below $1,000). The GAVI Alliance offers five kinds of support. The first type of support is for immunization services. Countries can apply for an annual grant of $20 per additional child targeted for immunization in the "investment phase" (the first two years of the country's multiyear plan). In the "reward phase" (the third year to the end of the multiyear plan), countries receive a further $20 per additional child immunized (measured against the total number of children immunized the previous year with diphtheria-tetanus-pertussis vaccine, or DTP3). The second kind of support that GAVI offers is for new and underused vaccines. Countries can apply if they have a national coverage rate of 50% for the full infant course of DTP3. The specific new and underused vaccines available to eligible countries are hepatitis B, *Haemophilus influenzae* type b, pneumococcal, and rotavirus vaccines. All 72 countries can apply for the yellow fever vaccine, regardless of DTP3 coverage rates. Countries that are eligible according to WHO criteria can also apply for measles vaccination (second dose). GAVI offers three other kinds of support, and all 72 countries can apply for these: injection safety support, health system strengthening, and civil society organization support.

Some critics have questioned whether GAVI's focus on new and underutilized vaccines like hepatitis B is the best strategy. They have argued that GAVI's priority should be on increasing the coverage of traditional EPI vaccines.[55] Critics have also charged that, through its partnership with the private sector, GAVI is creating profitable new markets for multinational vaccine manufacturers for the more expensive vaccines such as hepatitis B vaccine (recombinant) and that GAVI has not been tough enough with these companies in negotiating prices.[56] Godal, GAVI's first executive secretary, rebuts these accusations as "nonsense," stating, "If the public sector can work to help make the developing-country vaccine environment more attractive to vaccine manufacturers, children living in the poorest countries will have access to better and more effective vaccines."[57]

Critics have also charged that GAVI is making it difficult for developing countries to manufacture vaccines locally. They point out that GAVI has resisted requests by countries with generic-drug industries (including Brazil, India, and Indonesia) for supporting the transfer of patented vaccine technology.[58] Respect for intellectual property rights, however, was agreed on at the first GAVI Alliance Partners' meeting in 2000 as a condition for developed country industry involvement. The GAVI Alliance supports the developing world vaccine industry through procurement of vaccines (if prequalified by WHO) and the allocation of one rotating seat on GAVI's board. At the heart of these questions are concerns about the role of the private sector in global health partnerships and specific worries about sustainability, transparency, and accountability of public-private partnerships in health.

While these debates continued, GAVI made a significant impact on access to hepatitis B vaccine in developing countries through financing both the introduction of the vaccine and the infrastructure needed to support vaccination. GAVI's activities especially affected the adoption and affordability of hepatitis B vaccine. As of June 2004, 85% of all countries with adequate delivery systems had introduced the hepatitis B vaccine into their routine systems (149 countries). In addition, 82% of the GAVI Fund–eligible countries with adequate delivery systems had introduced the vaccine into their routine systems (61 countries). Figure 4.1 shows that coverage with three doses of hepatitis B vaccine has risen steadily since 1990, reflecting increased national adoption into routine immunization programs and also growing coverage within some countries. Coverage levels in many countries remain low, however, and addressing this problem is a main challenge facing hepatitis B vaccine advocates.

Because prices of hepatitis B vaccine remain higher than the traditional EPI vaccines, continued access to the vaccine in developing countries depends on the sustainability of the GAVI model. In its first phase of operation (2000–2005), GAVI decided it would help a country introduce a new or underutilized vaccine such as hepatitis B for free for five years. The logic behind this approach was that during those five years, vaccine prices would decrease, and then developing country governments and donors would take on the financing of procurement.[59] GAVI has found, however, that prices have not declined as expected (prices of combination vaccines with hepatitis B have in fact increased), countries are not able to afford procurement, and other donors have not stepped in to help.[60] GAVI subsequently reformed its business model in order to support countries to gain long-term financial sustainability. This new model requires countries to co-pay for vaccine procurement from the beginning but does so over a longer time period than in its first phase to promote sustainability (GAVI's second phase is from 2006–2015). A country's level of co-pay depends on its ability to pay. Success of this new model will have a strong influence on creating access to the vaccine in developing countries in the short and medium term.

Figure 4.1 | Coverage of hepatitis B vaccine (globally and in selected WHO regions)

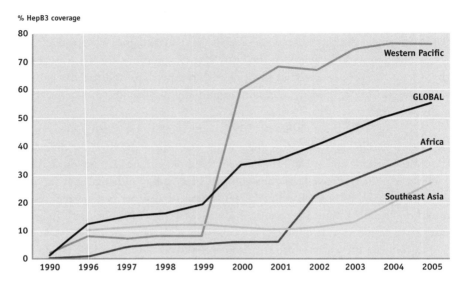

% HepB3 coverage

Note. The data for this figure come from WHO and UNICEF estimates of national immunization coverage between 1980 and 2005. These estimates are based on officially reported data by Member States to WHO, a historical database maintained by UNICEF, the published literature (particularly coverage survey results and methods), and unpublished surveys from ministries of health. Coverage levels are calculated by dividing the number of children receiving their third dose of hepatitis B vaccine by the number of children surviving to their first birthday. Data from *WHO Vaccine-Preventable Diseases: Monitoring System. 2006 Global Summary* by WHO, 2006, Geneva, available at http://www.who.int/vaccines-documents/.

Conclusions

This story of access for the hepatitis B vaccine demonstrates the close linkages between architecture, availability, affordability, and adoption (see Table 4.4 for a summary of the access barriers and strategies). For decades, problems in affordability blocked access, as the price of hepatitis B vaccine remained too high for developing countries to include in their national immunization programs. As a result, demand outside of industrialized countries was low. Product adoption was also hampered by safety concerns about plasma vaccines and a limited understanding by global and national actors about the burden of hepatitis B in many countries. With low demand, manufacturers refused to increase production capacity for the vaccine, product prices remained high, and vaccine availability was limited.

New players in the architecture of hepatitis B vaccine successfully addressed the problem of limited availability, affordability, and adoption through several key strategies. The Task Force, an effective product champion for hepatitis B vaccine both at the global level and in developing countries, achieved decreases in the vaccine's product prices by fostering competition and showing companies that a market for the vaccine existed in developing countries. But the Task Force also had limitations. Problems persisted of low national adoption in developing countries due to numerous pressing health problems and inadequate financing of hepatitis B vaccine for mass immunization programs. While the Children's Vaccine Initiative tried in the 1990s to address these problems of access to underutilized vaccines like hepatitis B, this organization lacked sufficient political and financial power. These experiences show the importance of establishing a robust architecture for fulfilling access goals.

The establishment of the GAVI Alliance changed the architecture in ways that helped solve the problems of limited availability, affordability, and adoption. By financing the procurement of hepatitis B vaccine for developing countries through the GAVI Fund and forecasting demand across countries, GAVI showed vaccine producers that a viable international market for hepatitis B vaccine existed. GAVI's actions also further facilitated the entry of new manufacturers, an increase in manufacturing capacity, a rise in price competition, and the creation of a steady vaccine supply. Giving industry a seat equal to UN agencies within GAVI's board of directors created closer public-private collaboration. But this model also has its critics. They have argued that industry's integral involvement in GAVI kept recombinant hepatitis B vaccine prices higher than necessary, thereby limiting access in poor countries and raising questions about long-term sustainability.

This case demonstrates several other factors that facilitated the entry of vaccine producers into the hepatitis B vaccine market. For instance, the Task Force's role as a product champion helped to develop early relationships with several Korean companies and persuaded them of the growing demand for the vaccine in developing countries. In addition, work by WHO staff, government officials, and the vaccine industry to improve national drug regulating authorities and clinical testing capacities assisted the entry of vaccine producers with quality products. The expiry of patents also facilitated the entry of new manufacturers. Finally, the flow of global financing for immunization programs changed the calculus of affordability for countries. The financial support from the Bill & Melinda Gates Foundation and other donors made a huge difference in making the GAVI architecture effective. GAVI's support for the procurement of vaccines and the strengthening of health systems in developing countries helped create the basis for improved access to hepatitis B vaccine around the world.

The global architecture of hepatitis B vaccine—involving the Task Force, WHO, and the GAVI Alliance—thus successfully addressed problems of limited availability, affordability, and adoption of this technology in developing countries. A major issue now is how to improve vaccination rates in countries with low coverage. Continuing access to the vaccine in the future also remains a major problem. Solving these problems will depend on whether national governments and donors continue to finance the vaccine and on related factors, including product price, the sustainability of GAVI, and government and donor funding priorities.

Table 4.4 | Hepatitis B vaccine access table

	BARRIER	STRATEGY	SPECIFIC ACTION
ARCHITECTURE	Lack of effective global product champion for developing countries	Identify effective leadership and design partnerships for the technology	Establishment of the International Task Force on Hepatitis B Immunization to address problems in availability, affordability, and adoption
			Establishment of the GAVI Alliance to address problems in availability, affordability, and adoption
ADOPTION	Safety concerns for plasma vaccines (affecting national and end-user adoption)	Conduct safety evaluations that can be disseminated to policy makers and end-users	WHO conducted safety assessments of the plasma hepatitis B vaccine
		Develop second generation of hepatitis B vaccine	Academic researchers and companies developed new hepatitis B vaccines using DNA-recombinant technology
	Limited understanding of burden of disease for hepatitis B (affecting global and national adoption)	Facilitate international meetings that can promote consensus on the disease and the vaccine	The Task Force and WHO convened an international meeting to encourage the integration of hepatitis B vaccine into national immunization programs
		Seek global recommendation on hepatitis B vaccine	WHO secured a World Health Assembly recommendation on the integration of hepatitis B vaccine into national immunization programs

Table 4.4 | Hepatitis B vaccine access table (continued)

	BARRIER	STRATEGY	SPECIFIC ACTION
AFFORDABILITY	High product price (affecting government affordability)	Promote lower prices through expanded competition and entry of new manufacturers into the market	The Task Force promoted lower product prices by working with existing manufacturers, identifying new manufacturers, and seeking to foster competition
			Through procurement and forecasting activities, the GAVI Alliance encouraged entry of new manufacturers by showing that a viable market for the vaccine existed.
		Lower product cost to governments by providing them with procurement funds	The GAVI Alliance provided funding to governments for vaccine procurement
AVAILABILITY	Difficulties in producing large quantity of plasma vaccine because of need for blood from hepatitis B carriers	Develop second generation of hepatitis B vaccine	Academic researchers and companies developed new hepatitis B vaccines using DNA-recombinant technology
	Delivery challenges from weak immunization programs and problems in administering birth dose	Show that delivery methods can be implemented effectively	The Task Force financed demonstration projects in a number of countries to develop effective delivery methods and identify problems
		Support health system improvement	The GAVI Alliance provided funding for strengthening immunization systems and broader health systems as part of vaccine financing

Endnotes

1   World Health Organization, *Hepatitis B Immunization* (Geneva: WHO, 2001, WHO/V&B/01.28); and GAVI Alliance, "Hepatitis B," http://www.gavialliance.org (retrieved March 6, 2008).

2   Brian J. McMahon, W. L. Alward, D. B. Hall, William L. Heyward, T. R. Bender, D. P. Francis, and J. E. Maynard, "Acute Hepatitis B Viral Infection: Relation of Age to the Clinical Expression of Disease and Subsequent Development of the Carrier State," *Journal of Infectious Diseases* 151 (1985): 599–603.

3   World Health Organization, *Hepatitis B Immunization*.

[4] Margie Patlak, *Beyond Discovery: The Path from Research to Human Benefit. The Hepatitis B Story* (Washington, DC: National Academy of Science, 2000), http://www.beyonddiscovery. org (retrieved March 27, 2006).

[5] William Muraskin, *The War Against Hepatitis B* (Philadelphia: University of Pennsylvania Press, 1995), 3.

[6] Patlak.

[7] William Muraskin, *The War Against Hepatitis B*, 3.

[8] Patlak.

[9] Baruch S. Blumberg, *Hepatitis B: The Hunt for a Killer Virus* (Princeton, NJ: Princeton University Press, 2002), 139.

[10] Blumberg.

[11] Muraskin, The War Against Hepatitis B.

[12] Blumberg.

[13] Muraskin, *The War Against Hepatitis B*.

[14] Denise DeRoeck, *Immunization Financing in Developing Countries and the International Vaccine Market* (Manila: Asian Development Bank, 2001), http://www.adb.org/Documents/ Books/Immunization_Financing/default.asp (retrieved June 11, 2007).

[15] DeRoeck.

[16] Patlak.

[17] Richard T. Mahoney, "DNA Hepatitis B Vaccine: International Vaccine Institute, Korea," in *Executive Guide to Intellectual Property Management in Health and Agricultural Innovation: A Handbook of Best Practices*, eds. Anatole Krattiger, Richard T. Mahoney, and L. Nelsen, et al. (Oxford: MIHR and Davis, CA: PIPRA, 2007), CS22–23, http://www.ipHandbook.org (retrieved March 18, 2008).

[18] Mahoney, "DNA Hepatitis B Vaccine."

[19] DeRoeck.

[20] Robert E. Vryheid, Mark A. Kane, Nancy Muller, Gary C. Schatz, and Shewit Bezabeh, "Infant and Adolescent Hepatitis B Immunization up to 1999: A Global Overview," *Vaccine* 19 (2001): 1026–1037.

[21] Vryheid et al.

[22] Vryheid et al.

[23] Muraskin, *The War Against Hepatitis B*, 217.

[24] Vryheid et al.

[25] Vryheid et al.

[26] Muraskin, *The War Against Hepatitis B*.

27 Richard T. Mahoney, "Public-Private Partnerships in the Development of the Hepatitis B Vaccine in Korea: Implications for Developing Countries," *Science, Technology and Society* 10 (2005): 129–140.

28 Muraskin, *The War Against Hepatitis B*.

29 Muraskin, *The War Against Hepatitis B*, 92.

30 Vryheid et al.

31 DeRoeck.

32 Muraskin, *The War Against Hepatitis B*.

33 Pierre Van Damme, Mark A. Kane, and Andre Meheus, "Integration of Hepatitis B Vaccine into National Immunization Programmes," *British Medical Journal* 314, no. 7086 (1997): 1033–1036; and Mark A. Kane, "Status of Hepatitis B Immunization Programmes in 1998," *Vaccine* 16, suppl. (1998): S104.

34 Muraskin, *The War Against Hepatitis B*.

35 Kane.

36 Vryheid et al.

37 Muraskin, *The War Against Hepatitis B*.

38 UNICEF, *Vaccines for Children: Supply at Risk* (New York: UNICEF, 2002), http://www.unicef.org/publications/index_4442.html (retrieved March 20, 2007).

39 UNICEF.

40 DeRoeck.

41 DeRoeck.

42 Mahoney, "Public-Private Partnerships"; and Mahoney, "DNA Hepatitis B Vaccine."

43 Mahoney, "Public-Private Partnerships."

44 Mahoney, "Public-Private Partnerships."

45 Y. Madhavi, "Manufacture of Consent? Hepatitis B Vaccination," *Economic and Political Weekly*, June 14, 2003, 2417–2424.

46 William Muraskin, "The Last Years of the CVI and the Birth of the GAVI," in *Public-Private Partnerships for Public Health*, ed. Michael R. Reich (Cambridge, MA: Harvard Center for Development Studies, 2002), 115–168.

47 Muraskin, "The Last Years of the CVI."

48 Muraskin, "The Last Years of the CVI."

49 Muraskin, "The Last Years of the CVI."

50 Scott Wittet, "Introducing GAVI and the Global Fund for Children's Vaccines," *Vaccine* 19, no. 4-5 (2001): 385.

51 Wittet.

[52] Bill and Melinda Gates Foundation, "Ensuring The World's Poorest Children Benefit From Lifesaving Vaccines," http://www.gatesfoundation.org/whatwerelearning (retrieved March 20, 2007).

[53] Gates Foundation.

[54] Gates Foundation.

[55] See, for example: Anita Hardon and Stuart Blume, "Shifts in Global Immunization Goals (1984–2004): Unfinished Agendas and Mixed Results," *Social Science and Medicine* 60 (2005): 345–356.

[56] Rachel Zimmerman, "Some Question Whether Drug Makers Play Too Large a Role in Vaccine Fund?" *Wall Street Journal*, December 3, 2001, A12.

[57] Tore Godal, "GAVI, the First Steps: Lessons for the Global Fund," *The Lancet* 360 (2002): 175–176.

[58] Madhavi.

[59] Gates Foundation.

[60] Gates Foundation; and HLSP, *Lessons Learned from GAVI Phase 1 and Design of Phase 2: Findings of the Country Consultation Process* (London: HLSP, 2005), http://www.gavialliance.org/resources/Lessons_learned_Phase_1_July05.pdf (retrieved March 7, 2008).

CHAPTER 5

MALARIA RAPID DIAGNOSTIC TESTS:

Access to Diagnostics

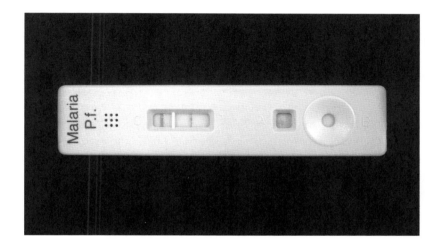

An estimated 40% of the world population today is at risk of malaria infection.[1] The disease, a parasitic infection spread from person to person by the bite of the female *Anopheles* mosquito, affects people in approximately a hundred nations. The World Health Organization (WHO) estimates that each year there are more than 300 million episodes of acute illness and at least a million deaths due to malaria worldwide.[2] In addition, more than 90% of the global burden is in sub-Saharan Africa. Children under five years of age are at greatest risk of death from malaria. Pregnant women and their unborn children are also vulnerable to the disease, which can lead to perinatal mortality, low birth weight, and maternal anemia. There are four types of human malaria: *Plasmodium falciparum*, *P. vivax*, *P. malariae*, and *P. ovale*. Of these, *P. falciparum* is the most deadly and the most common in sub-Saharan Africa.

The symptoms of malaria usually appear nine to fourteen days after the infectious bite of the mosquito, though this varies with the different *Plasmodium* species. Typical symptoms are fever, headache, vomiting, and other flu-like symptoms. Without effective treatment, malaria infection can lead to death by infecting and damaging red blood cells (anemia) and by blocking the capillaries that carry blood to the brain (cerebral malaria) or other essential organs.[3] Malaria treatment is complicated due to the widespread resistance of *P. falciparum* to common antimalarial drugs such as chloroquine, sulfadoxine-pyrimethamine (SP), and amodiaquine. Today, WHO recommends that all countries experiencing resistance to these common monotherapies use combination therapies for *P. falciparum* malaria, preferably those containing artemisinin derivatives (known as artemisinin-based combination therapies, or ACTs).[4] An artemether/lumefantrine combination therapy called Coartem, manufactured by Novartis, was the first fixed-dose ACT prequalified by WHO.

A major challenge for malaria treatment is the prompt and correct diagnosis of malaria infection. Diagnosis is critical because early treatment helps reduce morbidity and mortality. Malaria diagnosis has also become increasingly important due to the high price of ACTs. In 2008, governments could purchase Coartem for $0.80 per treatment for use in the public sector (where it is usually provided free to the end-user). End-users purchasing Coartem in the private sector pay a much higher price whereas they can purchase older treatments for $0.10–$0.20. Unfortunately, malaria diagnosis is often problematic and therefore presents a significant barrier to effective control of the disease.

The "gold standard" for malaria diagnosis is conventional light microscopy based on careful examination of a blood film by an expert microscopist. Microscopy is sensitive (it can detect densities as low as 5–10 parasites per microliter of blood), informative, and relatively inexpensive ($0.12–$0.40 per slide, though these figures do not reflect the full costs, which are higher).[5] Furthermore, as a general diagnostic technique, microscopy can be shared with other disease control programs and provides a permanent record of diagnostic findings. The method, however, is labor-intensive and time consuming (an estimated 20 to 60 minutes from specimen collection to result, depending on the available lab equipment). In practice, delays often occur in providing microscopy results to the clinician, so treatment decisions are commonly made before diagnostic results arrive. Finally, microscopy depends on good techniques, reagents, microscopes, and well-trained and well-supervised technicians. These conditions are often lacking at the lower levels of health systems in poor countries because microscopy has not been prioritized or supported by sustained financing.[6]

In settings where microscopy is unavailable or unreliable, health professionals typically use clinical judgment to diagnose malaria. Clinical diagnosis is inexpensive, requires no special equipment or supplies, and is often the only option in health units without laboratory support at the periphery of a health system. It is the most widely used approach to malaria diagnosis. The symptoms of malaria, however, are nonspecific and overlap with symptoms of other febrile illnesses, so patients with fever are often treated presumptively and include many persons who do not have malaria.[7]

Rapid diagnostic tests for malaria (RDTs) offer a new diagnostic alternative for health professionals and result from advances in molecular biology. These rapid tests are based on the detection of antigens, or proteins, derived from malaria parasites in lysed blood, using immunochromatographic methods. RDTs are relatively new products, and efforts to provide access to them are ongoing. This chapter traces the history of RDTs, beginning in the mid-1990s with the initial testing and commercial introduction of the first products and following through current efforts to scale up the technology. The case study highlights challenges of providing access to a new technology in an environment where external funding for procurement provokes rapid product uptake but where financing is lacking for other aspects of the access process, including information on product availability and quality. It also illustrates the important roles of a global coordinating body to arrange the architecture and promote the adoption and use of a new technology.

Product Development (Phase 1)

For many years, the World Health Organization and other global health agencies called for better diagnostic tools for settings with limited health infrastructure in developing countries. The goal was to develop simple and rapid diagnostic tests that could be used to guide treatment in these settings for various infectious diseases, including malaria, AIDS, and syphilis. These tests became known as point-of-care (POC) tests, and most of them used immunochromatography to identify antigens (proteins) or antibodies in dipstick or lateral-flow formats. (For definitions of antigens and antibodies, see the Glossary.) Immunochromatography relies on the migration of liquid across the surface of a nitrocellulose membrane and became a popular platform for rapid tests since its introduction in the late 1980s. POC tests have the advantages of being inexpensive to make, simple to use, and quick to produce visual findings. In addition, they often require no additional equipment.[8]

The POC tests developed for malaria became known as malaria rapid diagnostic tests (RDTs); they are also sometimes called "malaria dipsticks" or "malaria rapid diagnostic devices." Malaria RDTs use a dipstick or test strip carrying monoclonal antibodies to detect specific antigens produced by malaria parasites that are present in the blood of infected people. Health professionals are the end-users of malaria RDTs. The health worker obtains a patient's blood from a finger-prick and then places the blood sample on the RDT, as described in a WHO document.[9] Although variations exist among different malaria RDT products, the principles of the tests are similar. The test follow three basic steps, as presented in the WHO document (see Figure 5.1):

1) Dye-labeled antibody (Ab), specific for the target antigen, is present on the lower end of the nitrocellulose strip or in a well provided with the strip. Antibody, also specific for the target antigen, is bound to the strip in a thin (test) line, and either antibody specific for the labeled antibody or antigen is bound at the control line.

2) Blood and buffer, which have been placed on the strip or in the well, are mixed with the labeled antibody and are drawn up the strip across the lines of bound antibody.

3) If the antigen is present, some labeled antibody will be trapped on the test line. Other labeled antibody is trapped on the control line.

Products vary by format and are available as a dipstick (placed in wells containing blood and/or buffer), cassette (dipstick in a plastic holder), or in a card format. Cassettes are generally easier to use.[10] RDT tests for malaria typically use between two and six steps of test procedures and take five to thirty minutes.[11]

RDTs also vary by the kind of antigen (protein) detected by the product. Some products detect histidine-rich protein-2 (HRP2), others detect parasite-specific lactate dehydrogenase (pLDH), and still others react with pan-specific aldolase.[12] All tests detect proteins specific to *P. falciparum*, either HRP2 or

Figure 5.1 | Mode of action of common malaria RDT format

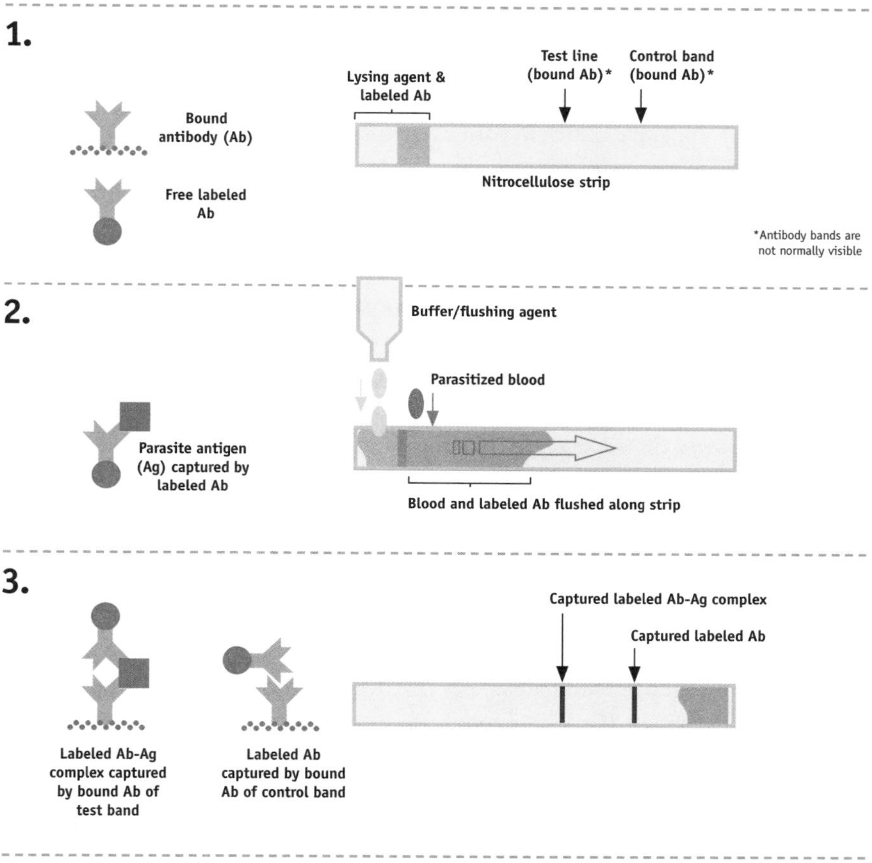

Note. From *The Use of Malaria Rapid Diagnostic Tests*, 2nd ed., by World Health Organization, 2006, Geneva: Author. Copyright 2006 by WHO. Adapted with permission.

pLDH. Some tests also detect pan-specific aldolase or pLDH; these can distinguish a non–*P. falciparum* infection from *P. falciparum* or mixed-species infections. One problem with the HRP2 tests is the persistence of the HRP2 protein following treatment—an estimated 14 days in a large proportion of people.[13] This characteristic means that HRP2 tests can show positive results even after clinical symptoms have subsided and parasitemia has disappeared in the host.[14] Emerging evidence also suggests broad antigenic variation in HRP2 from *P. falciparum* isolates within and between nations, likely influencing the accuracy of HRP2 tests at parasite densities below 500 per microliter blood.[15]

The ideal malaria diagnostic would always correctly identify whether patients have the disease. In practice, however, all diagnostic methods have some level of false-negative results (negative results in patients with malaria parasites) or false-positive results (positive results in patients without malaria parasites). Under good conditions, RDT products can achieve a low level of false-negative results, similar to levels commonly achieved by microscopy. This is important because false-negative results can lead to failure to treat a potentially fatal disease. To limit malaria treatment costs for governments and patients, RDTs also need to achieve a low level of false-positive results so health workers prescribe expensive ACT treatment only to patients with the disease. The measures of sensitivity (high sensitivity means there is a low level of false-negative results) and specificity (high specificity means there is a low level of false-positive results) are the two most widely used statistics to assess the accuracy of diagnostic tests (for definitions of these measures, see the Glossary). WHO recommends sensitivity of greater than 95% at parasite densities of 100 per microliter and specificity close to 90%.[16] Early field trials of the first commercially available RDT, the ParaSight-F test (Becton Dickinson), found sensitivity of 99% and specificity of 94%.[17]

Environmental conditions can affect the performance of RDTs.[18] The proteins identified by the tests are denatured by heat, causing some of their original properties to be diminished or eliminated. Exposure to low temperatures, 0°C and below, can also cause damage. Finally, high humidity can damage RDTs through the disruption of the nitrocellulose strip. Most manufacturers recommend RDT storage between 4°C and 30°C, requiring the maintenance of a "cool chain" for storage and distribution.[19] A cool chain for RDTs has a wider temperature range than a cold chain (the temperature-controlled supply chain for vaccines, ranging from 2° to 8°C). A major challenge with the cool chain for RDTs is that temperature control is required for extended periods at peripheral units in the health system.[20] If RDTs are stored at temperatures higher than the recommended limits, their shelf life and diagnostic accuracy will likely be affected. Packaging can help address temperature concerns, and some RDT manufacturers pay more attention to how their products are packaged than others. According to WHO, all tests should be individually packaged in sachets with two layers of foil and should remain sealed until use.[21] Careful attention to distribution procedures (including temperature-controlled transport and storage) and packaging characteristics of RDT brands is therefore important in ensuring the proper performance of RDTs.

Manufacturers' prices of RDT products depend in part on the quality of materials used (such as the nitrocellulose strip), internal quality control within the company, and an assessment of what the market can bear. On the international market, the price of most RDT brands in 2006 was between US$0.65 and US$2.50 per test.[22] Pan-specific tests are usually about 40% more expensive than products detecting *P. falciparum* only.[23]

In most developing countries, governments do not require regulatory approval for diagnostics like malaria RDTs, as they do for drugs and vaccines. Most manufacturers, therefore, choose not to enter the regulatory process for diagnostics. Of the multiple manufacturers producing RDTs in March 2008, only one company had approval from the U.S. Food and Drug Administration (FDA) or European regulatory agencies. This company is Binax, Inc., which worked in partnership with the U.S. Walter Reed Army Institute. Walter Reed wanted an RDT to use for its U.S. military personnel overseas, and since the product would be for purchase within the United States, it required FDA approval. Finding a company that was willing to seek FDA approval was difficult. It took years for Walter Reed to identify an appropriate partner, the American biotechnology firm Binax, a midsized company based in Maine. In looking for a commercial partner, Walter Reed staff learned that most diagnostic companies are small "mom-and-pop" businesses that do not possess the resources, know-how, or experience to navigate the FDA process.[24] They also discovered that larger companies were not interested in partnering because the technologies were not viewed as profitable enough for them.

By the early 1990s, laboratory and field trials showing high accuracy of malaria RDT products indicated that the technology could make an important contribution to malaria diagnosis. The RDTs could be particularly valuable for health workers in remote areas without reliable access to microscopy. In the next section, we examine how the technology was introduced globally and the challenges that arose.

Introduction of Rapid Diagnostic Tests (Phase 2)

Introduction of malaria RDTs began in the mid-1990s, when the first RDT, Para-Sight-F (Becton Dickinson), became commercially available. The first RDT kits detected HRP2 proteins and therefore could only diagnose *P. falciparum* malaria. RDTs detecting other proteins were still being tested in clinical and field studies and were not yet commercially available. The first-to-market HRP2 RDT kits were primarily purchased for national malaria control programs. Government agencies and non-governmental organizations and others also purchased RDTs for special situations such as complex emergencies, epidemics, and the diagnosis of malaria in returning travelers.[25] The total number of RDT tests sold in the mid- to late 1990s is unknown, but one manufacturer reported selling 3 to 6 million tests in this period.[26]

The early introduction of RDTs was not coordinated by any global organization and was driven by demand from developing-country governments and non-governmental organizations. Manufacturers introduced their products on the market as they became available, with little coordination among producers, potential purchasers, and global actors. In October 1999, a joint WHO/U.S. Agency for International Development (USAID) informal consultation in Geneva began to bring some global coordination to RDT introduction. At this meeting, developers, manufacturers, and potential users of malaria RDTs discussed the current status of the tests as well as future actions, research needs, and standards to ensure widespread access.

Participants in the meeting identified three priority areas for action.[27] First, some of the technical characteristics of RDTs needed improvement, such as reducing false-negative and false-positive results, assistance to end-users (such as clear instructions in appropriate languages), and temperature stability. Second, the meeting called for the establishment of a system of international quality control and quality assurance outside the commercial sector. Participants agreed that the WHO or another agency should act as the global coordinating body for RDTs on quality assurance issues. Quality assurance for RDTs includes all processes for ensuring and sustaining high quality performance, from the manufacture of diagnostic components to their use and interpretation by RDT end-users, health workers in developing countries.[28] The third area for action was the need for multidisciplinary analysis on such issues as the cost of deploying RDTs, the potential for RDTs to reduce malaria mortality and morbidity and delay drug resistance, and the use of diagnostic results by health workers.

Participants also discussed the affordability of RDTs. Many believed that national and global actors perceived product price as the most important obstacle to widespread use. The price was higher for RDTs ($0.65–2.50 per test) than for microscopy ($0.12–0.40 per slide).[29] Participants discussed possible ways to decrease the cost of RDTs for governments, such as reducing distribution costs, import fees, and local taxes through government intervention; promoting technology transfer or local production; and encouraging bulk purchasing.[30] Overall, participants agreed that even at a reduced purchase price of $0.30–0.50 per test, widespread use of RDTs was unlikely to occur or continue without substantial and sustained external assistance.

In the early 2000s, the use of RDTs increased rapidly as did the number of products available. WHO estimates that procurement nearly doubled from 2000 to 2004.[31] Reported procurement of RDTs in 2005 was 12 million units. WHO notes that these procurement figures are incomplete because of a lack of private-sector data and incomplete reporting by procurement agencies.[32] Global RDT production figures are perhaps a more accurate measure of uptake because manufacturers usually only produce RDTs when they receive procurement orders. Figure 5.2 shows that global RDT production in 2005 was 28 million units. Increased funding for malaria control programs through the Global Fund to Fight AIDS, TB, and Malaria (Global Fund) fueled the rising procurement of RDTs. The number of countries adopting RDT use and budgeting for them in malaria control activities rose from 1 country in 2000 to 32 countries in 2005. In particular, the public sector in countries of South America, Southern Africa, and

Figure 5.2 | Country RDT procurement and manufacturer production data

Number of RDTs (millions)

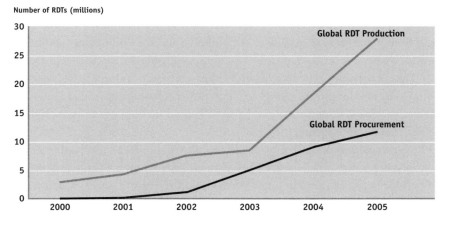

Note. WHO calculated RDT procurement data from Global Fund to Fight AIDS, Tuberculosis and Malaria documents, the WHO World Malaria Report, UNICEF and MSF procurement information, and the WHO Global Atlas Query. These estimates are incomplete because they lack private-sector data and complete reporting by procurement agencies. RDT production figures may provide a better measure of RDTs obtained in developing countries, as manufacturers usually only produce RDTs when they receive orders. WHO calculated RDT production by taking the total amount of anti-HRP2 antibody supplied to manufacturers and dividing by 0.7 micrograms (the average amount of antibody used per RDT). WHO then calculated total annual RDT production assuming that HRP2 RDTs represent 8% of the RDT market. Data from "Forecasting Global Procurement of Malaria Rapid Diagnostic Tests: Estimates and Uncertainties," by World Health Organization, available at http://www.wpro.who.int/sites/rdt.

Southeast Asia purchased RDTs on a large scale. The non-governmental organization Médecins Sans Frontières (MSF) also increasingly used RDTs in its operational programs.

In this period of rapid uptake, three challenges associated with RDTs emerged: (1) varying performance of RDT products in field use and study findings, (2) confusing range of products on the market, and (3) limited health worker and patient adoption of malaria diagnostic results. We discuss these challenges next.

Varying Performance of RDT Products

Health workers in developing countries using RDT products reported performance problems with some products. In particular, a high level of false-negative results appeared with a range of products and sometimes necessitated product lot replacement.[33] The specific reasons for these problems remain unclear. One explanation could be poor quality of product manufacturing, possibly related to overly rapid expansion of production. Poor quality of manufacturing can also result when procurement orders have short delivery times and require manufacturers to increase production at short notice, placing pressure on quality assurance processes.[34]

A second reason for performance problems could be that products were exposed to temperatures exceeding the recommended 4°C to 30°C range during transport and storage. One study that assessed temperatures in the distribution chain from manufacturer to villages in Cambodia and the Philippines found that the RDTs were frequently exposed to conditions outside the recommended limits.[35] The authors suggested that health workers use cheap and simple evaporative cooling boxes for long-term storage in villages. They also recommended a study of whether vaccine vial monitors (see chapter 7) could be used to indicate product damage due to temperature.

Problems with product performance could also arise from how health workers use RDTs. Often, the absence of clocks and timers in health clinics makes it difficult for health workers to know when to read the test results.[36] Reading the test results too late can result in back-flow of blood and buffer appearing as a positive line, leading to false-positive results on previously negative strips.[37] Furthermore, using too much blood for an RDT can result in a false-negative result because it becomes difficult to read the positive line on the test.[38] Operational difficulties such as these can decrease RDT performance. Health worker use is closely linked to the technical characteristics of the RDT product. Improving product characteristics (such as providing clear instructions and including timers) can improve health worker performance. Better training of health workers can also improve product performance and appropriate use of RDTs, as shown in various field trials.[39]

These problems with product performance created considerable uncertainty among local, national, and global actors about whether and where RDTs should be used in health systems in developing countries. For example, when is it appropriate to use RDTs instead of improving microscopy in a particular setting? In what situations are RDTs cost-effective? Should RDTs be used in both the public and private sectors? Are RDTs effective for self-diagnosis by individuals (such as travelers)?

The publication of a wide range of field and laboratory studies on RDT products, often with conflicting or inconsistent results, added to the uncertainty. Some published studies report diagnostic accuracy for *P. falciparum* well below that required for operational use. The studies also report results on individual products with widely divergent findings.[40] Publications have not suggested methods for improving RDT performance; rather they have created confusion for potential purchasers and have not provided evidence needed for guiding scaling up. With no global coordinating body in place during early introduction to help make sense of the confusing range of field experiences and research findings, potential purchasers' decisions about whether and what kind of RDTs to procure were difficult.

Confusing Range of Products

The growing range of commercial products also created confusion among purchasers of malaria RDTs. In the late 1990s, only three tests were available commercially: ParaSight-F (Becton Dickinson), ICT Malaria Pf (ICT Diagnostics), and OptiMAL (Flow, Inc.). By early 2008, 40 branded products could be purchased commercially.[41] Two of the three original tests, ParaSight-F and ICT Malaria Pf, were no longer available, and many other manufacturers had taken their products off the market. This shifting range of products is not surprising since RDTs are a new technology with a low profit margin. This situation, however, makes the assessment of products by buyers (developing-country governments and non-governmental organizations) both confusing and difficult.

Limited Health Worker and Patient Adoption

Even in contexts where RDTs are available and used, some health workers do not base their malaria treatment decisions on RDT results. As reported by WHO, "Experience indicates that some health care providers treating a patient with suspected malaria will ignore negative RDT results and give antimalarial drugs regardless."[42] The same phenomenon occurs with malaria diagnosis by microscopy. A study in Zambia found that results from microscopy had little influence on how clinicians treated patients with fever; from 20 to 54% of patients with negative blood slides were prescribed antimalarial drugs.[43] In this study, despite the availability and use of microscopy for diagnosis, many health workers continued to rely on their personal experience and intuition about clinical diagnosis in making decisions about patient management.

Health workers resist RDT results for multiple reasons, including the varying quality of available products and inconsistent evidence about their accuracy. In addition, RDTs are heat- and humidity-sensitive, and health workers at the clinic level have no way to know about the environmental exposure of kits during transport and storage. Also, when resupply systems are not in place at the national level, stock-outs may occur at health clinics, creating further frustration for health workers.[44] Another explanation is that many health workers have always relied on clinical diagnosis of malaria and find it difficult to change their diagnostic habits. A study in Malawi that assessed two RDTs found that providers were unwilling to believe negative RDT results when their clinical diagnosis was positive for malaria.[45] In this instance, they wished to run a second test to confirm the different result from clinical diagnosis. Finally, health workers may not adopt RDT results because of patient expectations about treatment when presenting with fever. The Malawi study found that patients were happy with RDT diagnostic results when the test confirmed they had malaria; if the results were negative, they were not happy with the product.[46] Public education about the benefits of test-based treatment, whether using microscopy or RDTs, could help health workers use these diagnostic methods in their patient management decisions.

Emergence of WHO as Coordinating Entity for Scaling Up (Phase 3)

High product demand and a sufficient number of manufacturers characterized the market for malaria RDTs in the early 2000s. Unlike other technologies analyzed in this book, product champions were not faced with the need to stimulate demand and encourage the entry of new manufacturers. Instead the challenges involved information, product performance, and adoption. Building a global architecture for RDT access—specifically, identifying a global coordinator to provide information, set up quality assurance systems, and bring together partner organizations—was required to address these access barriers.

The WHO/USAID meeting in 1999 recommended that WHO take on a global coordinating role for RDTs. Two years later, in 2001, WHO began an initiative to develop policies defining the place of RDTs in malaria management. The initiative also sought to address the uncertainties that had arisen about the technology and their impacts on adoption and availability. These uncertainties included the role of RDTs in health systems, quality problems, product delivery problems, and perceptions of health workers and patients. Three groups in WHO became involved in this initiative: the Roll Back Malaria Partnership (RBM) and the UNDP/World Bank/ WHO Special Programme for Research and Training in Tropical Diseases (TDR), both in Geneva, and the Western Pacific Regional Office (WPRO) of WHO in Manila. In early 2002, WPRO hired David Bell as the "global focal point" for malaria RDTs and charged him with heading the preparation of WHO guidelines on the use of this technology. He sat in WPRO's office in Manila because at the time this region had the highest use of RDTs.[47] By 2006, however, sub-Saharan Africa had become the leading user of RDTs, while Bell remained in Manila.

Early on, Bell and his WHO colleagues planned a large field trial to assess the performance of RDTs. But this field trial never occurred because of its expense (and the lack of budget) and the rapidly changing RDT products. The rapid turnover of products in the global market meant that those tested in the field trial would probably be irrelevant by the end of the trial.[48] Bell decided to shift his focus to quality assurance issues because of increasing reports about complications in field use. A meeting on Field Trials and Quality Assurance on Malaria Rapid Diagnostics Tests (funded by USAID, the U.K. Department for International Development, and Australian AID) was held at WHO's WPRO office in Manila in January 2003 to assess progress since the 1999 meeting and consider ways forward. In the meeting, participants emphasized that quality assurance processes enhance the value of RDTs because they provide "the evidence necessary to permit greater reliance on RDT results as a guide to treatment."[49]

Participants at the 2003 meeting recognized the "limited progress" in addressing the priorities identified in 1999 and "some confusion as to WHO's position in addressing them."[50] To focus WHO's position, Bell and his WHO colleagues moved forward on three strategies.

- *Policy development*: Specify policy for when and where RDTs should be used
- *Information dissemination*: Provide information about RDT products and suppliers
- *Quality assurance*: Establish quality assurance mechanisms to ensure performance of RDT products

Below we discuss these strategies and progress on them.

Policy Development

WHO efforts at policy development helped shape global consensus on RDT adoption by specifying when and where RDTs should be used.[51] The policy states that the tests should be used as a guide for decisions on the presence of clinically significant malaria infection, particularly when microscopy is not available. According to the policy, RDTs can improve malaria management if: (1) a clear plan of action has been prepared to deal with the test results (i.e., drug treatment or appropriate further investigation), (2) a clear benefit is demonstrated in health outcomes, (3) the RDTs are affordable, and (4) adequate systems exist to ensure RDTs are in good condition and are used correctly.[52] Global experts also recognized that microscopy must remain an important tool for patient management because of its many diagnostic applications and that microscopy should be supported where possible.[53] WHO policy therefore specifies that RDTs should be used in areas where good quality microscopy does not exist or cannot be maintained.

WHO staff and other technical experts also sought consensus on the role of RDTs in areas of high malaria transmission. In these areas, people acquire immunity to malaria after continued exposure to malaria parasites over time. This immunity protects most people from the severe effects of the disease, though not complete protection from malaria parasites. As a result, in high-transmission areas, children under five years are most at risk of malaria mortality and acute morbidity, while individuals over five years are relatively protected against the disease. Consequently, WHO policy states that in high transmission areas, all children under five years with a clinical suspicion of malaria (i.e., with fever) should be treated presumptively rather than tested with RDTs or microscopy. This policy recognizes that the mortality risk of misdiagnosis with RDTs (from a false-negative result) exceeds the costs and risks of overtreatment (from a false-positive result) that can occur in clinical diagnosis.[54] For children over five and adults, however, WHO recommends that treatment only be provided following parasitological diagnosis, either from microscopy or RDTs, in order to reduce the wastage of malaria treatments.

Information

To address the problem that potential RDT purchasers lack information about the range of products available, Bell and his WHO colleagues have undertaken several activities. First, they developed a website with information on trials, manufacturers, and large-scale users of RDTs (http://www.wpro.who.int/rdt). The website improves information flows and communication among end-users of RDTs (health workers), researchers, purchasers, and manufacturers, and assists policy development.[55]

WHO staff have also disseminated information to potential purchasers on the range of available RDT products and their manufacturers. WHO, in collaboration with UNICEF, Population Services International, and Management Sciences for Health made this list available in its first report of *Sources and Prices of Selected Products for the Prevention, Diagnosis and Treatment of Malaria*, which provides market information on malaria-related products from manufacturers worldwide.[56] The report gives names, format, and contact details of all diagnostic manufacturers, but the authors do not endorse or evaluate any of the products. Activists from the MSF Access Campaign complained in a January 2005 online discussion forum, E-drug, that listing the RDTs makes it inevitable that readers will assume they are endorsed by WHO and that it is "irresponsible" not to give information on the quality or performance of these tests.[57] In his reply the next day, Bell explained, "It is impossible for WHO to verify the quality of such data at present," and "WHO is continuing to develop a transparent evidence-based product testing/prequalification system."[58]

In early 2007, the WHO RDT website began to post a list of products and manufacturers that was regularly updated. The list does not represent WHO endorsement of a specific product but is restricted to manufacturers with evidence of quality manufacturing standards. Also on the website was a report from August 2005 including "interim notes" for national malaria control programs on how to select an RDT in relation to the occurrence of different parasite species. Bell sees it as the organization's role to advise countries on what kind of product would respond best to the country's epidemiological situation.[59] For instance, choosing the appropriate RDT depends on whether the purchaser's region is a low-, moderate-, or high-transmission context and which malaria species (i.e., *P. falciparum* or *P. vivax*) is predominant. These information activities helped to fix some of the market failures that have affected global sales of malaria RDTs, especially as the market expanded rapidly in the past five years.

Quality Assurance

A main focus of WHO's work as the RDT coordinating body has been the development of quality assurance methods for RDT products. WHO's initiative on quality assurance began in 2002 and functions in collaboration with the UNICEF/UNDP/ World Bank/WHO Special Programme for Research and Training in Tropical Diseases (TDR) and the Foundation for Innovative New Diagnostics (FIND). These organizations are focusing their work in three areas: product testing, lot testing, and testing at the level of the end-user. In the early years, WHO had limited funding to implement these quality assurance activities; this changed with a December 2006 grant ($9.8 million) from the Bill & Melinda Gates Foundation (through FIND) and funding from Australian AID (through WPRO) and TDR.

WHO and its partners in the quality assurance initiative have prioritized activities that ensure high quality RDTs because they believe this is a precondition to addressing other elements of RDT use, such as health worker use and interpretation. Product testing has been a primary focus. Partners in the initiative have developed a global specimen bank of antigen and parasite samples (housed in the U.S. Centers for Disease Control and Prevention) to support product testing. The laboratory-based product assessment involves testing on sensitivity, specificity, stability, and ease of use. The goal of this product testing is to generate performance data on commercially available RDT products. The data can then be used to guide UN procurement and WHO recommendations to government procurement agencies, and will provide a basis for future WHO prequalification of RDT products.[60] Lot testing (the testing of product conformity to expected standards at time of purchase) has also been conducted by the WHO quality assurance initiative through a network of laboratories around the world.

WHO and partner organizations have also begun quality assurance activities that address health worker use of RDTs. The Quality Assurance Project, funded by USAID, conducted quality-design research in the Philippines and the Lao People's Democratic Republic. The project sought to develop a generic RDT "job aid" that could be used with different products and in varying cultural contexts.[61] Job aids provide "simplified words and pictures on a card to explain each step in the correct application of the test," helping to train health workers in contexts with limited resources.[62] These job aids can improve health worker performance, particularly for procedures that involve concrete, predefined steps that must be followed each time the procedure is carried out, as is the case for RDTs.

Conclusions

The malaria RDT is a new diagnostic technology whose use has steadily increased since the early 2000s. WHO estimates that RDT procurement will continue to increase and that over 460 million RDTs will be purchased in the next 10 years.[63] In this period of scaling up, the product has faced several challenges that have affected availability and adoption, especially problems with product performance in field use, a confusing array of products, and resistance by health workers to use test results in patient management (see Table 5.1 for a summary of access barriers and strategies). Unlike most of the other health technologies discussed in this book, the global introduction phase for RDTs did not happen through product advocacy, a global architecture, or carefully planned access phases. Product introduction occurred mainly through commercial channels, beginning with the first malaria RDT product (from Becton Dickinson) in the mid-1990s. Other RDTs appeared in the global market as companies brought their new products forward. Commercial demand for this product was fueled by new external financing for purchasing malaria diagnostics—especially from the Global Fund—leading to a rapid expansion of the RDT market.

The provision of global financing for malaria control thus drove the technological innovation and global adoption of these rapid diagnostic tests. A major challenge for countries that have adopted malaria RDTs is future affordability. How will they build sustainable funding sources to purchase and use RDTs in the future if the external funds (from global aid) start to decline and dry up? As with many health technologies discussed in this book, the world's poorest countries do not have the internal resources to purchase the product or would be unwilling to purchase the product given other competing demands on their limited national budgets.

Market expansion of malaria RDTs thus occurred before a global-level architecture existed to support the scaling up of the new technology. It took WHO two years after a formal recommendation in 1999 to establish a "global focal point" for RDTs to address the challenges of making the diagnostic widely available. Moreover, the "global focal point" took the form of an individual, David Bell of the WHO regional office in Manila. Product champions for diagnostics within WHO usually consist of a single person, as the diagnostic field tends to be underfunded compared to other types of health technologies.[64] Though Bell is doing an excellent job as the global focal point for RDTs, he initially operated with extremely limited resources. This stands in stark contrast to the increased funding for RDT procurement through the Global Fund, which is expected to continue rising in the near future. This case study emphasizes that for new health technologies for poor countries, well-financed, effective global coordinating bodies are important for addressing market failures (such as information and quality problems) that arise in attempts to provide access. Furthermore, these global coordinating bodies are more effective if they are in place early, before rapid market expansion occurs.

This case study also demonstrates the importance of ensuring a good quality product from manufacturers. This availability issue arises in particular for diagnostics because most developing countries do not require regulatory approval for diagnostics, as is required for drugs and vaccines. As of March 2008, only one malaria RDT product had U.S. FDA approval. Alternative methods to assess quality—through quality assurance and prequalification systems—required time to put in place for malaria RDTs so that purchasers often had little guidance or independent information on the quality or appropriateness of products they considered. The development of assessment systems for product quality thus enables adoption at the global and national levels, as well as by end-users (in this case, health workers), since it helps create knowledge and trust about the diagnostic's performance during field use.

Finding a good partner for production in the private sector was not easy for one product developer of malaria RDTs, the Walter Reed Army institute, because the developer needed to find a company that would take the product to the FDA. After several years, Walter Reed located an appropriate partner in Binax, Inc., a midsized company. This experience shows that many diagnostic companies are unable to work through the FDA process because they do not possess the resources, know-how, or experience. Furthermore, large diagnostic companies may not be interested in partnering for the production of certain health technologies if the technologies are not viewed as sufficiently profitable.

The RDT access story emphasizes the importance of health systems in affecting adoption and use, even for relatively simple technologies such as rapid diagnostics. The operational use of RDTs requires good compliance with certain procedures and, depending on the product, appropriate infrastructure (such as a clock or timer) for producing accurate results. Suitable training, supervision, and clear instructions in the correct languages all influence the quality of RDT use by health workers. Health systems in poor countries thus require various kinds of targeted support if malaria RDTs are to produce the intended result of improved treatment of malaria cases.

Even if high-quality RDTs reach remote clinics and health workers have sufficient training to use the tests appropriately, other problems can affect whether the diagnostic is used in clinical decision-making. Some health workers have been hesitant to accept RDT results because of variable product quality, as well as their own diagnostic habits. Better product information and improved product quality will help address these challenges. But sometimes the problem arises from patient expectations of malaria treatment when presenting with fever. This case study highlights the importance of in-depth understanding by product developers of the challenges that end-users face. For malaria diagnostic products (and many other health technologies), this may require a paradigm shift in product development to involve people who understand operational realities at the field level in developing countries.[65]

The story of RDT access is still unfolding in malaria endemic countries around the world. Efforts to promote the product show that just developing a promising new technology is not enough to ensure access. Financing, global coordinating bodies, sufficient information flow, and quality assurance mechanisms all are important factors in promoting the adoption at global, national, and local levels, in assuring the high quality availability of the technology, and in securing the continued financing and affordability that can together ensure ongoing access to new malaria diagnostics. Even if RDTs reach health workers in the periphery of health systems in poor countries, the technology's influence on malaria mortality and morbidity ultimately depends on how end-users use test results in patient management decisions and on the availability and appropriate use of antimalarial medication. Future access efforts for this product will need to include contextually relevant strategies to address these ongoing challenges.

Table 5.1 | **Malaria rapid diagnostic tests access table**

	BARRIER	STRATEGY	SPECIFIC ACTION
ARCHITECTURE	Lack of effective global architecture for access in developing countries	Create global coordinator to promote the technology	Global focal point for malaria RDTs established in WHO regional office in Manila; the focal point consists of one individual who has limited funding for access activities
ADOPTION	Lack of global consensus about when and where RDTs should be used (affecting national and end-user adoption)	Promote global dialogue on appropriate policy and develop global policy guidelines	WHO held global meetings to discuss and develop guidelines on when and where RDTs should be used in health systems
	Limited global, national, and end-user adoption due to varying product performance in field use and study findings (performance affected by poor manufacturing quality, temperature exposure during storage and transport, and health worker use)	Facilitate international agreement on quality assurance system and supply stability	WHO collaborated with the Foundation for Innovative New Diagnostics to develop a quality assurance system for malaria RDTs
		Improve training for health workers on RDT use	WHO developed "job aids" for health workers to provide simplified and effective training that can be implemented in resource-poor health systems
	Limited health worker use of RDT results in decisions about patient management and treatment	Improve training for health workers on RDT use	WHO developed "job aids" for health workers to provide simplified and effective training that can be implemented in resource-poor health systems
AFFORDABILITY	High product price (affecting government affordability), especially compared to microscopy	Promote international financing to support government purchases of malaria RDTs	The Global Fund to Fight AIDS, TB and Malaria provided ample funds to countries to support increased procurement of malaria RDTs, thereby fueling market expansion
		Improve forecasting to take advantage of potential economies of scale	WHO has proposed a coordinated procurement and staggered delivery scheme but this is still in planning stages

Table 5.1 | Malaria rapid diagnostic tests access table (continued)

	BARRIER	STRATEGY	SPECIFIC ACTION
AVAILABILITY	Poor quality products, leading to performance problems of RDTs	Set up quality assurance system, improve forecasting, and ensure steady supply	WHO collaborated with the Foundation for Innovative New Diagnostics to develop a quality assurance system for malaria RDTs
			WHO has proposed a coordinated procurement and staggered delivery scheme but this is still in planning stages
	Shifting array of products on the global market, creating information problems for purchasers	Create information system on available products and prices	WHO focal point in WPRO (Manila) created website with regularly updated information on products and suppliers

Endnotes

1 Roll Back Malaria Partnership, *What Is Malaria?* (Geneva: World Health Organization, 2000), http://www.rbm.who.int/cmc_upload/0/000/015/372/RBMInfosheet_1.pdf (retrieved February 2, 2007); and UN Millennium Project, Task Force on HIV/AIDS, Malaria, TB, and Access to Essential Medicines Working Group on Malaria, Awash Teklehaimanot, Burt Singer, Andrew Spielman, Yesim Tozan, and Allan Schapira, *Coming to Grips with Malaria in the New Millennium* (London: Earthscan, 2005).

2 Roll Back Malaria Partnership.

3 Roll Back Malaria Partnership.

4 WHO in 2006 recommended the following combination therapies: (1) artemether/lumefantrine, (2) artesunate plus amodiaquine, (3) artesunate plus mefloquine, and (4) artesunate plus sulfadoxine/pyrimethamine. For more information, see: World Health Organization, *The Use of Malaria Rapid Diagnostic Tests*, 2nd ed., (Geneva: WHO, 2006), http://www.wpro.who.int/NR/rdonlyres/A30D47E1-1612-4674-8DF8FCA031CDB9BA/0/Reducedweb2_MalariaRDT_20062ndedition.pdf (retrieved February 2, 2007).

5 World Health Organization, *New Perspectives: Malaria Diagnosis: Report of a Joint WHO/USAID Informal Consultation, 25–27 October, 1999* (Geneva: WHO, 2000, WHO/CDS/RBM/2000.14/WHO/MAL/2000.1091).

6 World Health Organization, *New Perspectives*.

7 World Health Organization, *New Perspectives*.

8 David Mabey, Rosanna W. Peeling, Andrew Ustianowski, and Mark D. Perkins, "Diagnostics for the Developing World," *Nature Reviews. Microbiology* 2 (2004): 231–240.

9   World Health Organization, *The Use of MRDTs.*

10 Bevinje S. Kakkilaya, "Rapid Diagnosis of Malaria," *Lab Medicine* 8, no. 34 (2003): 602–608; and Anthony Moody, "Rapid Diagnostic Tests for Malaria Parasites," *Clinical Microbiology Reviews* 15 (2002): 66–78.

11 Kakkilaya; and World Health Organization, *New Perspectives.*

12 A water-soluble protein, HRP2 is produced by the asexual stages of young (but not mature) gametocytes of *P. falciparum*. PLDH is a soluble glycolytic enzyme produced by the asexual and sexual stages (gametocytes) of the live parasites and has been found in all four human malaria species. Pan-specific aldolase is an enzyme expressed by the blood stages of *P. falciparum* as well as the non-*P. falciparum* malaria parasites. Kakkilaya, 2003; World Health Organization, *The Role of Laboratory Diagnosis to Support Malaria Disease Management: Focus on the Use of Rapid Diagnostic Tests in Areas of High Transmission* (Geneva: WHO, 2006), http://www.who.int/malaria/docs/ReportLABdiagnosis-web.pdf (retrieved February 9, 2007).

13 World Health Organization, *The Role of Laboratory Diagnosis.*

14 Moody.

15 World Health Organization, *The Role of Laboratory Diagnosis.*

16 World Health Organization, *Malaria Rapid Diagnosis: Making It Work: Meeting Report of an Informal Consultation on Field Trials and Quality Assurance on Malaria Rapid Diagnostic Tests* (Manila: World Health Organization Regional Office for the Western Pacific, January, 2003).

17 Christine Beadle, Gary W. Long, Walter R. Weiss, Peter D. McElroy, S. Melissa Maret, Aggrey J. Oloo, and Stephen L. Hoffman, "Diagnosis of Malaria by Detection of *Plasmodium Falciparum* HRP-2 Antigen with a Rapid Dipstick Antigen-Capture Assay," *Lancet* 343 (1994): 564–568.

18 World Health Organization, *The Role of Laboratory Diagnosis.*

19 Pernille Jorgensen, Lon Chanthap, Antero Rebueno, Reiko Tsuyuoka, and David Bell, "Malaria Rapid Diagnostic Tests in Tropical Climates: The Need for a Cool Chain," *American Journal of Tropical Medicine & Hygiene* 74, no. 5 (2006): 750–754; World Health Organization, *Malaria Rapid Diagnosis*; and World Health Organization, *The Use of MRDTs.*

20 Jorgensen.

21 World Health Organization, *The Role of Laboratory Diagnosis.*

22 World Health Organization, *The Role of Laboratory Diagnosis.*

23 David Bell, *Is there a Role for Malaria Rapid Diagnostic Tests in Africa?* (Geneva: WHO/Roll Back Malaria, 2004).

24 Interview by author (Laura Frost) with anonymous official, March 31, 2006.

25 World Health Organization, *New Perspectives.*

26 World Health Organization, *New Perspectives.*

27 World Health Organization, *New Perspectives.*

28 World Health Organization and UNICEF/UNDP/World Bank/WHO Special Programme for Research & Training in Tropical Diseases (TDR), *Towards Quality Testing of Malaria Rapid Diagnostic Tests: Evidence and Methods* (Manila, Philippines: WHO/WPRO, 2006), http://www.wpro.who.int (retrieved March 22, 2008).

29 World Health Organization, *New Perspectives*.

30 World Health Organization, *New Perspectives*.

31 World Health Organization, "Forecasting Global Procurement of Malaria Rapid Diagnostic Tests: Estimates and Uncertainties," http://www.wpro.who.int/sites/rdt (retrieved April 12, 2008).

32 World Health Organization, "Forecasting Global Procurement."

33 World Health Organization, *Malaria Rapid Diagnosis*.

34 World Health Organization, "Forecasting Global Procurement."

35 Jorgensen et al.

36 Interview by author (Laura Frost) with anonymous NGO official, November 15, 2005.

37 World Health Organization, *The Role of Laboratory Diagnosis*.

38 Interview with anonymous NGO official.

39 A. H. Kilian, G. Kabagambe, W. Byamukama, P. Langi, P. Weis, and F. von Sonnenburg, "Application of the ParaSight-F Dipstick Test for Malaria Diagnosis in a District Control Program," *Acta Tropica* 72 (1999): 281–293; Z. Premji, J. N. Minjas, and C. J. Shiff, "Laboratory Diagnosis of Malaria by Village Health Workers Using the Rapid Manual ParaSight™-F test," *Transactions of the Royal Society of Tropical Medicine and Hygiene* 88 (1994): 418; and Mayfong Mayxay, Paul N. Newton, Shunmay Yeung, Tiengkham Pongvongsa, Samlane Phompida, Rattanaxay Phetsouvanh, and Nicholas J. White, "Short Communication: An Assessment of the Use of Malaria Rapid Tests by Village Health Volunteers in Rural Laos," *Tropical Medicine and International Health* 9 (2004): 325–329.

40 World Health Organization, *Malaria Rapid Diagnosis*.

41 World Health Organization, "Forecasting Global Procurement."

42 World Health Organization, *New Perspectives*, 36.

43 Lawrence Barat, James Chipipa, Margarette Kolczak, and Thomas Sukway, "Does the Availability of Blood Slide Microscopy for Malaria at Health Centers Improve the Management of Persons with Fever in Zambia?" *American Journal of Tropical Medicine and Hygiene* 60 (1999): 1024–1030.

44 World Health Organization, *The Role of Laboratory Diagnosis*.

45 Paula Tavrow, Elisa Knebel, and Lynne Cogswell, "Using Quality Design to Improve Malaria Rapid Diagnostic Tests in Malawi," *Operations Research Results* 1, no. 4 (2000).

46 Tavrow et al.

47 Interview by researcher (Jennifer Nanni) with anonymous official, October 28, 2005.

48 Interview with anonymous official, October 28, 2005.

49 World Health Organization, *Malaria Rapid Diagnosis*, 1.

50 World Health Organization, *Malaria Rapid Diagnosis*, 3.

51 World Health Organization, *The Use of MRDTs*.

52 World Health Organization, *The Use of MRDTs*.

53 World Health Organization, *The Role of Laboratory Diagnosis*.

54 World Health Organization, *The Role of Laboratory Diagnosis*.

55 World Health Organization, *Steps Towards the Development of a Global WHO Policy on Malaria Rapid Diagnostic Tests* (Geneva: WHO, 2002).

56 World Health Organization, UNICEF, Population Services International, and Management Sciences for Health, *Sources and Prices of Selected Products for the Prevention, Diagnosis and Treatment of Malaria* (Geneva: WHO, 2004), www.who.int/medicines/areas/access/ AntiMalariaSourcesPricesEnglish.pdf (retrieved February 5, 2007).

57 Daniel Berman (19 January 2005). Quality of Malaria Tests in WHO Sources & Prices [Msg 3]. Message posted to www.essentialdrugs.org/edrug/archive/200501/msg00064.php.

58 David Bell (20 January 2005). Quality of Malaria Tests in WHO Sources & Prices [Msg 4]. Message posted to www.essentialdrugs.org/edrug/archive/200501/msg00062.php.

59 Interview with anonymous official, October 28, 2005.

60 World Health Organization and TDR, *Towards Quality Testing of Malaria Rapid Diagnostic Tests*.

61 Waverly Rennie and Steven A. Harvey, *Field Report: Developing and Testing a Generic Job Aid for Malaria Rapid Diagnostic Tests (RDTs)* (Bethesda, MD: Quality Assurance Project, 2004).

62 World Health Organization, *The Role of Laboratory Diagnosis*, 23; and Elisa Knebel, *The Use of Manual Job Aids by Health Care Providers: What Do We Know?* (Bethesda, MD: Quality Assurance Project, 2000).

63 World Health Organization, "Forecasting Global Procurement."

64 Interview by author (Laura Frost) with anonymous official, January 4, 2007.

65 Interview with anonymous NGO official.

CHAPTER 6

NORPLANT:

Access to Contraceptives

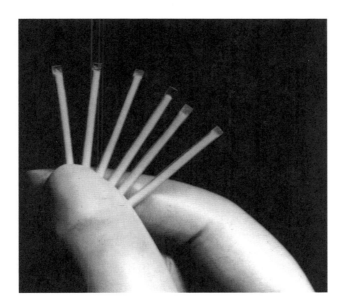

THE NORPLANT SYSTEM IS A SUBDERMAL FORM OF REVERSIBLE CONTRACEPTIVE that can prevent pregnancy for up to five years with an efficacy rate of over 99.9%. The implant system consists of six Silastic capsules that are inserted into a woman's upper arm and release the synthetic progestin levonorgestrel on a continual basis. The administration of Norplant requires a medical provider, specialized equipment, and 10 to 20 minutes for the insertion procedure. A medical provider is also necessary for Norplant removal, a procedure that can be conducted any time after insertion.

The Population Council, a New York–based nonprofit organization, began developing Norplant in the 1960s. The idea behind the development of an implant contraceptive was that its long-acting effectiveness and limited maintenance were ideal for women who lacked regular access to health services. Norplant fit this profile. It resembles the pill in that it inhibits ovulation but differs in its long-acting effectiveness. The implant contraceptive is also similar to the intra-uterine device (IUD) in that it is long acting, reversible, and highly efficacious, but unlike the IUD, Norplant does not require a gynecological procedure. Norplant was approved by the U.S. FDA in 1990, offering women a new choice for long-term contraception that generated excitement around the world.

This case study begins with the story of Norplant development and then examines the product introduction activities of the Population Council and its partners in the 1980s. The chapter then assesses efforts at scaling up global access to Norplant from the early 1990s to today. The Norplant story involves several key players: the Population Council, product developer and global coordinator of product introduction in developing countries; the U.S.-based company Wyeth-Ayerst Laboratories (now Wyeth Pharmaceuticals), provider of Norplant to the private sector in both developed and developing countries; the Finland-based manufacturer Leiras Oy (now Bayer Schering Pharma AG), provider of the Norplant system to the public sector in developing countries; as well as government and non-governmental organizations' family planning programs, health providers, and women who use the implants. The chapter pays particular attention to the Population Council's efforts to construct effective architecture for Norplant at the global and national levels.

The Norplant case study examines a technology that was repeatedly shown to have high safety, efficacy, and effectiveness in clinical trials and postmarketing surveillance but still encountered numerous access problems within countries. Some access barriers are related to the technical characteristics of Norplant that created problems of end-user adoption. These characteristics also affected availability, because as a provider-dependent technology, Norplant required trained health professionals for insertion and removal. Other barriers, such as cost, are less specific to Norplant and relate to broader issues of affordability in providing access to health technologies in poor countries. The lessons learned by the Population Council and its partners in promoting access to Norplant worldwide serve as a cautionary tale to access planners for other new health technologies.

Product Development of Norplant (Phase 1)

In the mid-1960s, Sheldon J. Segal, director of the Biomedical Division at the Population Council, and postgraduate fellow Horacio Croxatto proposed that subdermal capsules of polydimethylsiloxane (also known by Dow Corning's trade name Silastic) could be used for long-term, reversible, steroidal contraception. Silastic, a medical-grade plastic, is the polymerized form of a silicone-based compound. At the time Segal and Croxatto became interested in the compound, it had already been in medical use for over 15 years and was used, among other applications, as tubing to drain fluid building up around the brain into the abdominal cavity for children born with hydrocephalus. Silastic's most important property was its biocompatibility; it can be used in the human body without causing a reaction or an allergic response.[1]

According to Segal, the concept of a subdermal implant contraceptive was a "logical extension" of work at Children's Hospital in Boston. Judah Folkman, a pediatric surgeon, and his colleague David Long were using Silastic in experimental surgery and discovered that oil-soluble dyes slowly diffuse out of Silastic.[2] As Segal recalled after hearing about Folkman's findings, "I immediately thought, if oil-soluble dyes, why not oil-soluble hormones? Putting this together with biocompatibility, I could envisage a system placed subdermally, like the hydrocephalus shunts, that would slowly release a steroid hormone and serve as a long-acting contraceptive."[3] Segal envisaged a new contraceptive method that "would enable a woman to substitute one clinic visit for thousands of days of pill taking."[4]

To make this new concept a reality, Segal and his team at the Population Council needed to identify a suitable contraceptive compound, potent enough so that a small amount released each day could act as a contraceptive. They also needed to decide on the most appropriate form of Silastic implant to provide the desired safety and effectiveness for human use. Moving forward on these two activities required first securing the appropriate intellectual property rights on Silastic. Folkman's patent on the principle of steroid diffusion through Silastic had been assigned to the Dow-Corning Company of Midland, Michigan. Folkman agreed to waive royalty rights for any product that might come out of the Population Council's work, but this needed approval by Ira Hutchinson, an executive at Dow-Corning. Hutchinson agreed to the waiver after several visits to the Population Council, which assured him that the Council was not planning to use the patent for commercial purposes.[5] The issue of intellectual property rights, however, would have to be revisited once Segal and his team identified a suitable contraceptive compound since all the compounds under consideration belonged to different companies.

To move forward on the biochemical and clinical studies, Segal decided to work through a cooperative research group. As he states in his memoir, "Instead of hiring a large clinical research group, as was customary for product development efforts in pharmaceutical companies, I decided to form a team of talented people who would stay in their home academic positions and work with us on contraceptive development projects."[6] This cooperative research group became known as the International Committee for Contraceptive Research (ICCR).[7] The structure of this group resembles the model of a "virtual research organization" employed by some of today's public-private partnerships for product development, such as the Drugs for Neglected Diseases Initiative.

ICCR's search for the optimal contraceptive hormone to use with the implant confronted a series of challenges. The team first studied a progestin called megestrol acetate, owned by the British Drug House of the United Kingdom. After "considerable progress" with the compound, the research group faced a "discouraging setback" when the British Drug House withdrew the chemical because of adverse findings in beagle dogs.[8] The group then decided to test all progestins used in oral contraceptives or for other gynecological purposes. A major scientific advance proved vital to the research team's work—the discovery of a synthesis process to produce the progestin called norgestrel. This compound has a high potency per unit weight compared to other progestins and showed good diffusion characteristics from Silastic.

In 1974, ICCR began human studies of a six-capsule contraceptive drug delivery system comparing several different synthetic hormones. The research team finally chose norgestrel, belonging to Wyeth-Ayerst Laboratories of Radnor, Pennsylvania,[9] after conducting a randomized clinical trial in 1975 comparing norgestrel with a super-progesterone named R2010 from the Roussell-UCLAF Company of Paris. The study was conducted in six countries (Brazil, Chile, Denmark, Finland, the Dominican Republic, and Jamaica), and found that norgestrel had a higher level of contraceptive efficacy, although R2010 limited the amount of vaginal bleeding. While Segal wanted to pursue both hormones to give women more choice, budgetary constraints required ICCR to select only one compound, and norgestrel made the final cut based on efficacy, clinical acceptability, and safety.[10] Norgestrel's safety was further supported by animal studies and large-scale human studies conducted by Wyeth-Ayerst, which already produced oral contraceptives containing norgestrel.[11]

Intellectual property rights again emerged as an issue when the Population Council asked Wyeth-Ayerst to use their compound for the contraceptive implant. As Segal explains,

Ordinarily, companies are reluctant to release compounds that are used in their successful commercial products for other uses. An unexpected finding could be extremely damaging. By this time, Wyeth's line of oral contraceptives was the high-riding leader of the pack in the U.S., so there was a lot at stake. Once again, the credit belongs to an in-house executive who believed in the importance of the Population Council's work. At Wyeth, it was Dr. Richard Bogash, a chemist with a worldly view, who had risen to become a vice president of the company. He persuaded his company to enter into an "agreement to agree" with the Population Council so that we could proceed with our implant studies with assurance that, if successful, a product would be made available to women around the world.[12]

The Norplant system that resulted from the product development process consisted of six flexible, silicone-based capsules made of Silastic, each containing 36 milligrams of levonorgestrel (a more potent version of norgestrel). Each capsule was 34 millimeters long with a diameter of 2.4 millimeters. The wall thickness of Silastic controlled the rate of diffusion and was custom made for Norplant. The implants, inserted into a woman's upper arm in a "fan" pattern under local anesthesia, released levonorgestrel into a woman's circulation at a relatively constant rate over five years.

Product development for Norplant was not an easy road, as often happens with many health technologies. As Segal states, "It sounds so straightforward in retrospect, but we hit brick walls along the way. On at least two occasions I can recall, we came close to dropping the idea."[13] During the development process, ICCR scientists assessed as many safety problems as they could hypothesize (see Table 6.1 for a list of studies). With these studies completed and results satisfactory, Norplant was ready in the early 1980s for introduction in developed and developing countries.

Table 6.1 | Trials undertaken in development of Norplant

Clinical Trials in 15 Countries:	
1975-1979	Phase III multinational trials in Brazil, Chile, Denmark, Dominican Republic, Finland, Jamaica (PC/ICCR)
1980-1982	Trials begin in Colombia, Ecuador, Egypt, India, Indonesia, Thailand (PC)
1981	Phase II/III studies begin in the United States. Another multinational Phase III clinical trial begins in Chile. Dominican Republic, Finland, Sweden, and the United States (PC/ICCR)
1990-1995	Phase III clinical trials of soft tubing Norplant capsules and reformulated Norplant with two rods in Chile, Dominican Republic, Egypt, Finland, Singapore, Thailand, United States
Preintroduction Studies in 30 Countries (start dates):	
1984	Bangladesh, Brazil, Chile, China, Dominican Republic, Haiti, Kenya, Nepal, Nigeria
1985	Philippines, Singapore, Sri Lanka, Zambia
1988	Colombia, El Salvador, Ghana, Malaysia, Mexico, Pakistan, Peru, Senegal, South Korea, Tunisia, Venezuela, Zambia
1989	Bahamas, Rwanda, Zaire (now Democratic Republic of Congo)
1990	Bolivia, Madagascar
Private-Sector Training in 7 Countries (Leiras Oy):	
1988	Belgium, Bulgaria, former Soviet Union, France, Israel, West Germany, Taiwan
Postmarketing Surveillance in 8 Countries (WHO/HRP, PC, FHI)	
1988-1997	Bangladesh, Chile, China, Columbia, Egypt, Indonesia, Sri Lanka, Thailand
Training Curriculum Testing:	
	Nigeria, Rwanda, Kenya
International Training Centers:	
	Dominican Republic, Egypt, Indonesia
Regional Training Center	
	Kenya
Over 70 Acceptability Studies in 20 Countries (FHI, PC, PATH, clinics, health ministries):	
1987 (start date)	Bangladesh, Brazil, China, Colombia, Dominican Republic, Ecuador, Egypt, Haiti, Indonesia, Kenya, Mexico, Nepal, Nigeria, Peru, Philippines, Rwanda, Sri Lanka, Thailand, United States, Zambia

Note. FHI = Family Health International, ICCR = International Committee for Contraception Research, PATH = Program for Appropriate Technologies in Health, PC = Population Council. From *Contraceptive Research, Introduction, and Use: Lessons from Norplant* by Polly F. Harrison and Allan Rosenfield, eds., 1998, New York: National Academy Press, p. 109. Copyright 1998 by the National Academy of Sciences. Adapted with permission.

Introducing Norplant in Developing Countries (Phase 2)

In 1980, the Population Council turned its attention toward access for Norplant in developing countries. Staff members in the organization recognized that some of Norplant's characteristics would present challenges to access. For example, in many women Norplant can cause menstrual changes, including frequent, prolonged, or absent bleeding. Council staff knew that these changes would create inconvenience to some users. In addition, they knew that the product depended on quality health services. Norplant requires trained health staff for counseling, insertion, removal, and clinical management. As Spicehandler notes, "From the outset of the introduction program, it became clear that Norplant would be both a training-intensive and service-intensive method."[14]

The Population Council decided to undertake systematic planning for the introduction and scaling up of Norplant in developing countries. This effort marked the first time that a public-sector organization managed contraceptive introduction in this way.[15] As Spicehandler reports, the decision emerged from three concerns that Council staff had about worldwide access to Norplant.[16] The first concern related to lessons learned in earlier attempts to introduce the intrauterine device (IUD) into family planning programs. The IUD had been seen as a revolution in the contraceptive field because of its high efficacy in clinical trials. But once women began to use the technology, many reported problems with inadequate preinsertion checks and insufficient management of side effects. These difficulties, combined with growing rumors of IUD problems, led to high discontinuation rates and a drop-off in insertions. In her analysis of the IUD experience in India, Soni points out, "The [IUD] programme had, quite simply, been rushed through without organizational preparedness to cope with the known side effects, which in any case were higher than anticipated among a population containing many malnourished and anaemic women."[17] In his annual address in 1966, Population Council President Bernard Berelson commented that too much attention had been given to scaling up quickly and too little to communicating with women about difficulties they might experience with the IUD.[18]

The Council's second concern was the importance of addressing the perceived needs of contraceptive users in relation to a new technology. The Council understood that access to Norplant depended on the adoption of this technology by family planning organizations and by women interested in contraception. The organization's final concern related to misinformation about contraceptives. The Council knew that misinformation creates controversy, which can then limit contraceptive choice. The Council was acutely aware of the negative publicity over the faulty Dalkon Shield (an IUD associated with pelvic inflammatory disease and septic spontaneous abortion, leading to its market withdrawal in 1975) and of how the American public mistakenly linked that IUD with all others.

With an awareness of these three issues and a desire to ensure widespread access to Norplant, the Population Council began to design a comprehensive plan and architecture for Norplant. In its broader work, the Council focused on the goal of promoting increased use of family planning services instead of advocating for a specific contraceptive method. This meant that the organization would have to take a "nonpromotional approach to Norplant introduction."[19] The challenge for the Population Council was to introduce the new technology into family planning services without promoting the new method alone, so that women would have a full choice of contraceptive options.

The Population Council based its access plan in 1982 on six main strategies.[20] The first strategy was to ensure widespread availability of Norplant to the public sector at the lowest possible price. This required locating a company to produce, register, and distribute Norplant. Leiras Oy, an international pharmaceutical firm based in Turku, Finland, had collaborated with the Council during the last stages of product development. Together the two organizations worked out a licensing agreement for worldwide distribution of the product at a low price for public-sector family planning programs in developing countries. In 1984, Finland (the country of manufacture) became the first country to approve Norplant. Leiras Oy then began registration and distribution of Norplant in other countries. Meanwhile, the Population Council negotiated a licensing agreement with Wyeth-Ayerst allowing the company to manufacture and distribute Norplant in the private sector in the U.S. and other countries. The Population Council submitted the New Drug Application for Norplant to the U.S. FDA in 1988 and received approval in December 1990.

The Council's second strategy was to provide training to health providers through international training centers. Three centers (in the Dominican Republic, Chile, and Indonesia) were chosen, all of which had experience with the ICCR clinical trials. The centers offered a large caseload of both insertions and removals for training purposes and had knowledgeable staff familiar with the counseling needs specific to Norplant.[21]

The third strategy sought to promote adoption in specific countries by carrying out preintroduction trials. These trials would provide firsthand experience with the method and assessments of the effectiveness, safety, and acceptability of the method under local conditions. Undertaken during the product development phase, these studies represented an innovation in technology introduction.[22] They were important for several reasons. Sivin et al. point out that the studies helped national programs and health providers assess the method in their own settings and also provided local training.[23] In addition, in some countries regulatory approval required data on local experience with Norplant. The preintroduction studies provided these data. The studies also gave the Population Council and national governments a basis for assessment of end-user and health service needs in varying cultural and socioeconomic situations. Finally, the studies afforded the opportunity to fine-tune local management strategies for responsible introduction of the method into family planning programs and to distribute informational materials. In all, the Council and its partners conducted more than 30 preintroduction trials (as shown in Table 6.1).

The access plan's fourth strategy was to conduct end-user feedback research to assess women's satisfaction with the method. While the preintroduction studies focused on the clinic's experience with the method, the end-user research focused on the client's experiences and perceptions. This end-user research represented a critical component of the Council's Norplant access strategy.[24] The research studied whether and why women continued with Norplant despite menstrual irregularities and also the impact of these irregularities on daily life. Studies also looked at problems with access to removal on demand, sufficiency of information about Norplant, and competence of counseling and support when choosing the method.[25] The Council and its partners conducted over 70 user-acceptability studies in 20 countries (see Table 6.1 for a list of these countries).

The Council's fifth and sixth strategies related to communication activities designed to reduce negative publicity about the contraceptive. One communication activity was to inform national and local groups about Norplant and its service delivery requirements. These groups included government officials, women's groups, the medical community, counselors, and end-users. The other activity was to develop prototype informational and training materials for family planning programs to adapt to their particular contexts.

Implementing these strategies required staffing changes at the Population Council.[26] A larger management team was needed than in past Council programs. The Council decided to hire a core team of three professionals in New York and three full-time medical professionals in regional offices. In addition, two multidisciplinary advisory bodies provided input to the program's development: one on policy, biomedical, and regulatory matters, the second on end-user and health service needs. The Council also created a global architecture for Norplant based on partnerships with a number of non-governmental agencies (including Family Health International, the Program for Appropriate Technology in Health, and the Association for Voluntary Surgical Contraception). The groups had substantial expertise in training, clinical study, materials development, end-user acceptability research, and operations research.

During the introduction phase for Norplant, several global agencies began assessing the new contraceptive method. The World Health Organization (WHO) conducted a technical evaluation of Norplant in 1984 and stated that the contraceptive was "particularly advantageous to women who wish an extended period of contraceptive protection."[27] The United Nations Population Fund (UNFPA) also approved the method, and many professional organizations, including the American College of Obstetricians and Gynecologists and the American Society for Reproductive Medicine, reviewed safety and efficacy data and endorsed Norplant. These endorsements promoted both global and national adoption of the new technology.

Based on lessons learned from the introduction of the IUD and other contraceptives, the Population Council devised a comprehensive Norplant access plan for developing countries. As Council staff had anticipated, many of the access problems in countries were related to training and health service quality. However, other problems were unanticipated. The specific access barriers and facilitators that arose in the Norplant story are discussed below. We draw heavily on the experiences of the two countries with the most Norplant users in the mid-1990s: Indonesia, a developing country in which the government worked with the Population Council to provide Norplant to the public sector, and the United States, a developed country in which Wyeth-Ayerst provided the contraceptive to public and private clinics.

Scaling Up Global Access to Norplant (Phase 3)

In 1986, Indonesia became the first developing country to approve Norplant for national introduction. The National Family Planning Coordinating Board (known by its Indonesian acronym, BKKBN), with assistance from the Population Council and USAID, became the driving force for implementation of the Norplant system in Indonesia. The Indonesian government had a formal policy of emphasizing long-acting contraceptive methods. In introducing Norplant, the government sought to expand choice for women and offer a contraceptive alternative to sterilization, a procedure that is forbidden in Islam because it alters the body. Norplant promotion efforts were targeted to mothers aged 20–25 for birth spacing, mothers older than 30 to limit future births, and rural women.[28] Preintroduction trials beginning in 1981 facilitated Norplant's entry into Indonesia. Following Norplant's approval in the country, BKKBN moved from working on introductory trials to promoting nationwide access. Norplant use expanded rapidly, with sharp increases in both the late 1980s and in 1994–95.[29] By 1994, Indonesia claimed the most Norplant users per country, with 1.8 million women adhering to this method, representing 9.5% of all contraceptive users.[30] A 1998 study of end-users found that most women who were using Norplant came from rural areas, had some primary education, and had two or more children.[31]

In the United States, the FDA approved Norplant in December 1990, and Wyeth-Ayerst launched the product nationwide soon thereafter, in February 1991. The product's introduction took place rapidly. Wyeth-Ayerst handled all aspects of training, marketing, and distribution of the product in the U.S. as the Population Council focused its efforts on developing countries. The American public was enthusiastic about the new contraceptive. Even prior to FDA approval, Norplant was acclaimed as a major contraceptive breakthrough. This enthusiasm arose from positive reports in the press that emphasized Norplant's efficacy, convenience, and reversibility.[32] Many American women had high expectations for Norplant, even before its launch. Wyeth-Ayerst estimated that 100,000 women received Norplant implants in 1991, and by mid-1993, 750,000 implant kits had been sold.[33] The demand for the product initially surpassed Wyeth-Ayerst's projections, leading to supply shortages and waiting lists in parts of the country.[34] The company calculated in late 1992 that of the implant kits distributed, 48% went to private physicians, 33% to clinic-based practitioners, and the remaining 19% to other providers.[35]

In addition to Indonesia and the United States, Norplant was approved and launched in many other developing and developed countries. To ensure the new product's safety and effectiveness, the WHO conducted the first large-scale, longer-term prospective drug surveillance project in developing countries, known as the Post-Marketing Surveillance Study of Norplant.[36] This five-year follow-up study was conducted in 32 family planning clinics in eight countries from 1988–1997 (as shown in Table 6.1). This WHO study, like the preintroduction Population Council studies, confirmed high effectiveness rates with failure rates of less than 1% per year, essentially equal to that provided by nonreversible methods. The main side effect of Norplant, menstrual pattern changes, tended to stabilize by the end of the first year to a level that became acceptable to most women. The researchers concluded that the contraceptive is safe, well tolerated, and highly effective.[37] Despite these important findings, attempts to promote Norplant worldwide encountered three access barriers related to: (1) affordability, (2) end-user adoption, and (3) provider removal services. We show below that the relative importance of these barriers depended on the particular setting.

Affordability

As a result of licensing agreements between the Population Council and the two manufacturers of Norplant (Leiras Oy in Finland and Wyeth-Ayerst in the United States), a tiered pricing system determined the product's price in different markets. In the public sector in developed countries and the private sector worldwide, Wyeth-Ayerst provided Norplant at a relatively high price: $350 per implant kit in the United States and about half that in Europe. Leiras Oy offered the product at a much lower price, $23 per implant kit, for public-sector family planning programs in developing countries.

The price of the Norplant product and services to insert and remove it posed an access problem for end-users in the United States. Wyeth-Ayerst, the company that manufactured and marketed the product in the country, did not provide Norplant at a lower public-sector price, as it and other companies had done with oral contraceptives.[38] Though the price of a set of Norplant implants in the United States was $350, the total cost to users of the method, including the price of implants and clinic or physician fees, ranged between $500 and $1,000. Depending on the clinic or physician, there could also be an additional fee for removal. Many private insurance plans, however, did cover part or all of the costs of Norplant, as did Medicaid agencies in all 50 states. (Medicaid is the U.S. health program for low-income people.) But Medicaid did not guarantee coverage of Norplant removal if a woman became ineligible during the life of the contraceptive.[39] Although Medicaid paid for Norplant for the poor, and higher income women could either pay for it or their insurance covered it, low-income women ineligible for Medicaid were left without coverage for Norplant. For potential end-users in this latter group, Norplant access was limited because of a lack of product affordability. This affordability problem also influenced provider adoption. An Alan Guttmacher Institute nationwide survey of family planning agencies in 1992 found that some agencies did not promote Norplant because of its high cost.[40]

To address these problems with affordability in the United States, Wyeth-Ayerst established the Norplant Foundation to provide Norplant at no cost to women without insurance or Medicaid coverage. But the Foundation could not keep up with demand.[41] The Foundation also required that clinics order each kit separately, making it impossible for clinics to stockpile a small supply.[42] In addition, the Foundation limited providers to 10 kits a year and required that clinicians perform Norplant insertion without reimbursement.[43] Several years later, in December 1995, Wyeth-Ayerst decided to sell Norplant implants to public-sector providers at a reduced price, something that family planning advocates had been requesting since 1991.[44]

End-user Adoption

Following the launch of Norplant, concerns were raised in a number of countries about whether end-users were adopting the new contraceptive based on free choice. In Indonesia, some providers reportedly steered women in the direction of long-acting methods such as Norplant because government policy favored these methods. Choices about contraception thus occurred in the context of a hierarchical provider-client interaction and government focus on demographic objectives.[45] Hardee et al. recount how a women's group in Bangladesh raised questions about whether Norplant trials (which began in 1985) targeted poor, uneducated women because they could be intimidated.[46] While a study by an international research team found that illiterate rural women were not targeted by the clinical trials, political controversy surrounding allegations of Norplant coercion continued in Bangladesh in the mid-1990s.

In the United States, Norplant's launch generated enthusiasm, positive media reports, and high expectations. But there was also public discussion early on about the potential for coercive uses of the method. While many family planning advocates and policy makers believed that Norplant could reduce high rates of unintended pregnancy (particularly among young people and low-income women), others worried that the method might be forced on women who were not willing or fully informed (including women of color, young people, and low-income women).[47] Some potential end-users and family planning advocates, for example, were suspicious of the motivations for Medicaid funding for Norplant, feeling that this public funding might pressure women of color and low-income women into using the method.[48] Two days after the FDA approved Norplant, the *Philadelphia Inquirer* published an editorial called "Can Contraception Reduce the Underclass?" This began media commentary and public debate nationwide about using Norplant in the fight against black poverty.[49] After this editorial and ensuing public debate, many Americans began to view Norplant as a method of social control.[50] Beginning in 1991, legislators in 13 states proposed two dozen bills that made welfare payments conditional on Norplant use or offered financial incentives to welfare recipients who use the implant.[51] In addition, courts ordered at least four women convicted of child abuse to have Norplant inserted as a condition of probation. These actions singled out poor, single mothers, frequently black or Hispanic.[52]

In the end, none of the bills linking Norplant to welfare payments passed into law.[53] Furthermore, a study of 2,000 low-income women in the U.S. found no evidence of coercion in the use of Norplant in private interactions between women and their health care providers.[54] These researchers concluded that the public debate about Norplant was a "double-edged sword." On the one hand, it may have reduced the magnitude of coercion through increased vigilance; on the other hand, the debate stigmatized the method in the United States. The case illustrates the importance of having end-users make informed and free decisions about selecting and using technologies—for ethical reasons and also to protect the reputation of the technology and promote its proper use.

In the late 1990s, studies of Norplant end-users around the world showed a high level of satisfaction with the contraceptive.[55] Studies of Norplant continuation generally found high rates through the first two years of use, except in the United States, where discontinuation was associated with negative media coverage. In general, after five years of using Norplant (the approved term of use), approximately half of the women who originally chose the method were continuing use, with a significant proportion of discontinuation due to the desire to start a pregnancy. Findings from clinic-based studies also showed that most women who continued using Norplant were satisfied with the method, although they had not found it easy to get used to. A large majority of these end-users would recommend it to others. Satisfaction levels were slightly below levels for oral contraceptives and the injectable contraceptive known as Depoprovera. Importantly, women who decided to discontinue the method were much less positive, and only a few said they were "very satisfied." Many women in this group did not like Norplant because they experienced menstrual irregularities after insertion. Both groups of women pointed to convenience and effectiveness as Norplant's best features.

Studies also found that end-users were more satisfied with Norplant and more likely to continue using the contraceptive if they received sufficient information about the technology and potential side effects.[56] The three principal areas of limited awareness among end-users were Norplant's five-year efficacy, the right to early removal, and the common side effects. When unaware of Norplant's five-year efficacy, users would not seek removal and could become pregnant because of decreased effectiveness. The lack of communication about the right to early removal may have encouraged women to use the product longer than they would otherwise have done, which in turn decreased levels of satisfaction. In one study, less than one third of users could not name one common side effect associated with Norplant use.[57] Those who were not educated about potential side effects, particularly menstrual irregularities, became concerned about these changes and tended to request early removal. These end-users were likely to communicate their less than positive experiences with Norplant to other potential users in their social networks. As Widyantoro explains, "It has been found in Indonesia that clients who experience side effects without being forewarned are more likely to discontinue and will share their disappointment with others. In a society where personal recommendations from friends and family are important, the lack of full information can have a negative effect."[58] In response to these problems, the Indonesian government worked to improve the information given to Norplant users and, with the Population Council, created materials and held refresher training for providers.[59]

Provider Removal Services

After Norplant insertion, the contraceptive implant remains efficacious for five years; a provider must remove the implant within the five-year period. If a woman wishes to continue using Norplant, the provider can at the time of removal insert a new implant system. For several reasons, removal problems became major barriers to Norplant access in some countries, with negative implications for the product's reputation, appropriate use, and customer satisfaction. End-users encountered difficulties in obtaining removal services and also experienced problems with the quality of removal services.

The high price of the product reportedly made some providers reluctant to remove Norplant before the full five years of efficacy. Tuldahar et al. report that some Indonesian providers refused early removal and justified their position by stating that removal before five years for reasons other than a desire to conceive was trivial and a waste of government resources.[60] Women dealt with this problem by lying about their motivation for removal (saying they wanted to conceive even when this was not their reason for early removal), going to unqualified practitioners, or even removing Norplant themselves. In Bangladesh, Hardee et al. state that removal problems occurred in a handful of centers due to a few providers who felt that Norplant was costly and should not be removed at will.[61] This resistance by providers meant that some women could not have the implant removed on demand.

Problems also arose with provider training on the technical aspects of insertion and removal, and on the management of side effects and medical problems. Harrison and Rosenfield point out that the speed of Norplant's scale up exacerbated the problems of training:

Introduction of any new medical technology typically requires new learning and education in its use. Although many new medical devices and surgical techniques are introduced gradually, often through academic medical centers, that was not so with Norplant. The implant system was introduced countrywide and its initial market penetration grew so rapidly that the base of deliverers, although broad, was not deep; this was true in the United States and in the very large Indonesian program. The combination of speed and lack of depth became especially problematic when removals became an issue.[62]

Despite attempts to train providers by the Population Council and national governments in developing countries, and by companies in developed countries (such as Wyeth-Ayerst in the U.S.), the result was often uneven. AGI's survey of family planning agencies across the United States in 1992 found the lack of a trained clinician often explained why the agency did not promote Norplant to its clients.[63] In Indonesia, only a few practitioners had been trained in removal at the time Norplant was introduced nationally since the initial training program had focused only on insertion techniques.[64] Provider culture and attitudes contributed to the training problems as well. Physicians in many countries felt that this new technology did not require special training and resisted spending time on training.[65] In addition, successful Norplant training required that practitioners prove competency in both insertions and removals, something that the training programs did not always require.

In the United States, intense public controversy arose around the quality of removal services for Norplant. A class action lawsuit was filed in mid-1994 against Wyeth-Ayerst on behalf of 400 women who contended that they suffered severe pain and scarring when their doctors removed the implants. The suit was then extended to include a number of side effects about which the women claimed they were not adequately informed. It also included accusations that Wyeth-Ayerst withheld information from users that the implant's capsules or rods are made of Silastic, a material that some women claimed prompted immune-system problems.[66] The suit alleged that Wyeth-Ayerst failed to adequately warn women and their physicians of dangerous side effects of Norplant. The plaintiffs collectively argued that they experienced almost a thousand different side effects since the method went on the U.S. market in 1991.[67] Side effects included memory loss, muscle pain, depression, autoimmune disorders, infections, seizures, blindness, cancer, and heart attacks. By 1995, 50,000 women had joined Norplant lawsuits. The lawsuits against Norplant were brought by many of the same lawyers who previously sued the makers of silicone breast implants (and won a $4 billion settlement).[68]

With the lawsuits, the tone of media coverage in the United States shifted from enthusiasm to negativity. In May 1994, a TV report on *Eye to Eye with Connie Chung* presented the first broad public airing of Norplant problems, focusing on women who had experienced difficult implant removals. That year, requests for Norplant insertions began to drop, and discontinuation rates rose dramatically. In 1995, Norplant sales in the United States dropped from 800 to 60 units per day.[69]

In August 1999, Wyeth-Ayerst agreed to pay a $1,500 settlement to any American woman who had filed suit before March 1 of that year. Over the next three years, about 32,000 plaintiffs accepted the offer, and another 2,960 either rejected it or failed to respond.[70] In August 2002, a federal judge in Texas dismissed the claims of most of the remaining women, stating that they had "not produced a shred of evidence or expert testimony that supports an association between Norplant and any of the exotic conditions."[71] Meanwhile, Wyeth-Ayerst spent more than $40 million defending itself against Norplant claims. In July 2002, the company decided to discontinue marketing Norplant in the United States, although the company stated that its decision was due to the short supply of certain components of the product and not the litigation. Harrison and Rosenfield point out that problems with implant removal combined with rumors about serious side effects and complications created a critical mass of opinion and events, leading to decreased Norplant use in the U.S.[72] The story of Norplant in the United States demonstrates how litigation and the media can shape public perceptions about a technology in ways that a company finds difficult to control, leading to stigma, declining use, and ultimately withdrawal from the market.

Norplant's Legacy

Given the withdrawal of Norplant in the United States in 2002, many view the product's experience as a "disaster."[73] Yet millions of women around the world became Norplant users. By the end of 1992, 24 countries had granted regulatory approval to Norplant; by mid-1997, that number reached 58. By the end of 1996, over 5 million implants had been distributed worldwide, with about 3.6 million of those in Indonesia and close to a million in the United States.[74] As of 2002, an estimated 10.5 million units had been distributed worldwide.[75] In 2003, an estimated 6 million women were using the contraceptive.[76] Norplant also paved the way for a new generation of long-acting contraceptive implants. Two new implant products have U.S. FDA approval (Jadelle and Implanon), a third product (Nestorone) has approval in Brazil, and one other is in development (Uniplant). In 2003, Norplant, Jadelle, and Implanon were approved in 60 countries and were being used by an estimated 11 million women around the world.

The new implants differ from Norplant in having a smaller number of rods or capsules, which makes insertion and removal easier for providers. The primary advantage of the new implants over other contraceptives remains their high degree and long duration of efficacy. Like Norplant, however, the new implant products require a surgical procedure for insertion and removal, calling for trained providers. Also, in some contexts the implants remain costly. In addition, the new implant products are like Norplant (and other progestogen-only contraceptives like the injectable Depoprovera) in that end-users can experience menstrual problems. Oral contraceptive pills use a combination of a progestin and estrogen, so women do not have the same type of menstrual irregularities. Scientists have turned to basic research to try to understand the mechanisms underlying normal endometrial bleeding in order to improve progestogen-only contraceptives.[77]

Norplant also changed the way that international family planning agencies work with developing countries to provide access to contraceptives. Beginning in 1991, the UNDP/UNFPA/WHO/World Bank Special Programme of Research, Development, and Research Training in Human Reproduction (HRP) developed a new process—based on lessons learned in the Norplant experience—for considering whether new contraceptive methods should be added into service settings.[78] The HRP process has three main premises: (1) contraceptive introduction must focus on the needs of actual and potential users; (2) policy and operational decisions should concentrate on the institutional capacity to provide contraceptive methods with attention to service quality; and (3) decisions about contraceptive introduction must be placed in the context of all potentially relevant contraceptive methods, instead of focusing on only one method.

The government of Vietnam and WHO used the HRP process in 1994 to assess government plans to introduce Norplant and Depoprovera. Research found that the health system in Vietnam lacked adequate capacity to support Norplant use. These research findings fed directly into government policy, leading to a reversal of the decision to introduce Norplant at that time. As Ruth Simmons and

Peter Fajans, two of the creators of the HRP approach, state, "Decisions not to introduce or to reverse introductory plans are just as important outcomes as is the decision to introduce new methods. Previous technologically and demographically focused approaches to introduction would not have reached such a conclusion."[79] In sum, Norplant's legacy is both a wider array of implant contraceptives available to women and a strategic rethinking about how to introduce (and not introduce) new contraceptive products worldwide.

Conclusions

In 1988, at the 12th World Congress of the Federation for International Gynecology and Obstetrics, the then-director of the HRP said of Norplant, "Probably no other contraceptive on the market has been developed by research done on such a large scale and reported step-by-step to the scientific community."[80] By 1988, more than 50,000 women in 44 countries took part in Norplant trials, and more than 400 articles were published in peer-reviewed scientific journals. Yet the Norplant story demonstrates that having a large research record and a highly safe and efficacious technology is not enough to ensure successful access and appropriate use by providers and clients. (Table 6.2 presents a summary of barriers to Norplant access.) A key lesson is that a technology's problems can be extrinsic to its safety and efficacy.[81] The perception of a technology by end-users and providers can shape its ultimate fate in access. In addition, the end-user's ability to obtain quality services on demand is also an important access factor. The Norplant case also shows how affordability problems can create barriers for public providers and end-users in settings where the product is not offered at a lower public-sector price. For Norplant, these availability, affordability, and adoption issues played major roles in the contraceptive's lack of sustained success in many developed and developing countries.

The Population Council became the product champion for Norplant worldwide and created a largely effective architecture for access. The organization managed the 25-year product development phase and then promoted the adoption, availability and affordability of Norplant in developing countries. Wyeth-Ayerst and Leiras Oy also played core roles in Norplant's access architecture. Total expenditures on product development and access activities by these three actors exceeded $110 million.[82] The Population Council's costs on research ($23.5 million) and access activities ($16 million) came from public-sector funding from the U.S. government and from some private foundations. Leiras Oy spent $23 million to develop manufacturing procedures, while Wyeth-Ayerst spent $50 million to introduce the contraceptive into the private market and also donated levonorgestrel to the Population Council for development of the Norplant system.

The Population Council coordinated both product development and access activities, allowing the development team to work closely with the access team to ensure full understanding of the technical aspects of the product. But some analysts have suggested that problems arose because the Council acted as Norplant's champion. In Indonesia, some researchers argue, the Population Council and other international experts underestimated problems with counseling and implant removal.[83] These researchers maintain that the issues could have been addressed more effectively if the Council and its partners had collected and analyzed more research from different perspectives. The Council's deep commitment to Norplant may have blinded the organization to anticipating and addressing some of the difficulties encountered in adoption and availability for both providers and end-users.

A key feature of the Norplant experience was the creation of an introduction phase for the new technology. The Population Council conceived of this phase as a bridge from research, development, and clinical trials to Norplant's entry into national family planning programs in developing countries. The activities included introductory trials, acceptability studies, and service delivery research, with the goal of identifying management and technical issues affecting method delivery. The concept was to move beyond a focus on the technology itself as the solution and place the technology within the broader context of health service quality and user perspectives. Although the methodologies used in Norplant introduction provided extensive empirical knowledge about the method, they did not always adequately prepare the national service system for widespread access.[84] The introduction phase in some countries did not provide a systematic link between research and policy, and service delivery research did not inform the planning of large-scale access.[85] As described in the previous section, the lessons learned from Norplant led the HRP to develop a new approach to contraceptive introduction that consists of a staged process of research and policy development.

The scaling-up phase of Norplant involved transitioning from the introductory bridging activities to making the technology widely available. This case study demonstrates that for provider-dependent methods such as Norplant, which require proper training and service quality, the pace of scaling up needs to be coordinated with the strengthening of system capacity. The experiences in Indonesia and the United States demonstrate that rapid scaling up may increase the availability of a technology but can also result in poor service quality, which can negatively influence user satisfaction, long-term use, and product reputation—and thereby undermine access.

The price of Norplant and related services in the United States affected affordability in negative ways, especially the inability of some end-users to pay for insertion and removal. In many settings, product cost also affected provider practices. In the United States, many potential users and family planning experts questioned the product's tiered pricing structure, particularly in terms of the implant's high price in the private sector, when much of the product development costs were borne by the American public sector and private foundations. Family planning experts raised these questions even while recognizing that the profit requirements of industry and their exposure to risk need to be reflected in the price of the product to the consumer.[86]

End-user adoption of Norplant was influenced by many factors, depending on the particular sociocultural and historical context. Islamic women in Indonesia viewed Norplant as an acceptable alternative to sterilization, which was forbidden by Islam. In the United States, the introduction of Norplant to low-income women led to concerns about social coercion based on previous experiences with sterilization. The Norplant story emphasizes the need to understand—for ethical, practical, and reputational reasons—the social and historical context within which decisions about technology access are being made.[87] The case study also demonstrates the challenges of learning from past experiences. The Population Council, for example, identified several critical lessons from previous efforts at contraceptive introduction (such as the IUD) but was unable to effectively implement all those lessons in its promotion of access to Norplant.

The Norplant story provides important lessons about access for other contraceptives and technologies. A major finding is that assuring safety and efficacy for a product is not sufficient to create access. Critical determinants of access also include affordability for both governments and end-users. Important availability barriers involve provider training and competency on insertion and removal as well as assuring adequate health system capability to deliver quality services—especially for technologies (like Norplant) that depend on health system performance. The technology must also respond to the perceived needs of end-users. Finally, the Norplant story demonstrates the role of end-user adoption factors, particularly the importance of providing end-users with information about the new technology and potential side effects, and also the role of the media and litigation in influencing a product's reputation and fate.

Table 6.2 | Norplant access

	BARRIER	STRATEGY	SPECIFIC ACTION
ARCHITECTURE	Need for a global champion for Norplant	Identify effective leadership and design partnerships for the technology	The Population Council assumed the role as product champion and coordinator for the development, introduction, and scaling up of Norplant in developing countries
ADOPTION	Problems with end-user adoption and continuation due to side effects, poor information about the technology and its side effects, stigma, and negative media coverage	Produce acceptance of the technology at the global and national levels, while creating demand among providers and end-users	The Population Council and its national partners improved training courses for providers and information for end-users in developing countries; these actions addressed adoption barriers in some contexts
			Wyeth-Ayerst decided to settle lawsuits filed in the U.S. by women claiming damages due to side effects from Norplant; the company later withdrew the product from the market
AFFORDABILITY	Limited government funds to purchase Norplant in some developing countries	Assure affordable price for government purchasing agencies	Tiered pricing arrangement for developing country markets
	High price of Norplant for end-users in developed countries	Assure affordable price for individual end-users	Wyeth-Ayerst established the Norplant Foundation in the U.S. but was unable to keep up with demand; the company later decided on a reduced price for public-sector providers
AVAILABILITY	The challenge of dividing different markets to provide access in developing countries while meeting private company interests in the U.S.	Assure adequate quality and quantity of production for different markets	The Population Council assumed responsibility for all activities in developing countries, with a manufacturer in Finland, while Wyeth-Ayerst assumed responsibility for the U.S. market
	Problems in obtaining quality removal services, due to product service and cost, and inadequate provider training	Manage provider activities and provision of removal services to end-users	The Population Council and Wyeth-Ayerst upgraded its training courses for providers and its information for end-users which improved removal services in some settings; in other contexts, removal services remained poor quality

----

Endnotes

[1] Sheldon J. Segal, *Under the Banyan Tree: A Population Scientist's Odyssey* (New York: Oxford University Press, 2003).

[2] Sheldon J. Segal, "The Development of Norplant Implants," *Studies in Family Planning,* 14 (1983): 159; and Judah Folkman and David M. Long, "The Use of Silicone Rubber as a Carrier for Prolonged Drug Therapy," *Journal of Surgical Research,* 4 (1964): 139–142.

[3] Segal, *Under the Banyan Tree,* 89.

[4] Segal, *Under the Banyan Tree,* 159.

[5] Segal, *Under the Banyan Tree.*

[6] Segal, *Under the Banyan Tree,* 91.

[7] ICCR has since been responsible for developing a wide range of products in contraceptive and reproductive health. Staff at the Future's Group calculated that in the year 2000, products developed by the ICCR since its inception in 1971 accounted for 50.9% of reversible contraceptive methods used in developing countries. More than 120 million women in the developing world were using products developed through the research group. See: Segal, *Under the Banyan Tree.*

[8] Segal, *Under the Banyan Tree,* 92.

[9] Wyeth-Ayerst Laboratories, now Wyeth Pharmaceuticals, moved its corporate headquarters from Radnor, Pennsylvania to Madison, New Jersey in 2003.

[10] Segal, *Under the Banyan Tree*; and Irving Sivin, Harold Nash, and Sandra Waldman, *Jadelle Levonorgestrel Rod Implants: A Summary of Scientific Data and Lessons Learned from Programmatic Experience* (New York: Population Council, 2002).

[11] Sivin et al.

[12] Segal, *Under the Banyan Tree,* 94.

[13] Segal, *Under the Banyan Tree,* 94.

[14] Joanne Spicehandler, "Norplant Introduction: A Management Perspective," in Sheldon J. Segal, Amy O. Tsui, and Susan M. Rogers, *Demographic and Programmatic Consequences of Contraceptive Innovations* (New York: Plenum Press, 1989), 204.

[15] Spicehandler.

[16] Spicehandler.

[17] Veena Soni, "The Development and Current Organisation of The Family Planning Programme," in *India's Demography: Essays on the Contemporary Population,* eds. Tim Dyson and Nigel Crook (New Delhi: South Asian Publishers Pvt. Ltd., 1984), 191, cited in Spicehandler, 200.

[18] Spicehandler.

[19] Spicehandler, 203.

[20] Spicehandler.

[21] Spicehandler.

[22] Sivin et al., 3.

[23] Sivin et al.

[24] Spicehandler.

[25] Spicehandler.

[26] Spicehandler.

[27] World Health Organization, Special Programme of Research, Development and Research Training in Human Reproduction, "Facts about an Implantable Contraceptive: Memorandum from a WHO meeting," *Bulletin of the World Health Organization* 63 (1985): 491.

[28] Jayanti Tuladhar, Peter J. Donaldson, and Jeanne Noble, "The Introduction and Use of Norplant Implants in Indonesia," *Studies in Family Planning* 29 (1998): 291–299.

[29] Tuldahar et al.

[30] Central Bureau of Statistics, National Family Planning Coordinating Board, Ministry of Health and Macro International, Inc., *Indonesian Demographic and Health Survey: Preliminary Report* (Jakarta: Central Bureau of Statistics, 1995), cited in Karen Hardee, Sandor Balogh, and Michelle T. Villinski, "Three Countries' Experience with Norplant Introduction," *Health Policy and Planning* 12 (1997): 199–213.

[31] Tuladhar et al.

[32] For analysis of these reports, see: Heather Boonstra, Vanessa Duran, Vanessa Northington Gamble, Paul Blumenthal, Linda Dominguez, and Cheri Pies, "The 'Boom and Bust Phenomenon': The Hopes, Dreams, and Broken Promises of the Contraceptive Revolution," *Contraception* 61 (2000): 9–25.

[33] Boonstra et al.; and Jennifer J. Frost, "The Availability and Accessibility of the Contraceptive Implant from Family Planning Agencies in the United States, 1991–1992," *Family Planning Perspectives* 26 (1994): 4–10.

[34] Hardee et al.

[35] The Alan Guttmacher Institute, *Norplant: Opportunities and Perils for Low-Income Women*, Special Report no. 1, (New York: Alan Guttmacher Institute, 1992); and Frost.

[36] Ian S. Fraser, Aila Tiitinen, Biran Affandi, Vivian Brache, Horacio B. Croxatto, Soledad Diaz, Jean Ginsburg, Sujuan Gu, Pentti Holma, Elof Johansson, Olav Meirik, Daniel R. Mishell, Jr., Harold A. Nash, Bo von Schoultz, and Irving Sivin, "Norplant Consensus Statement and Background Review," *Contraception* 57 (1998): 1–9.

[37] Fraser et al.

[38] Frost.

[39] Frost.

[40] Frost.

[41] Hardee et al.

[42] Barbara Feringa, Sarah Iden, and Allan Rosenfield, "Norplant: Potential for Coercion," in *Dimensions of New Contraceptives: Norplant and Poor Women*, eds. Sarah E. Samuels and Mark D. Smith (Menlo Park, CA: Henry J. Kaiser Family Foundation, 1992), 53–64.

43 Frost.

44 Frost.

45 Ruth Simmons and Peter Fajans, "Contraceptive Introduction Reconsidered: A New Methodology for Policy and Program Development," *Journal of Women's Health* 8 (1999): 163–173.

46 Hardee et al.

47 Boonstra et al.

48 Boonstra et al.; and Frost.

49 "Poverty and Norplant: Can Contraception Reduce the Underclass?" *The Philadelphia Inquirer*, December 12, 1990, p. A18.

50 Andrew R. Davidson and Debra Kalmuss, "Topics for Our Times: Norplant Coercion—An Overstated Threat," *American Journal of Public Health* 87 (1997): 550–551.

51 Polly F. Harrison and Allan Rosenfield, eds., *Contraceptive Research, Introduction, and Use: Lessons from Norplant* (New York: National Academy Press, 1998).

52 Kristyn M. Walker, "Judicial Control of Reproductive Freedom: The Use of Norplant as a Condition of Probation," *Iowa Law Review* 78 (1993): 779–812.

53 Davidson and Kalmuss.

54 Davidson and Kalmuss.

55 Polly F. Harrison and Allan Rosenfield, "Research, Introduction, and Use: Advancing from Norplant," *Contraception* 58 (1998): 323–334.

56 Margot Zimmerman, Joan Haffey, Elisabeth Crane, Danusia Szumowski, Frank Alvarez, Patama Bhiromrut, Vivian Brache, Firman Lubis, Maher Salah, Mamdouh Shaaban, Badria Shawky, Ieda Poernomo Sigit Sidi, "Assessing the Acceptability of Norplant Implants in Four Countries: Findings from Focus Group Research," *Studies in Family Planning* 21 (1990): 92–103.

57 Tuldahar et al.

58 Ninuk Widyantoro, "The Story of Norplant Implants in Indonesia," *Reproductive Health Matters* 3 (1994): 26.

59 Hardee et al.

60 Tuldahar et al.

61 Hardee et al.

62 Harrison and Rosenfield, "Research, Introduction, and Use," 326–327.

63 Frost.

64 Simmons and Fajans.

65 Harrison and Rosenfield, "Research, Introduction, and Use."

66 Hardee et al.

67 American Lawyer Media, "Ruling Ends Many Norplant Claims," *The Legal Intelligencer* 226, no. 43 (2002): 4.

[68] Gina Kolata, "Will the Lawyers Kill Off Norplant?" *The New York Times*, May 28 1995, pp. 1, 5.

[69] Kolata.

[70] American Lawyer Media.

[71] American Lawyer Media, 4.

[72] Harrison and Rosenfield, "Research, Introduction, and Use."

[73] Harrison and Rosenfield, "Research, Introduction, and Use," 324.

[74] Harrison and Rosenfield, *Contraceptive Research*.

[75] Sivin et al.

[76] John Maurice, "Contraceptive implants come of age," *Progress in Reproductive Health Research* 61 (2003): 1.

[77] Maurice.

[78] Ruth Simmons, Peter Hall, Juan Diaz, Margarita Diaz, Peter Fajans, and Jay Satia, "The Strategic Approach to Contraceptive Introduction," *Studies in Family Planning* 28 (1997): 79–94.

[79] Simmons and Fajans, 170.

[80] Harrison and Rosenfield, "Research, Introduction, and Use," 324.

[81] Harrison and Rosenfield, "Research, Introduction, and Use."

[82] Harrison and Rosenfield, *Contraceptive research*.

[83] Tuladhar et al.

[84] Simmons and Fajans.

[85] Simmons and Fajans.

[86] Harrison and Rosenfield, "Research, Introduction, and Use."

[87] Harrison and Rosenfield, "Research, Introduction, and Use."

CHAPTER 7

VACCINE VIAL MONITORS:

Access to Devices

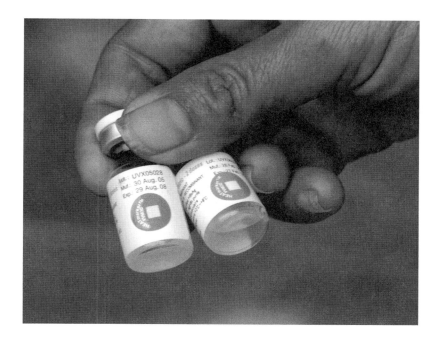

THE COLD CHAIN SYSTEM, DEVELOPED IN THE 1970S BY THE WHO EXPANDED PROGRAMME ON IMMUNIZATION (EPI), is an international protocol dictating procedures for maintaining the recommended conditions for storing and transporting vaccines from manufacture to use. These conditions include near-constant refrigeration that is often costly and cumbersome.[1] In climates where extreme heat occurs, the cold chain is considered "fragile." If health workers suspect either heat damage or extended storage in a nonrefrigerated container, the cold chain protocol requires the disposal of entire batches of vaccines to ensure damaged vaccines are not administered to children.[2] Though these safeguarding rules have been effective in ensuring that immunization programs administer only vaccines not exposed to heat, the inability to confirm vaccine damage often leads to vaccine wastage. Vaccine wastage is costly for cash-strapped ministries of health in developing countries and can result in fewer vaccinated children. Furthermore, maintaining the recommended conditions for storing and transporting vaccines is often difficult for health workers in poor countries, especially in remote areas. As a result, multiple problems in following the cold chain protocol reduce access to vaccines that prevent debilitating diseases in children.

The vaccine vial monitor (VVM) is a miniaturized time-temperature technology that can help health workers reduce vaccine wastage and assure coverage in hard-to-reach areas. This technology adds value to an existing technology (vaccines) in order to address a specific barrier to access (vaccine availability in areas where the cold chain is fragile). A VVM is a low cost indicator (ranging from US$0.0328–0.055) that is printed onto the label of a vaccine vial, attached to the vaccine vial cap, or affixed on the ampoule neck. The indicator changes color when the vial has been exposed to warm temperature over an extended period of time. The technology allows health workers to assess vaccine heat damage from production through delivery, greatly improving the reliability of the cold chain system. The VVM does not measure the actual potency of the vaccine inside the vial but instead indicates if unacceptable heat exposure has occurred and probably damaged the vaccine in that specific vial.

This case study examines the story of creating access for vaccine vial monitors. It begins with calls in 1979 to create a new kind of technology for monitoring temperature exposure of individual vaccine vials, then follows the phases of product development, introduction on the oral polio vaccine (beginning in 1996) and scaling up for other vaccines (beginning in 2001). The case shows how VVMs contributed to decreased vaccine wastage and improved health workers' ability to vaccinate hard-to-reach populations based on changes in the cold chain protocol.

In detailing the technology's flow from product development to use by health workers in poor countries, the narrative highlights the challenges encountered and strategies used to address barriers to access. In this instance, access depended crucially on assuring the availability of high-quality VVMs designed for different kinds of vaccines and the adoption and use of VVMs by global vaccine producers. The success achieved in creating access for VVMs relied on the efforts of product champions within the immunization program of the World Health Organization and the non-governmental organization Program for Appropriate Technology in Health (PATH) in Seattle. Even here, however, the VVM success has occurred for UNICEF-supplied vaccines but not for two other important vaccine markets for developing countries (vaccines provided by PAHO and those sold by developing country domestic manufacturers). Challenges to full VVM access thus persist, as we explain below.

Discovery and Testing of Vaccine Vial Monitors (Phase 1)

Staff at WHO's Expanded Programme on Immunization (EPI) first began thinking about a heat exposure indicator for individual vaccine vials in 1979 after recognizing the success of using heat exposure indicators on cartons of vaccines during shipping.[3] EPI staff proposed the idea of creating similar temperature monitors for use at lower levels of the cold chain—a new technology for each vaccine vial that would extend monitoring to delivery levels where temperature control was most fragile.[4] WHO thus became an early advocate of VVMs by articulating the need for a new technology.

PATH responded quickly to WHO's call for creating a vaccine vial monitor product. The organization began seeking a potential technology and identified the diacetylene indicator technology that was under development at Allied Chemical Corporation. (Allied Chemical Corporation was established in 1920 as an amalgamation of five American chemical companies. In 1985 the company became AlliedSignal and today is part of Honeywell International, Inc., in Morristown, New Jersey.) Ray Baughman, a materials scientist within Allied, conceived the idea of using color changes associated with diacetylene polymerization for time-temperature indicators and made advanced indicator prototypes with his team.[5] Their initial focus was on a PTS (p-toluene sulfonate) diacetylene. Baughman headed the Color Responsive Materials Group within Allied, and he and his colleagues began visiting pharmaceutical and other companies to discuss potential applications of time-temperature technology to blood, vaccines, and perishable foods.

The efforts of Baughman and his team to interest companies in the technology were initially unsuccessful. PATH, however, learned of their work and sent two representatives—PATH president Gordon Perkin and Patrick Tam—to Allied to discuss the technology's possible application to vaccine vials. As a result of these discussions, Allied granted PATH a license to use the PTS chemical. In 1979, the same year as WHO's call for a new technology, PATH began developing first generation prototypes of a VVM for the measles vaccine. To do this, PATH used funding from various sources, including Alberta AID, the Edna McConnell Clark Foundation, the International Development Research Centre of Canada, and Oxfam.[6]

Between 1982 and 1985, PATH, WHO, and ministries of health conducted field tests to validate PATH's VVM prototypes in 10 countries (Argentina, Brazil, Egypt, Kenya, Nepal, Pakistan, Peru, the Philippines, Yemen, and Zimbabwe). Introductory field trials followed between 1987 and 1990 in five countries (Indonesia, Kenya, Sierra Leone, Thailand, and Zambia).[7] The validation and introductory field trials highlighted three problems with the prototypes based on PTS diacetylene technology: (1) the reaction rate was too slow for use with the least heat stable vaccines such as the oral polio vaccine (OPV); (2) the indicator created problems of dermal toxicity for some workers; and (3) the label with temperature indicator had some printing difficulties.[8] The slow reaction rate was particularly significant because during this period WHO decided that the new technology should be introduced first on OPV. The growing momentum of the polio eradication campaign provided a good opportunity to demonstrate the product's value since OPV is the most heat-sensitive vaccine.[9]

PATH used a subproject in its USAID-funded Technologies for Health (HealthTech) program to begin looking for a more suitable technology than PTS for the extremely heat-sensitive OPV. In 1988, while introductory field trials for PTS prototypes for the measles vaccine were ongoing, PATH staff identified a new technology owned by New Jersey–based Temptime Corporation (previously LifeLines Technology, Inc.) also based on diacetylenes. The Temptime researchers working on this new technology were actually the same people who previously developed the PTS technology at Allied. Temptime was a new company, formed in 1987 by staff from Allied Chemical Corporation after management at Allied decided that the diacetylene technology was not commercially significant for the company. Staff within Allied's Color Responsive Materials Group then decided to spin off and form a new company. Staff members at Temptime shifted their work from the PTS technology to devices based on alternative diacetylenes.[10] While the

PTS chemical in the first product changed color abruptly when a critical accumulated time-temperature exposure was exceeded, the color changes of the diacetylenes used in the new Temptime technology were more continuous. The new technology, therefore, could be applied to all vaccines. Furthermore, the new diacetylenes were easier to manufacture and print and also addressed the dermal toxicity issue.[11] This new technology became the basis for Temptime's broader business of time-temperature indicators for food and other applications.

With Temptime's identification of this second technology, PATH took on a new role in VVM development. Instead of seeking to develop its own prototypes, PATH began working with Temptime in 1989 to modify the company's core technology for use with all vaccines in developing country immunization programs. After months of failing to achieve technical success with the VVM, Temptime informed PATH that the company had decided to give up on the program. According to Ted Prusik, senior vice president of Temptime, PATH representatives visited the company, explained the global significance of the VVM, and persuaded Temptime to continue its work, even without additional funding.[12]

Shortly thereafter, Temptime succeeded in developing a VVM technology that worked well and called it HEATmarker. (In the rest of this chapter, any reference to the VVM is specifically to the HEATmarker product unless otherwise stated.) PATH began field trials of HEATmarker in 1990 in eight countries (Bangladesh, Bolivia, Cameroon, Indonesia, Kenya, Sierra Leone, Thailand, and the United States). The HEATmarker product consists of a circle with an inner square made of heat sensitive material that is light colored at the starting point and becomes darker with thermal exposure. The combined effects of temperature and time cause the inner square to gradually and irreversibly grow dark. (Table 7.1 shows the start and end points of the Temptime VVM.)

The end point is reached when the inner square is the same color as the outer circle. The inner square continues to darken with heat exposure until it is much darker than the outer circle. Whenever the inner square matches or is darker than the outer circle, the individual vaccine vial should be discarded. The technology only monitors heat exposure and does not indicate whether a vaccine has been exposed to freezing.[13]

It took 12 years of product development (1979–1991) before a suitable vaccine vial monitor was ready for introduction. PATH used funding from USAID and other sources to explore potential core technologies and work with Temptime to achieve success in product development. Having conceived of the initial idea for the technology, WHO staff collaborated throughout product development by

Table 7.1 | VVM start and end points

Start point	◻	**Square lighter than circle** (Use vaccine vial if expiry date not reached)
End point	●	**Square matches the circle** (Discard vaccine vial)
End point exceeded	◼	**Square darker than the circle** (Discard vaccine vial)

Note. From *PQS Performance Specification for Vaccine Vial Monitors* by World Health Organization, 2006, Geneva: Author. Adapted with permission.

providing product specifications to potential VVM manufacturers, including Temptime. With product development nearing completion, WHO, PATH, and Temptime confronted the next challenge—introducing the new product so that it would be used and achieve its objectives.

Introducing VVMs on the Oral Polio Vaccine (Phase 2)

During the final stages of product testing in laboratory and field studies, PATH and WHO staff members began formulating plans to introduce VVMs on the oral polio vaccine (OPV). They focused initially on gaining product adoption by the UNICEF Supply Division and WHO-prequalified OPV producers. Responsible for UNICEF's global procurement operation, the Supply Division purchases all vaccines for the global campaign to eradicate polio (as well as purchasing vaccines for other global campaigns, UNICEF-supported programs, and the GAVI Alliance). In 1990, WHO and PATH staff met with OPV producers to present the VVM and persuade the producers to add the new technology to their product labels.[14] (The eight vaccine producers in the 1990 meeting were Connaught Laboratories, Conpharma Vaccines, Evans Biologicals, Interexport, Pasteur Merieux, Sclavo, SmithKline Beecham, and Swiss Serum.) Vaccine producers then received HEATmarker prototypes for evaluation. The following year, WHO, 10 vaccine producers, and the Pan American Health Organization (PAHO) participated in a further appraisal of "live" HEATmarker VVMs. (The ten producers included the same eight as before, minus Conpharma Vaccines, plus Human Institute, Institute of Immunology, and MAIMEX.)

A number of other actions helped promote VVMs around this time. In 1990, UNICEF organized a Technology Introduction Panel in New York to discuss VVM technology for OPV. A year later, during a second meeting at UNICEF, WHO staff asked UNICEF representatives to include VVMs for OPV in the global tender (an invitation to submit a competitive bid) for the 1992–1994 vaccine supply. UNICEF responded by including a clause in the tender announcement requesting producers to add VVMs to their OPV labels. UNICEF went a step further in the next tender announcement in 1993 for the vaccines to be supplied in 1994–1995 and requested that bids for measles vaccine and OPV include VVMs on the labels. Despite UNICEF's efforts, however, only a few vaccine producers responded with bids that included VVM labeling.[15]

Vaccine producers resisted VVMs for two reasons. First, they were concerned that no one had independently validated the HEATmarker VVM. To address this concern, WHO hired the Maryland-based firm of Strasburger and Siegel, Inc., Food Testing Laboratories to conduct an independent evaluation of the Temptime product. This laboratory evaluation was completed in 1992.

Second, OPV producers did not want to purchase new labeling equipment to print the VVMs. To solve this issue, PATH provided a loan to Temptime in 1993 for the purchase of special labeling equipment. The new equipment allowed Temptime to print VVMs directly on vaccine producers' vial labels. This technical innovation allowed producers to use a single label printed with both the VVM and the vaccine's traditional label information, rather than incur additional costs from two separate labeling processes. Debra Kristensen, senior technical officer of PATH, pointed out that Temptime's willingness to go "the extra mile" in resolving producers' labeling concerns was key to securing acceptance by OPV producers.[16]

In 1994, WHO, UNICEF, and the OPV producers met and decided that following pilot introduction in Tanzania and Vietnam starting in April 1995, all OPV would include VVMs as of January 1996. WHO released official specifications for VVMs for OPV in 1995 that stipulated the purpose, design, and use of VVMs. One year later, all five OPV suppliers to UNICEF (SmithKline Beecham, Biocine, Pasteur Merieux Connaught, Chiron Behring, and PT Bio Farma) provided OPV with VVM labels.

Once VVMs appeared on OPV in immunization programs, research focused on health worker acceptance and experience with the technology and on assuring the technology's impacts in the field. WHO conducted four impact studies in conjunction with ministries of health during national immunization days in Kenya, Nepal, Tanzania, and Turkey (completed in 1997). An additional impact study was conducted in the Kingdom of Bhutan (1998). In Turkey, the study compared wastage due to heat exposure in a first-round National Immunization Day without VVMs (the baseline), with that in a second round after VVM implementation. Wastage due to heat exposure declined a remarkable

77%.[17] In addition, EPI managers in the study reported that most staff found VVMs easy to recognize and interpret, though systematic data on perceptions and practices were not collected.[18] In the Bhutan study, a Knowledge, Attitudes, Practices Survey found that health workers understood the purpose of VVMs and correctly interpreted the new technology.[19] Finally, a study of vaccine wastage during a polio campaign in India found that VVMs played an important role in health workers' decisions to discard vials exposed to heat.[20]

Overall, the process of making VVMs available on OPV required six years, from the moment WHO and PATH began their introduction strategy (1990) to compliance by all OPV suppliers to UNICEF (1996). As PATH's Debra Kristensen stated, "At the time, we felt that it had taken a long time to introduce VVMs on OPV. But we had no idea how much longer it would take when we enlarged the program to all EPI vaccines."[21]

Scaling Up Vaccine Vial Monitors on EPI Vaccines (Phase 3)

In 1998, WHO officials and researchers presented the VVM impact studies for OPV at the WHO Technical Network for Logistics in Health (TechNet) meeting held in Copenhagen. TechNet is a WHO initiative that links experts and organizations working in logistics for health, mostly in the area of national immunization programs and primary health service delivery in developing countries. The Bhutan impact study generated particular interest because in addition to the Knowledge, Attitudes, Practices Survey, it assessed whether VVMs on OPV vials could be used to monitor heat exposure to other vaccines transported with OPV. The authors recommended against this practice given the strong probability that other vaccines could be exposed to temperature conditions different from OPV even when transported together.[22] In response to this conclusion from the Bhutan study and evidence of reduced vaccine wastage from several studies, TechNet formally recommended that all vaccines use VVMs on individual vials as soon as possible.

Implementing VVMs on all EPI vaccines required Temptime to modify its temperature indicators for different categories of vaccines. This scaling up to other vaccines also required processes of policy development by WHO and the UNICEF Supply Division, as well as product adoption by a larger group of vaccine producers. PATH continued to lead the advocacy efforts for VVMs during this scaling-up period, providing assistance to WHO and Temptime. PATH financed these activities with funds from its HealthTech project (funded by USAID) and other sources such as the U.S. Centers for Disease Control and Prevention (which jointly funded scaling up VVMs on the measles vaccine along with HealthTech).

Product Modification

WHO staff specified the need for four categories of VVMs because of the different temperature and time sensitivities of EPI vaccines:

1 VVM2 for the least stable vaccines (2 days to end point at +37°C)
2. VVM7 for moderate stability vaccines (7 days to end point at +37°C)
3. VVM14 for medium stability vaccines (14 days to end point at +37°C)
4. VVM30 for high stability vaccines (30 days to end point at +37°C).

In 1998, WHO sent a letter to all WHO prequalified vaccine producers requesting their reaction to the proposed new VVM specifications. At the same time, Temptime modified its VVM product to meet the requirements of these four categories of stability. Independent third parties, mostly under WHO contract, then conducted conformity tests of the new HEATmarker types.[23] These product modifications represented an essential step in expanding adoption of VVMs to other vaccine producers.

Global Adoption and Policy Development

Global adoption of VVMs in the scaling-up phase depended on specific actions by WHO and the UNICEF Supply Division. WHO assumed responsibility for deciding on VVM specifications and assigning each WHO prequalified vaccine to one of the four VVM categories (VVM2, VVM7, VVM14, or VVM30). The UNICEF Supply Division included VVMs in its tender specifications and discussed VVMs with vaccine producers.

The UNICEF Supply Division expressed two major concerns about availability in scaling up VVMs to all EPI vaccines. First, Temptime was the sole supplier of VVMs with no competitors. UNICEF's policy is to avoid working with sole suppliers (unless no other option exists) because if the monopoly company encounters problems with its supply, then UNICEF has no other sources of product.[24] Both PATH and WHO had encouraged other companies to develop competitive VVM products, including Albert Brown, Ltd. (U.K.), 3M (U.S.), Rexam/Bowater (U.K.), CCL Label (U.S.), and Sensitech (U.S.). WHO and UNICEF invited all potential suppliers to meetings about VVMs, and PATH provided start-up funding through its USAID HealthTech project to potential VVM suppliers.[25] None of the companies, however, succeeded in developing a product that met the performance requirements of WHO and UNICEF and that could compete with the price of Temptime's HEATmarker VVM.[26] Their inability to develop competitive products may be related to these firms' choice of different core technologies as well as Temptime's comparatively low overhead.[27]

UNICEF's second concern about availability related to the global vaccine market, which at that time had a limited number of producers. The main goal of UNICEF's Supply Division is to procure sufficient vaccines for developing country immunization programs. In this context of limited vaccine supply, UNICEF needed to purchase all vaccines produced, regardless of whether they included VVMs.

These two leading international agencies wielded enormous market power by setting global norms (WHO) and procuring global vaccines (UNICEF). Despite their concerns about the availability of VVMs and the availability of vaccines, WHO and UNICEF issued a joint policy statement in 1999 advocating the use of VVMs on all vaccines. The statement read, "All agencies purchasing vaccines should request manufacturers to supply all vaccines with VVMs that meet WHO specifications."[28] In UNICEF's invitation to bid for the 2001–2003 global tender for vaccines, UNICEF included VVMs among the minimum requirements for vaccines to be procured by UNICEF. That same year, the Global Alliance for Vaccines and Immunization (GAVI) included VVMs among the minimum requirements for vaccines in its first Request for Proposals for underused vaccines, related products, and contributions. The inclusion of VVMs in these official policy statements and tender announcements gave great impetus to the global adoption of this technology.

Vaccine Producer Adoption

Yet vaccine producers still lagged in adopting VVMs. Following the WHO and UNICEF announcements in 1999, only three vaccine suppliers to UNICEF fully met the terms to include VVMs on vaccine labels (Japan BCG, Pasteur Dakar, and Chiron). In response, UNICEF asked vaccine producers to explain why they had not incorporated VVMs into their labels. WHO reviewed the replies, provided UNICEF with an assessment of each technical concern, and revised the VVM specifications and test procedures.[29] Despite these efforts, only two more prequalified producers (Bio Farma and LG Chemical Inv., Ltd.) fully complied with the VVM requirement for EPI vaccines (apart from OPV). Eighteen WHO-prequalified vaccine producers (supplying yellow fever, measles, measles-rubella, measles-mumps-rubella, hepatitis B, tetanus toxoid with Uniject, and Bacillus Calmette-Guérin vaccines) did not comply, with some asking for additional time to make adjustments.[30]

WHO staff next sent a letter to all prequalified vaccine producers requesting feedback on the revised VVM specifications and test procedures. They compiled a list of all the issues and prepared a question-and-answer document to address the concerns one by one.[31] The 20 issues covered five categories: validation, logistics, regulatory, program, and commercial (see Table 7.2). In March 2002, WHO hosted a technical review of VVM implementation in Geneva to discuss the issues and included representatives from PATH, the UNICEF Supply Division, vaccine producers, Temptime, and other potential VVM suppliers.

Vaccine producers expressed disquiet about three issues in particular. First, like UNICEF, vaccine producers were uneasy having Temptime as the sole supplier of VVMs. To address this problem, UNICEF agreed to specify in contracts with vaccine producers that if Temptime could not provide the needed VVMs, the vaccine producers would not be liable for the absence of the technology on their vaccine labels.[32]

Second, vaccine producers questioned the need to introduce a different labeling system for VVMs into their existing vaccine production. As discussed above, Temptime and PATH had worked together to improve the labeling system so that one label, instead of two, could be used on the oral polio vaccine product. VVMs for OPV and other liquid vaccines can be placed on custom labels. But for freeze-dried vaccines such as measles and yellow fever, labeling with VVMs is more complex because the product must be removed during the reconstitution process. VVMs for freeze-dried vaccines in *vials* are placed on the top of the vial. VVMs for freeze-dried vaccines in *ampoules* are placed on the ampoule's neck. At the time of the March meeting, two companies who were early VVM adopters had already developed new methods for the labeling process for freeze-dried vaccines: Japan BCG for ampoule neck labeling and Chiron for top labeling on vials.[33] At the WHO meeting, Temptime agreed to work with each producer to identify the best solutions for their particular label applications and to seek solutions that would have minimal investment and production costs for the producers.[34]

VVMs subsequently became available in both full label and dot formats. The full label format is for liquid vaccines and is specific to each vaccine producer. Temptime prints the VVMs onto the vaccine producer's labels and sends the labels (with VVM) to the vaccine producer. The full label format therefore does not require an additional investment in VVM application by the vaccine producer.[35] The dot format, designed for all freeze-dried vaccines, requires additional equipment by the producer to apply the dot to the existing vaccine label.[36] Temptime agreed to work with each company to tailor the VVM product to each firm's particular labeling system.[37]

The vaccine producers' third main concern focused on issues of legal and financial responsibility. Who would be responsible when a vial or shipment is

Table 7.2 | **Questions and concerns raised by vaccine producers**

Validation issues

1. The shelf life of the VVM is less than the shelf life of the vaccine.

2. Will WHO conduct correlation studies for VVMs and vaccine potency for all vaccines?

3. Can the VVM consistently reflect the true stability of each vaccine?

4. What data exist to show how the VVM is validated?

5. Is there some typical specification for VVM adhesion?

6. Chemical temperature indicators produce a high percentage of false readings.

Logistics issues

7. Concerns exist about introducing a different labeling system for a portion of production.

8. How can suppliers maintain the logistics of import and inventory control?

9. There are different multilingual, multiproduction, and multipacked quantities.

10. Additional capital expenditures are incurred to implement VVMs.

11. Does the current GMP requirement prohibit preprinted labels or require an on-line printer with a blank roll?

Regulatory issues

12. Does VVM attachment to the vaccine vial need to be approved by the national regulatory authority?

13. Who is legally and financially responsible when a vial or shipment is rejected because the status of the VVM(s) indicates excessive heat exposure?

14. Does the manufacturer's obligation cease at the time that the shipment is accepted in country?

Program issues

15. What is the benefit of having a VVM on a vaccine that is very heat stable, such as hepatitis B?

16. Is the VVM color change clear and does it convey the information to the field worker in a form that is easy to understand?

Commercial issues

17. Temptime Corporation is the sole supplier of VVMs. There is no competitor.

18. Why doesn't the Temptime warranty mirror the minimum shelf life required of the vaccine suppliers (18 months from the date of shipment from the vaccine supplier)?

19. Why does Temptime have a +/− 10% tolerance on the quantity of VVMs delivered?

20. Why does a minimum VVM order quantity have to be set?

Note. From *Technical Review of Vaccine Vial Monitor Implementation* by World Health Organization, 2002, Geneva: Author. Adapted with permission.

rejected following a VVM indication of excessive heat exposure? WHO staff explained that the vaccine producer is responsible for the product and for its transportation to the country using a number of monitoring devices, of which the VVM is only one. Once accepted by the buyer, the responsibility shifts to the buyer. Since VVMs are subject to strict controls before use, it is unlikely that a faulty VVM lot would reach the field. Should this happen, two scenarios are possible: (1) the faulty VVM would reach the end point early, leading to vaccine disposal and perhaps wastage but no increased liability; or (2) the VVM would fail to reach the end point in time, with the potential risk of health workers using a vaccine exposed to heat.[38] This latter scenario is the only one in which a potential liability exists. However, WHO staff pointed out that in "six years of experience and over 10 billion doses corresponding to more than 500 million VVMs used, it has never been documented that a faulty VVM lot has led to the use of vaccines of unacceptable potency."[39] The March meeting concluded that liability issues exist with or without the use of VVMs and that VVMs would not create additional liability; instead, VVMs should reduce producer liability because the technology helps health workers avoid administering heat-damaged vaccine to children.[40]

Though not articulated at the March 2002 meeting, vaccine producers may have resisted VVMs because the firms had no incentive to use the technology. At the time of scaling up VVMs, many vaccines were in short supply. UNICEF sought to purchase the entire available supply, and firms knew that they could sell their vaccines even if they did not use VVMs. Later, more companies began supplying most EPI vaccines (though not all), giving UNICEF more choices and decreasing vaccine producers' power in the market. These changing market dynamics may have contributed to greater compliance with VVM use by vaccine producers.

Gaining acceptance for the VVM technology by vaccine producers proved to be a major barrier in scaling up the technology to all EPI vaccines. Many vaccine producers who raised concerns about VVMs at the March 2002 meeting were already using the product on OPV. PATH and WHO employed a series of strategies to persuade EPI vaccine producers to adopt VVMs. The strategies included proving the technology's effectiveness through impact studies, requiring its use in vaccine specifications and tenders, making adjustments to the technology and labeling procedures, and conducting a series of international meetings with vaccine producers to provide ample opportunity for open discussion of issues. WHO and PATH also made explicit efforts to analyze and address producers' concerns, in preparation for the March meeting. All these factors contributed to the turn-around by vaccine producers in agreeing to use VVMs on other vaccines.

The ultimate success in scaling up VVMs to EPI vaccines supplied through UNICEF thus resulted from a series of factors: the energies of PATH and WHO as product champions, the funding by USAID and other donors to PATH, policy development by WHO and the UNICEF Supply Division, the willingness by Temptime to continue making technological innovations to the product, and the changing vaccine market. These efforts by the product champions and the manufacturer paid off. In 2004, almost one third of the doses of non-OPV vaccines purchased and supplied by UNICEF suppliers had a VVM label. UNICEF estimated in 2004 that by the end of 2005, there would be 100% implementation of VVMs on seven of the twelve UNICEF-supplied vaccines.[41] UNICEF also expected three other vaccines to be at or above 80% implementation, leaving only two with lower implementation rates. As of August 2005, these estimates were surpassed; only one UNICEF supplier, Sanofi Pasteur, was not using the VVM on non-OPV vaccines. (Sanofi Pasteur does use the VVM on its OPV product.)

Impact of Vaccine Vial Monitor Scale-Up

Success in scaling up VVMs on EPI vaccines provided through the UNICEF Supply Division has affected developing countries' immunization programs in two major ways. The first is that VVMs have decreased vaccine wastage and costs. As previously discussed, VVMs allow health workers to discard only those vaccines with a VVM reading showing excessive heat exposure. VVMs have also reduced vaccine wastage by helping health workers better manage the cold chain. As an indicator of cumulative heat exposure, the device allows health workers to assess which vaccines in their stocks have experienced some heat exposure but are still effective and should be used first.[42] Ümit Kartoglu, project manager for VVMs at WHO, points out that learning to "incorporate the VVM into the whole management cycle is an art" and is harder than simply reading a VVM.[43] This aspect of VVM use, therefore, is the main focus of WHO's training of health workers.

Another way VVMs have decreased vaccine wastage is that they have assisted implementation of WHO's multidose vial policy of 1995 (revised in 2000). This policy allows health workers to use opened vials of some vaccines for more than one day (instead of discarding them).[44] The presence of VVMs on EPI vaccines allows health workers to decide if open vials should be used the next day if the VVM has not reached its end point.[45] The previous policy required health workers to discard all open vials at the end of the day's immunization session. This new multidose vial policy has implications for vaccine wastage and costs. WHO estimates that the policy could reduce wastage rates by up to 30%, with annual vaccine cost savings of $40 million worldwide.[46] A study carried out by PATH and the Kingdom of Bhutan, which assessed the impact of the multidose vial policy and VVMs on liquid vaccines, found wastage decreases of 48.8% for OPV, 27.1% for diphtheria-tetanus-pertussis, 55.5% for tetanus toxoid, and 23.8% for hepatitis B vaccine (PATH, 1999).

Health worker adoption of the VVM sometimes encountered obstacles when VVMs were introduced in tandem with the new multidose vial policy. In Turkey, for example, it was difficult to convince some health workers, who had received training on the old policy, not to discard OPV at the end of the day (so that remaining vaccine could be used the next day) if the VVM had not reached its end point.[47] These health workers felt that a VVM that had not darkened by the end of the day was "defective" because "it does not darken as fast as it should."[48] The authors of the study in Turkey recommended that WHO clarify the reasons for the multidose vial policy and provide clear answers to questions raised by management and health staff to improve implementation by these workers in the field.

Analysts are currently studying whether VVMs can further reduce vaccine wastage by protecting against freezing of vaccines. Hepatitis B and tetanus toxoid vaccines (aluminum adjuvant-based vaccines) are heat stable but freeze sensitive, especially in the cold chain.[49] A baseline study in Indonesia found that 75% of hepatitis B vaccines were exposed to freezing temperatures.[50] Freezing problems decreased when the vaccine was transported and stored at ambient temperatures. In 2005 WHO staff drafted a policy paper proposing procedures to transport all vaccines without ice in order to prevent freezing of vaccines like hepatitis B and tetanus toxoid. The policy's success will depend in part on how effectively VVMs can be used to ensure against heat damage for vaccines transported without ice.[51]

The second major impact of VVMs is that they have allowed a more flexible cold chain strategy so that health workers can take vaccines out of the cold chain for longer periods to travel to remote settings. In 2000, WHO developed a strategy for using VVMs in this way to achieve better coverage of hard-to-reach populations in polio eradication efforts.[52] The success of this new strategy required health worker training on both VVMs and the new policy, but also depended on adoption by the parents of children to be immunized. Many mothers in developing countries know vaccine protocols well and expect vaccines to come directly from the refrigerator. Therefore, some mothers were wary when the OPV vials were transported at room temperature as a result of the new WHO policy.[53]

In sum, the VVM has led to decreases in vaccine wastage (and reduced costs to governments) and has had a paradigm-shifting impact on the cold chain protocol (resulting in more immunized children in remote areas).[54] PATH estimates that over the 10-year period of 2005–2015, VVMs will allow health workers to recognize and replace more than 230 million doses of inactive vaccine and to deliver 1.4 billion more doses in remote areas.[55] The organization believes that using this technology could save more than 140,000 lives and lead to morbidity reductions for many others. In terms of cost savings, UNICEF and WHO estimate that the use of VVMs on basic vaccines can save the global health community US$5 million per year (based on typical vaccine wastage rates).[56]

Current Challenges

To fully realize the VVM's potential impacts on vaccine wastage, vaccine costs to governments, and vaccine coverage in areas with a fragile cold chain, the device needs to be scaled up on all vaccines used in immunization programs. The major limitation on these impacts has been low adoption of VVMs outside the UNICEF Supply Division. While VVM use is now close to 100% on EPI vaccines procured through UNICEF, the device is underused on vaccines financed by the PAHO Revolving Fund for Vaccine Procurement and on those purchased directly by developing-country government procurement agencies (and not procured through UNICEF). As Stephen Jarrett, deputy director of UNICEF's Supply Division, said, "The uptake of the device on other [non-UNICEF procured] vaccines has been slower than originally anticipated. . . . One of the reasons has been that UNICEF is the only committed buyer of vaccines with VVMs."[57]

The PAHO Fund has never recommended the use of VVMs in its region (North and South America and the Caribbean). At the March 2002 meeting on VVM implementation, a PAHO representative stated that the agency had not adopted VVMs because initially the device was used only for OPV, and polio had already been eradicated in the Americas at the time of VVM introduction. He then explained that the subsequent delay in adopting VVMs had been due to PAHO's desire to introduce VVMs on all vaccines; now that these VVMs were more widely available, PAHO would revisit its decision.[58] As of November 2006, however, PAHO still had not recommended the use of VVMs to vaccine suppliers or purchasers. While PAHO did contribute to early VVM research, the agency did not support later trials in the region. As a result, there has been no opportunity to evaluate whether the technology would be cost-effective in the region or well received by health workers.[59] PAHO's resistance to VVMs adds a layer of complexity to the production processes of vaccine producers who provide vaccines to both the UNICEF Supply Division and the PAHO Fund. These producers require two different types of labels to produce both VVM-labeled and nonlabeled vaccines.

Like the PAHO Fund, many developing-country government procurement agencies have not required VVM use. John Lloyd of PATH asserts that this has led to "a huge proportion of domestically supplied non-polio vaccines in vaccine-producing countries [that] are still being distributed without VVMs."[60] Without a government requirement, vaccine producers have little incentive to use VVMs.[61] For them, affordability remains an important problem. Though the VVM is low cost, these vaccine producers are understandably reluctant to pay the additional costs of VVMs in a competitive market where the technology is not requested by the purchaser for all producers, where other producers are not using VVMs, and where the government is not interested in paying the additional costs.

In 2007, WHO and UNICEF issued a joint statement requesting countries to include VVMs among the minimum requirements for vaccine purchasing agreements with all producers.[62] The government procurement agencies in two countries, Indonesia and India, now require VVMs on all vaccines. WHO has had discussions with other government procurement agencies and national vaccine producers about using VVMs, but with limited success. While there is a potential cost savings to immunization programs that use VVMs (through decreased vaccine wastage), and the device can also help increase vaccine coverage in remote areas, most governments have been slow to require the product. Debra Kristensen of PATH explains that one model that has been successful in getting national producers to adopt VVMs is the use of an advocate/consultant with a mandate from the government and some funding.[63] In India, for example, the United Kingdom Department for International Development (DFID) gave money to the Indian government in the mid-1990s to scale up VVMs on all OPV in the country, including vaccines supplied by national manufacturers. DFID also provided financing and technical assistance to manufacturers for VVM implementation and paid for a one-time procurement of OPV from each of the manufacturers. This project succeeded because there was both sufficient funding and a concerted effort, led by an advocate, to include the government and all producers in the country. But PATH currently has no funding dedicated to support VVM adoption in developing countries. While PATH continues to provide technical assistance to WHO on VVMs, its focus has moved to other new technologies. As a result, the architecture steering the adoption process for VVMs by individual developing countries has stalled.

Conclusions

The VVM story, spanning 27 years and still ongoing, demonstrates that bringing new technologies through product development, introduction, and scaling up is a "long and arduous journey."[64] The process requires focused effort by public and private agencies, plus sufficient financing and patience. Each access phase for VVMs required years of concerted effort: twelve years for product development, six years for the first introduction on oral polio vaccine, and nine years for scaling up to EPI vaccines supplied by WHO prequalified producers. Data are not available for VVM coverage on vaccines delivered in developing-country immunization programs, but sales data from Temptime show a marked increase in VVM uptake over time. Between 1996 and 2007, Temptime's sales of VVMs for oral polio vaccine rose more than three-fold to nearly 200 million vials per year and for other EPI vaccines sales rose from nothing to over 100 million vials per year (see Figure 7.1). By the end of 2005, close to 100% of WHO-prequalified vaccine producers used the technology. Significant challenges, however, still remain in expanding VVM access in the PAHO region and in developing-country vaccine markets.

Efforts to promote access to VVMs encountered barriers (as shown in Table 7.3)—particularly adoption problems—and these differed in the introduction and scaling-up phases. When VVMs were first introduced on OPV, the technology was new and the most pressing needs were to demonstrate the effectiveness of VVMs on OPV and to require their use through policy development. The primary barriers involved a number of vaccine producers' concerns that were eventually addressed through open discussion in meetings, technical changes, and validation studies. In the scaling-up phase to all EPI vaccines, the number of vaccine producers that became potential VVM users increased significantly. As the number of actors multiplied, so too did the number of barriers encountered in trying to achieve adoption by vaccine producers. To address these blockages, WHO and PATH held a series of technical meetings with vaccine producers and Temptime, UNICEF specified and enforced VVM requirements in vaccine tenders, and Temptime modified the technology and worked with vaccine producers to develop new labeling processes.

This chapter shows how actors can have widely diverging views of new health technologies, affecting product adoption. For example, for WHO staff and health workers, the technology meant improvements to the functioning of the cold chain and decreases in vaccine wastage. For the UNICEF Supply Division, VVMs challenged their policy on sole suppliers and created stress in their relationships with vaccine producers. For vaccine producers, attaching VVMs to their vaccines sold

Figure 7.1 | Sale of Temptime's VVM products, 1996-2007

VVMs, in millions

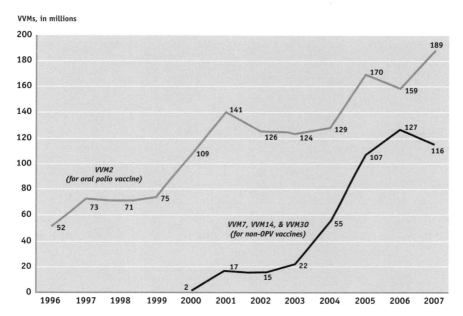

Note. Temptime has four categories of VVMs. The first is the VVM2 (for the least stable vaccines) that is used for the oral polio vaccine. The other three categories are the VVM7 (for moderate stability vaccines), VVM14 (for medium stability vaccines), and VVM30 (for high stability vaccines). The VVM7, VVM14, and VVM30 are used for EPI vaccines other than the oral polio vaccine. From *Implementation Update on VVM* by Temptime Corporation, 2005, Morris Plains, NJ. Adapted with permission.

to UNICEF meant a number of legal, logistical, and commercial challenges to their business. Providing access for VVMs required a concerted effort—and a significant amount of time—to bring these diverse groups together. VVM product champions in WHO and PATH steered the process step by step from initial development to introduction on OPV to scaling up to other EPI vaccines. WHO and PATH staff members worked together in an informal partnership on VVM-related activities (testing, impact studies, meetings with vaccine producers) and also had separate responsibilities (WHO was responsible for training, PATH provided technical support to Temptime). WHO served as the coordinating body for VVM access, though once vaccine producers began to use VVMs, the time WHO staff spent in coordination diminished. PATH's role has been one of providing technical expertise to WHO and the VVM manufacturer. Kartoglu, the project manager for VVMs at WHO, stated that since he arrived at WHO in 2001,

PATH staff provided mentoring and other crucial support throughout the VVM access process.[65] PATH and WHO, together with the UNICEF Supply Division, created an effective architecture for VVM access; the focused effort and time commitment given by staff in these organizations were critical factors in assuring VVM implementation on vaccines procured through UNICEF.

VVM product champions, especially PATH, worked hard to create a close relationship with Temptime as a central part of the architecture for VVM access. PATH established a relationship with Temptime early in the access process by encouraging the company to develop the product. PATH provided continuing support to Temptime, urging the company to continue working on the VVM product from an early stage when the company questioned whether to move forward. For Temptime, PATH staff gave the company the end-user's point of view and a vision for the overall program.[66] Temptime invested more than $10 million to develop the VVM[67] and did not begin to make a profit on the product until 2001.[68] The company responded to repeated requests to modify the original VVM technology according to evolving WHO specifications and the needs of particular vaccine producers. Importantly, Temptime relied on product champions PATH and WHO to market the technology, rather than carrying out these activities on its own. As a midsized company with no background in public-sector or global health work, Temptime was unprepared to market the VVM and required the support and guidance of WHO and PATH staff in this realm.

The champions for VVMs gave special attention to product adoption by different groups. For example, PATH provided loans that facilitated Temptime's purchase of custom labeling equipment so that vaccine producers could begin using VVMs on OPV. Product champions also tried to find other manufacturers for VVMs in order to address concerns among vaccine producers and UNICEF about Temptime's role as sole manufacturer—but without success. As a result, this issue continues.

Product champions also worked to convince procurement agencies of the need for VVMs on all EPI vaccines. These relationships represented important components of the VVM architecture. Requiring VVMs in UNICEF tender specifications for vaccines and enforcing these requirements was vital to achieving adoption by vaccine producers.[69] UNICEF enforced the VVM requirements gradually over time, due in part to the limited supply of some vaccines and the organization's need to purchase all available products, regardless of whether they had VVMs. A continuing problem has been the resistance to VVMs by PAHO and many developing-country government procurement agencies. The lack of adoption by these groups has limited access to VVMs in the PAHO region and in countries that procure their own vaccines (often from domestic sources) but do not require VVMs on all vaccines.

The work of VVM product champions depended on adequate financing. For VVMs, these funds came to PATH mainly through USAID's HealthTech Program. USAID's willingness to provide long-term funding for HealthTech (1987–2006) was particularly important. This gave PATH the unusual opportunity of providing long-term support to WHO, Temptime, and other groups. In addition to USAID funds, PATH financed its VVM work through other sources, such as its Loan Fund, the U.S. Centers for Disease Control and Prevention, and other donors.

The story of VVMs demonstrates that creating access to this innovative technology required much more than simply putting a label on a vaccine vial. Producing access to VVMs on vaccines procured through UNICEF has been successful and has created far-reaching impacts—reducing vaccine wastage, allowing health workers to take vaccines to remote areas, pinpointing weak links in the cold chain, implementing a multidose vial policy, and ultimately expanding the reach of immunization programs—to improve health and save lives in developing countries. Achieving these impacts has required diverse agencies to work together, overcome logistical issues, address limited uptake by vaccine producers, and embrace new ways of thinking about the cold chain and vaccine management. This could only be achieved through the efforts of dedicated product champions like PATH and WHO collaborating with public and private actors to achieve access and technology uptake. Achieving the full potential cost gains and health gains offered by the VVM, however, will require continued advocacy by product champions to expand access to the device for all EPI vaccines used in developing-country immunization programs.

Table 7.3 | **Vaccine vial monitors access table**

	BARRIER	STRATEGY	SPECIFIC ACTION
ARCHITECTURE	Need for a global champion for VVMs	Identify effective leadership and design partnerships for the technology	PATH used funds from USAID and other sources to work with WHO as product champions and collaborated with Temptime to develop the technology and push it through product development, introduction, and scaling up
ADOPTION	Concerns by vaccine producers about lack of independent validation, labeling process, sole VVM supplier, and liability (vaccine producer adoption)	Assure adequate quality and quantity of the product to persuade producers to adopt the technology	WHO funded an independent validation of VVMs to demonstrate its effectiveness; PATH worked with Temptime to modify the technology to meet WHO specifications, develop new labeling processes and address concerns of individual vaccine producers; UNICEF addressed liability and sole supplier issues in contracts with vaccine suppliers; WHO and PATH held technical meetings with Temptime and vaccine producers
	Concerns of UNICEF Supply Division about sole VVM supplier and the limited global vaccine supply (UNICEF adoption)	Produce acceptance of the technology at the global level	PATH and WHO worked to assure adoption by UNICEF Supply Division
	PAHO has not required VVM use (PAHO adoption)	Produce acceptance of the technology at the global/ regional levels	WHO conducted impact studies to demonstrate how VVMs reduced vaccine wastage in developing country settings, but PAHO has resisted adoption
	Many developing countries have not required national vaccine producers to use VVMs (national adoption)	Produce acceptance of the technology at the national levels	This problem has not been adequately addressed, in part because PATH has lacked funding to work with governments and producers in developing countries to facilitate national adoption

Table 7.3 | Vaccine vial monitors access table (continued)

	BARRIER	STRATEGY	SPECIFIC ACTION
AFFORDABILITY	Concerns by producers that VVM labeling process would require new equipment (and costs)	Assure vaccine producers that the technology will not impose major additional costs	Temptime developed a new labeling process that did not require vaccine producers of liquid vaccines to purchase new labeling equipment; producers of freeze-dried vaccines do require additional equipment to apply the VVM, but Temptime agreed to work with each company to tailor the VVM to its particular labeling system
AVAILABILITY	Concerns of UNICEF and vaccine producers that Temptime was the sole supplier of VVMs.	Assure adequate quantity of production	PATH and WHO encouraged and funded other companies to develop competitive products, but none were successful; UNICEF addressed sole supplier issue in contracts with vaccine producers, and WHO and PATH held technical meetings with Temptime and vaccine producers

Endnotes

1   World Health Organization-UNICEF, *Quality of the Cold Chain: WHO-UNICEF Policy Statement on the Use of Vaccine Vial Monitors in Immunization Services* (Geneva: World Health Organization, 1999, WHO/V&B/99.18).

2   GAVI, *GAVI Sixth Board Report* (Ottawa, Canada: GAVI, 2001).

3   PATH, *HealthTech Historical Profile: Vaccine Vial Monitors* (Seattle: PATH, 2005). Other temperature indicators for vaccines are temperature data loggers (monitoring international transport), Cold Chain Monitor cards (monitoring transport between levels), and Stop!Watch (monitoring refrigerator temperatures). The VVM is the only tool that is available at all times during distribution and delivery.

4   PATH.

5   Ray Baughman (Robert A. Welch Professor of Chemistry and Director of Alan G. MacDiarmid NanoTech Institute, University of Texas in Dallas), interview by author (Laura Frost), August 19, 2005.

6   PATH.

7   PATH.

8   PATH.

9   Ümit Kartoglu (Scientist, World Health Organization), interview by author (Laura Frost), August 17, 2005.

10 Baughman interview.

11 PATH.

12 PATH; and Ted Prusik (Senior Vice President, Temptime Corporation) and Chris Caulfield (Director of Sales, Temptime Corporation), interview by author (Laura Frost), August 3, 2005.

13 CliniSense Corporation has developed an electronic time-temperature indicator called LifeTrack for monitoring both vaccine heat exposure and freezing. This indicator, however, costs $3.00–5.00 at high production volumes and is therefore too expensive to attach to each vaccine vial. See: Stephen E. Zweig, "Advances in Vaccine Stability Monitoring Technology," *Vaccine* 24 (2006): 5977–5985.

14 PATH.

15 PATH.

16 Debra Kristensen (Senior Technical Officer, PATH), interview by author (Laura Frost), August 16, 2005.

17 Oya Zeren Asfar and Birhan Altay, *Vaccine Vial Monitors Impact Study During 1997 National Immunization Days in Turkey* (Geneva: World Health Organization, 1998, WHO/EPI/TECHNET.98/WP.23).

18 Asfar and Altay.

19 PATH, Kingdom of Bhutan, and World Health Organization, *Vaccine Vial Monitor Impact Study Results: Kingdom of Bhutan* (Seattle: PATH, 1999).

20 Ajit Mukherjee, Tej Pal Ahluwalia, Laxmi Narayan Gaur, Rakesh Mittal, Indira Kambo, Nirakar Chandra Saxena, and Padam Singh, "Assessment of Vaccine Wastage During a Pulse Polio Immunization Programme in India," *Journal of Health, Population, and Nutrition* 22 (2004): 13–18.

21 Kristensen interview.

22 PATH, Kingdom of Bhutan, and World Health Organization.

23 The Consumer Association Research and Testing Centre (UK) carried out a conformity test of VVM2 samples, and Precision Measurements and Instruments Corporation (U.S.) carried out conformity tests of VVM7, VVM14, and VVM30 under a WHO contract.

24 Interview by author (Laura Frost) with anonymous source, September 29, 2005.

25 Kristensen interview.

26 PATH.

27 Kristensen interview.

28 World Health Organization-UNICEF, *Quality of the Cold Chain*.

29 PATH.

30 World Health Organization, *Technical Review of Vaccine Vial Monitor Implementation* (Geneva: WHO, 2002).

31 World Health Organization, *Q&A: Technical Session on Vaccine Vial Monitors* (Geneva: WHO, 2002).

32 Kristensen interview.

33 Kartoglu interview; and World Health Organization, *Technical Review.*

34 World Health Organization, *Technical Review.*

35 World Health Organization, *Q&A.*

36 World Health Organization, *Q&A.*

37 Prusik and Caulfield interview.

38 World Health Organization, *Technical Review.*

39 World Health Organization, *Technical Review*, 20.

40 World Health Organization, *Technical Review.*

41 GAVI, "VVM Uptake: Accelerating in International Markets," *Vaccine Forum* 1 (2004): 1–3.

42 PATH.

43 Kartoglu interview.

44 The policy applies to multidose vials of the following vaccines: oral polio, diphtheria-tetanus-pertussis, tetanus toxoid, diptheria-tetanus, hepatitis B and liquid formulations of *Haemophilus influenzae* type b vaccine. It does not apply to the vaccines that are reconstituted—Bacillus Calmette-Guérin, measles, yellow fever, and some formulations of *Haemophilus influenzae* type b vaccine. See: World Health Organization, *WHO Policy Statement: The Use of Opened Multi Dose Vials in Subsequent Immunization Sessions* (Geneva: WHO, 2000, WHO/V&B/99.18).

45 World Health Organization, *WHO Policy Statement.*

46 World Health Organization, *WHO Policy Statement.*

47 Asfar and Altay.

48 Asfar and Altay, 7.

49 PATH.

50 Carib M. Nelson, Hariadi Wibisono, Hary Purwanto, Isa Mansyur, Vanda Moniaga, and Anton Widjaya, "Hepatitis B Vaccine Freezing in the Indonesian Cold Chain: Evidence and Solutions," *Bulletin of the World Health Organization,* 82 (2004): 99–105.

51 PATH.

52 World Health Organization, *Making Use of Vaccine Vial Monitors: Flexible Vaccine Management for Polio* (Geneva: WHO, 2000, WHO/V&B/00.14).

53 Prusik and Caulfield interview.

54 PATH, 10.

55 PATH.

56 World Health Organization-UNICEF, *Quality of the Cold Chain.*

57 GAVI, "VVM uptake," 1.

58 World Health Organization, *Technical Review.*

59 Kristensen interview.

60 GAVI, "VVM uptake," 2.

61 Kristensen interview.

62 World Health Organization-UNICEF, *WHO-UNICEF Policy Statement on the Implementation of Vaccine Vial Monitors: The Role of Vaccine Vial Monitors in Improving Access to Immunization* (Geneva: WHO, 2007, WHO/IVB/070.04).

63 Kristensen interview.

64 Kristensen interview.

65 Kartoglu interview.

66 Prusik and Caulfield interview.

67 Temptime Corporation, *Implementation Update on VVM* (Morris Plains, NJ: Temptime Corporation, 2005).

68 Prusik and Caulfield interview.

69 PATH.

CHAPTER 8

FEMALE CONDOMS:

Access to Dual Protection Technologies

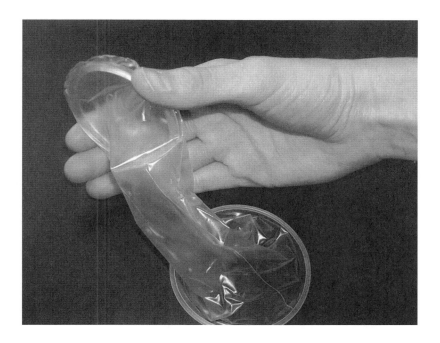

With Beth Anne Pratt

IN 2006, AN ESTIMATED 39.5 MILLION ADULTS WERE LIVING WITH HIV INFECTION worldwide, almost half of whom were women. The percentage of women with HIV has increased steadily over the years, from 35% in 1985 to 48% in 2006.[1] In 2006, two thirds of all adults and children with HIV lived in sub-Saharan Africa, of whom 59% were women.[2] These numbers reflect women's higher biological vulnerability to HIV infection relative to men, as well as gender inequalities in many societies that limit women's ability to protect themselves from HIV.

These vulnerabilities have prompted the search for female-initiated HIV prevention methods. The main female-initiated methods under consideration include female condoms, diaphragms, and microbicides. Studies on the diaphragm's efficacy in preventing HIV and other sexually transmitted infections (STIs) are still ongoing, as are efforts to develop microbicide products.[3] As of mid-2006, the only method available on the market with proven efficacy in preventing both pregnancy and STIs was the female condom.[4] Because of its ability to protect against both pregnancy and STIs, the female condom is known as a "dual protection" technology.

Introduced in 1992, the female condom has been launched in almost 100 countries worldwide. While the technology generated high levels of initial enthusiasm, adoption by end-users, providers, national governments, and donors has remained low. This chapter examines the low uptake and limited access for the female condom from its development in the mid-1980s through its introduction in the 1990s to efforts in the mid-2000s to address the multiple barriers to access. The female condom story highlights the challenges of creating access to a technology when barriers are encountered at many different levels—global, national, local—and when advocates are unable to create an access architecture and strategic plan for addressing these barriers. In this chapter, we describe current attempts to build architecture and access strategies to address persistent problems of product availability and affordability, as well as its adoption by many actors: end-users, providers, national governments, and global agencies. Whether advocates can create successful access for the female condom remains to be seen.

Product Development (Phase 1)

Lasse Hessel, a Danish physician, developed the female condom in 1984. Mary Ann Leeper, senior vice president of Wisconsin Pharmacal Co., Inc. (a company that primarily manufactured chemical products such as home cleaners and institutional health care products), heard about Hessel and his invention. In October

1987, Leeper and Hessel discussed the female condom and agreed that Wisconsin Pharmacal would develop the product to meet U.S. Food and Drug Administration (FDA) requirements in exchange for marketing rights in the United States, Canada, and Mexico. Hessel agreed to develop the manufacturing technology for the female condom. He sought a U.S. patent for the female condom, which he acquired in 1988. Wisconsin Pharmacal created a new division, the Female Health Company, to take responsibility for the female condom work. The company embarked on the studies required to gain FDA approval for the technology, with Leeper leading the effort. By the end of 1988, Leeper was ready to submit a clearance application for FDA approval, believing that the product met approval criteria.[5] At this same time, the FDA made a decision to use stricter criteria to evaluate all new condoms—based on a Citizen's Petition filed by the National Women's Health Network. The Network, though advocating for the development of new methods for HIV protection, believed that the developers of new male and female condoms needed to provide more effectiveness data than originally required by the FDA.[6] Based on the Network's petition and subsequent discussion within the FDA, the regulatory agency classified the female condom as a Class III medical device, requiring more extensive safety and efficacy studies for Wisconsin Pharmacal's product than Leeper originally thought necessary.[7] These studies would require more time and investment from Wisconsin Pharmacal. To raise capital for female condom development, the company went public in 1991.

Meanwhile, Hessel was experiencing financial and technical problems in his efforts to develop the manufacturing technology for the female condom. To solve these problems, he sold the female condom's world rights (outside the United States) to a Dutch investor. In 1989, this investor established Chartex Resources, Ltd., a London-based company, to manufacture the female condom and market it outside of North America. With resources from the investor (millions of dollars) and also a nonprofit Danish foundation, Chartex developed state of the art production processes for the technology and received permission to market the device in a number of countries outside the United States.

The FDA approved Wisconsin Pharmacal's application to market and distribute the female condom in the United States in 1993, and one year later, it approved the Chartex manufacturing facility. The FDA stated that it accelerated the approval process for the female condom because the device was the only existing female-initiated barrier method. But the agency also expressed concerns about the device's effectiveness in the field at preventing pregnancy and protecting against STIs. Because of these unresolved questions, the agency required product labeling stating that male latex condoms appeared to offer better protection against pregnancy and disease.[8] As FDA Commissioner David A. Kessler said at the time of approval, "The female condom is not all we would wish for, but it is better than no protection at all. . . . I have to stress that the male latex condom remains the best shield against AIDS and other sexually transmitted diseases."[9] FDA approval allowed Wisconsin Pharmacal to begin importing large quantities of the female condom for sale in the United States.

The product approved by the FDA in 1993 is a transparent polyurethane sheath the same length as a male condom with a flexible ring at each end. Polyurethane, invented in the 1940s, is a polymer whose molecules consist of a long repeating chain of smaller units called monomers. The polyurethane material used in female condoms is produced by combining two monomers (a diisocyanate and a polyol), creating a thin and odorless material that transfers heat better than the latex used in male condoms. The inner ring of the female condom is used to insert the device and secure it in place during intercourse, while the softer outer ring remains outside the vagina. The female condom can be inserted several hours prior to intercourse. It is prelubricated with a silicone-based, nonspermicidal lubricant. The FDA initially approved a shelf life of three years for the device but later revised this to five years.

Laboratory-based studies of efficacy show that the female condom provides protection against both pregnancy and sexually transmitted infections with no known side effects.[10] Early field research of contraceptive effectiveness under conditions of typical use shows an estimated 79% effectiveness for female condoms, compared to 85% for male condoms.[11] More recently, preliminary results from the first multisite study to compare contraceptive effectiveness of female and male condoms, supported by the World Health Organization (WHO), show effectiveness rates in Panama, China, and Nigeria as 94–98% for the female condom and 92–96% for the male condom.[12] Studies in Kenya, Thailand, and the United States also indicate that female condoms provide as much protection from STIs as male condoms.[13] Moreover, while they note that there is an absence of clinical trial data on the female condom's efficacy and effectiveness in preventing HIV infection,[14] the American Foundation for AIDS Research states that "the female condom is 94–97% effective in reducing the risk of HIV infection if used correctly and consistently."[15]

In its early years, the female condom generated great excitement in the United States and around the world. The product's approval received prominent attention in the media. Both specialists and the general public had high expectations.

One advocate describes her excitement about the new technology:

I had . . . high hopes for this new technology—it was effective, easy to learn to use, had no side effects, and wasn't tied to the existence of sophisticated medical facilities, unlike other technologies such as the pill or diaphragm. Most exciting, to me at least, the female condom could be used by a woman acting alone, a great advance over its male equivalent. This feature struck me as an unambiguously good thing—now women could take charge of their own reproductive health; now they could be freed from their dependence on their male partner's willingness to use the male condom in order to protect them from disease.[16]

But sales of the female condom did not take off right away. By 1995, Wisconsin Pharmacal had limited funds to market the product, and the company decided to restructure its business. First, in 1995 it purchased Chartex, and the next year it split into two companies, with the Female Health Company relocating to Chicago and remaining public. O. B. Parrish remained chief executive officer of the Female Health Company, and Leeper took over as president and chief operating officer in 1996. These changes gave the Female Health Company full ownership of all intellectual property related to the female condom. Its subsidiary, Chartex, continued as the sole manufacturer of the technology.

The Female Health Company refers to its product as the FC Female Condom. The product is known as Reality in North America and elsewhere as the Female Condom, Femidom, Femy, Preservativo Feminino, El Condon Femenino, and MyFemy. As of early 2008, the FC is the only female condom with FDA approval. It has been the primary female condom manufactured, marketed, and used in studies worldwide from 1992 until 2005, when the Female Health Company released a second-generation product, the FC2.

Introducing the Female Condom (Phase 2)

By the early 1990s, the Female Health Company was poised to introduce its innovative dual protection technology around the world. The company first launched its product in Switzerland in 1992. The device subsequently was registered by the U.S. FDA, the European Patent Convention, and by regulatory agencies in 11 additional countries. During the 1990s, the Female Health Company supplied female condoms to public agencies in over 80 countries (for public distribution and social marketing campaigns) and sold them commercially in 17 others. The product's main advocate since its introduction has been the manufacturer, the

Female Health Company, whose only product is the female condom. The company established the Female Health Foundation in 1996 to promote global women's health projects related to female condom use, including economic empowerment projects, sexual negotiation skills training, and reproductive health education. The foundation's partners include UN agencies (UNAIDS, UNFPA, WHO), national governments, non-governmental organizations, and community-based organizations.

Efforts to introduce the female condom showed some success in a number of countries where the product was actively promoted to try to achieve high levels of adoption, such as South Africa, Zimbabwe, Brazil, and India. For example, in Zimbabwe in the mid-1990s, more than 30,000 women petitioned the government to make female condoms accessible so women could protect themselves against HIV infection and STIs.[17] Population Services International (PSI) began a social marketing project in 1997 (funded by USAID and the United Kingdom Department for International Development) and marketed the device under the brand name Care as a "contraceptive sheath" rather than a condom in order to avoid stigmatizing associations with STI prevention.[18] Sales of female condoms were higher than PSI and its partners expected. In its first year (1997), the program sold 120,720 condoms. Sales figures rose steadily, and in 2002, the program sold 683,700 female condoms.

Despite successes in these few countries, most efforts to introduce the female condom between 1992 and 2005 showed only low levels of uptake. The high expectations of enthusiasts for the female condom were not easily realized. Many supporters believed "that if women were offered a method over which they had greater control, they would adopt it readily."[19] That simply never happened. Attempts to introduce the female condom worldwide encountered five access barriers at the global, national, and local levels: (1) limited affordability, (2) low end-user adoption, (3) lack of provider adoption, (4) insufficient global consensus, and (5) inadequate architecture.

Limited Affordability

The high price of the female condom is often cited as the primary obstacle to access. Family Health International's AIDS Control and Prevention Project (AIDSCAP) organized a meeting in October 1993 on the potential role of the female condom in international AIDS prevention.[20] Participants at the meeting discussed the problems of price as a barrier to access. Product price has remained a topic at all subsequent meetings on the female condom.

The commercial price to end-users in developing countries of the Female Health Company's product at introduction was approximately $2.00–$3.00 per condom. To make the product more affordable for governments and end-users, UNAIDS and the Female Health Company in 1996 negotiated a public-sector pricing agreement, reducing the price for developing country governments to approximately $0.58 per condom for bulk purchases. This public-sector price was reportedly only 10% above the cost of production.[21] Governments that purchase the female condom at this price provide the product free to end-users in public clinics or make the product available at low prices to end-users through social marketing programs. Despite this much lower public-sector price, the female condom is still much less affordable for governments than a male condom (the price of which, by contrast, is about $0.02 per condom for bulk purchases on the world market). Whether the product is affordable for the end-user depends on whether she is able to obtain the product through a public sector program where it is either free or available at subsidized prices.

One strategy used by some advocates of the female condom to address affordability issues was to seek global consensus for allowing end-users to use the product multiple times. When the U.S. FDA approved the female condom, it did so for one-time use. But advocates argued that since the polyurethane material used to make the female condom is stronger than latex, it could retain its structural integrity for repeated use. If end-users could utilize the product multiple times, this would reduce product cost per use. A number of studies were conducted on this issue, some of these supported by USAID. These studies found that indeed the female condom can be washed and reused multiple times without causing serious damage to its structural and microbiological integrity.[22]

The issue of reuse was debated at the global level during the female condom's introduction phase. WHO held consultations in 2000 and 2002 to review the evidence on reuse and make recommendations. Subsequently WHO issued a statement that did not recommend or promote the reuse of female condoms based on existing evidence.[23] The agency stated that unresolved safety questions about reuse remained and called for additional clinical and laboratory testing. The agency however recognized the diversity of contexts and personal circumstances and stated that the final decision on reuse should be made by each national government. WHO prepared a protocol for handling and preparing female condoms for reuse to be used by program managers who decided to evaluate the feasibility of reuse in local settings. This compromise suggests that advocates did not adequately address the affordability problems of female condoms through the reuse strategy. But interest in the reuse issue has persisted. A recent review of the research on female condom effectiveness, for example, called for more reuse studies because the possibility of reuse makes the female condom a much more affordable option.[24]

Affordability problems have depressed end-user adoption in settings where the product is only available through individual purchase.[25] In many countries, however, governments or non-governmental organizations make the product free to women at health facilities through donor-funded programs or provide it at subsidized prices in outlets such as pharmacies, clinics, supermarkets, and convenience stores. In these settings, the female condom's high price from the manufacturer is less problematic for end-users, but it continues to pose a barrier to governments, non-governmental organizations, and donors who purchase the product in bulk.

The high price of the female condom has affected adoption by global and national actors in other ways as well. Some analysts argue that high prices have distorted demand for the product and undermined donor and national government support. As Friel states, "One cannot miss the play of a familiar vicious cycle: because of perceived low demand, donors are unwilling to invest in female condom programming and procurement, women do not find the product accessible and the apparent low demand is perpetuated."[26]

Low Adoption by End-Users

Certain technical characteristics of the female condom can give negative first impressions to some users and pose continuing barriers to end-user adoption.[27] Some women consider the female condom to be large and bulky, aesthetically unappealing, prone to slippage and twisting during sexual intercourse, stiff in its internal rings, and difficult to insert, as well as unpleasantly noisy and smelly.[28] Studies have shown a high frequency of misuse and low levels of acceptability on the first attempt at use. Following repeated attempts, user confidence and satisfaction increase, as do users' skill at correct insertion and removal.[29] Without adequate training and counseling, women may lose interest after initial failed attempts or may expose themselves to risks of STIs and unplanned conception through mishandling of the female condom.[30]

Cultural attitudes also affect end-user adoption of the female condom. Women may feel shame and inadequacy if the female condom causes awkward problems during intercourse.[31] In some countries, female condom adoption is held back by negative cultural perceptions about touching or placing something within a woman's vagina.[32] A study conducted among refugees in Kenya noted a major gap in respondents' knowledge of reproductive anatomy to the extent that some refugees questioned advocates' assurances that condoms (both male and female) would not disappear permanently into an individual's body cavity resulting in illness or death.[33] Another acceptability study in Burundi noted users' beliefs that the female condom was "incompatible" with a special sexual technique ("ruganga"), prevalent among many communities around the Lake Victoria basin, involving clitoral stimulation with a man's penis.[34]

The politics of sexual relations can also create barriers for women who seek to use the female condom. Some studies show that men are far more willing to use either male condoms or female condoms with casual sex partners, particularly commercial sex workers, than they are with regular partners. For example, a study conducted among commercial sex workers in Mombasa, Kenya, demonstrated an increase in the number of protected sex acts with clients but no change in unprotected sex with boyfriends—regardless of female condom availability.[35] Men may interpret a woman's request to use a female condom as a symbol of a woman's infidelity or that a woman is suffering from an STI. In a study from South India, 56% of women reported that requesting the use of a condom resulted in violence from their husbands.[36] The association of the female condom with commercial sex workers in some settings, as opposed to a regular family planning measure for married couples, further compounds the problem of women's efforts to use the device.

Finally, female condoms have sometimes been used for other purposes by end-users. In Zimbabwe, where the government makes female condoms available for free in clinics and hospitals, there are reports of traders removing the rubber rings from the female condom, painting them, and selling them as bangles in the marketplace.[37] Though this practice is not widespread, the example illustrates how health technologies can be used in unexpected ways and can appear in unexpected places.

Lack of Provider Adoption

Efforts to introduce the female condom at the local level encountered a number of barriers to provider adoption. Some providers found themselves without the capacity, support, and training to implement female condom programs and therefore could not provide instruction, counseling, and follow-up to their clients.[38] Some providers lacked sufficient health infrastructure to promote the method. For example, many clinics had no female pelvic models on which to demonstrate female condom use.[39] An absence of provider support led to high discontinuation rates among clients in female condom programs.[40] This discontinuation, in turn, led circularly to the perception among providers of a lack of end-user demand for the female condom. Providers were therefore reluctant to promote the female condom, especially when provider-preferred substitutes existed for contraception and STI prevention, notably the more cost-effective, easy-to-use, and often publicly subsidized male condom.[41]

Cultural attitudes and patterns also affected provider adoption. Provider training and counseling efforts often focused on female clients, with little information directed toward male partners and little effort made at encouraging open communication between partners about protection methods. Without male cooperation and support or training for women in sexual negotiation skills, female end-users may be unable to assert their right to an independent choice of contraception.[42] Moreover, the provision and promotion of female condoms, even with male cooperation and involvement, do not necessarily translate into increased use if existing cultural, educational, or political inequalities prohibit female control over reproductive health decisions.[43] Providers are often unwilling or unable to intervene in these gender-based patterns of decision-making among couples. In addition, cultural stereotypes have affected provider preferences; the female condom has been viewed as a "method of last resort" for commercial sex workers when male condoms are unavailable.[44]

Provider adoption has also been affected by problems in availability—especially inconsistency of supply—at the local level. In some areas, oversupply has been reported for public service agencies and nongovernmental organizations (NGOs), resulting in wastage and expired stock.[45] Other NGOs and private pharmacies have found themselves stocked out of the female condom or anticipate female condom shortages when funding stops from pilot projects.[46] These problems with supply undermine provider adoption. Some providers believe that government or donor agencies are not serious about their long-term commitment to the female condom. As a result, some providers view female condom programs as an externally driven, unsustainable experiment for which government, donor, and consumer interest will inevitably wane over time.[47]

Insufficient Global Consensus

Efforts to introduce female condoms have also suffered from a lack of global consensus about the need for the technology and its relationship to other family planning and HIV prevention technologies. Several international agencies—especially WHO, UNFPA, and UNAIDS—all have signaled their support for female condoms through financial and administrative investments in research, programs, and advocacy activities. But individuals and organizations in the broader global health community have expressed sharply diverging views of the technology.

As the female condom is a dual protection technology, decisions about its promotion have required the collaboration of different global health policy communities—especially those dedicated to family planning and those focused on HIV prevention. These groups have tended not to communicate well with each other,[48] and their views of the female condom have differed because their work seeks distinctly different global health goals. Family planning groups, which seek to promote the most effective contraceptive, have been reluctant to promote the female condom because it is less effective than hormonal contraceptive methods. HIV prevention activists, by contrast, advocate a harm-reduction model that emphasizes the minimization of risk through a combination of strategies with varying degrees of effectiveness. Bringing these different groups together in global health requires concerted communication and hard work, and this did not occur for these policy communities in the introduction phase of the female condom.[49]

Splits also arose between women's health advocates and other health researchers. In his review of a 1997 AIDSCAP meeting on "The Female Condom: From Research to the Marketplace," Friel notes,

'Women's advocates' were said to be pushing for the female condom now; 'researchers and donors,' on the other hand, said it was too expensive until more research shows it to be effective in slowing the AIDS epidemic. The dilemma was and is real: if we don't invest in it, how can the female condom show success?[50]

The strongest advocates for the technology came from the international women's health community. Their support for the female condom resulted in part from evidence showing that heterosexual intercourse, rather than women's intravenous drug use, put women at greater risk of HIV infection than men. They concluded that women needed methods under their own control to protect themselves against HIV infection.[51] Some analysts have argued recently that international women's health advocates' efforts to promote the technology diminished after a period of initial excitement, once the technical and design problems became apparent in the introduction phase.[52] These advocates did not give up on the female condom, but some began focusing on other technologies such as microbicides.[53] Microbicides are seen as a preferable female-initiated HIV prevention method compared to female condoms because microbicide gels are supposedly "invisible." Women therefore would not have to obtain their partners' cooperation in order to use the technology.[54] Recent microbicide studies, however, have questioned whether gels will indeed be invisible to male partners. Other research points out that in many cultures, women will always seek male partners' consent and cooperation about the use of reproductive health technologies, even if the technology's design allows for "invisible" application.[55] Furthermore, optimistic estimates suggest it will be 2010 before an acceptable microbicide will be on the market.[56] As a result, the female condom is the only technology currently available (other than the male condom) that can protect against both pregnancy and STIs.

Significant gaps in the evidence base about the female condom also hampered global adoption. Female condom research has focused on acceptability studies and pilot studies conducted in different countries. These studies have been important for assessing both end-user perceptions of the new technology and field experiences in using the technology in small-scale interventions. But large-scale epidemiological studies on the female condom that could provide good evidence for moving the technology from introduction to scale-up have not yet been carried out.[57]

Large-scale epidemiological studies could encourage global adoption in several respects. First, large studies of actual female condom use, with outcome data such as pregnancy, STIs, or HIV infection, could help convince implementing organizations, donors, and other reluctant groups that they should invest in the technology.[58] The potential for the female condom to affect HIV incidence, for example, can only be shown in large-scale national programs. Data from large-scale studies could also help demonstrate whether scaling up female condom availability would result in significant and continued uptake. The focus on acceptability research and pilot studies has helped perpetuate the view of the female condom as still "in trial." Because doubts—both real and imagined—exist about effectiveness, many implementing agencies and national governments are unwilling to integrate the female condom into STI, HIV/AIDS, or family planning programs beyond a pilot project.[59] Similarly, many donors are reluctant to provide substantial funding for female condom programming and procurement.

Inadequate Architecture

Any new technology needs an effective champion to expand access. The female condom has its advocates, including international women's health groups, the

Female Health Company, and the Female Health Foundation. While the Female Health Foundation has promoted the product, the Foundation's efforts have focused mostly on local and national issues, rather than at the global level. Furthermore, the foundation is almost entirely funded by the Female Health Company, making some national and global actors uncomfortable and distrustful.[60] No other nonprofit organization has taken primary responsibility to promote access for the female condom at the global level. Nor has there been a global campaign for the female condom like the one for microbicides.

In its introduction phase, the female condom lacked an important component of architecture: an access plan to mobilize individuals and organizations behind the technology. At global meetings, experts discussed and identified important activities for scaling up. For example, the 1997 AIDSCAP meeting concluded with more than 40 "next steps to the marketplace." Six of these next steps emerged as consensus recommendations: (1) begin large-scale introduction in two to three countries in order to answer operational research questions, (2) promote the female condom for men as well as women, (3) market the female condom simultaneously through interpersonal and mass media strategies, (4) expedite research on whether the female condom can be used more than once, (5) provide incentives for alternative, less expensive product designs, and (6) disseminate information broadly, including to the media.[61] But none of these "next steps" or "consensus recommendations" became prioritized or written into a plan.[62] With no access plan, no global champion beyond the manufacturer and its foundation, and no strong architecture for partnership, the numerous problems discussed in this section persisted as barriers to access.

Rethinking Strategy for Scaling Up (Phase 3)

By early 2005, access to the female condom seemed to be leveling off worldwide (see Figure 8.1). In the nine years following the female condom's introduction, only 90 million units were sold.[63] Sales increased nine-fold between 1997 and 2003, but from a relatively low starting point.[64] Between 1996 and 2005, the Female Health Company operated at an annual net loss. According to the company's annual report in 2002, members of the board of directors needed to make substantial loans to help keep the company afloat.[65] By 2004, approximately 12.2 million units were sold per year, representing only 0.1–0.2% of the number of male condoms sold worldwide.[66] The company received a USAID contract in 2003 to provide female condoms to AIDS prevention initiatives in developing countries. But worldwide orders for female condoms did not change significantly

Figure 8.1 | Unit sales of the Female Health Company products (FC and FC2)

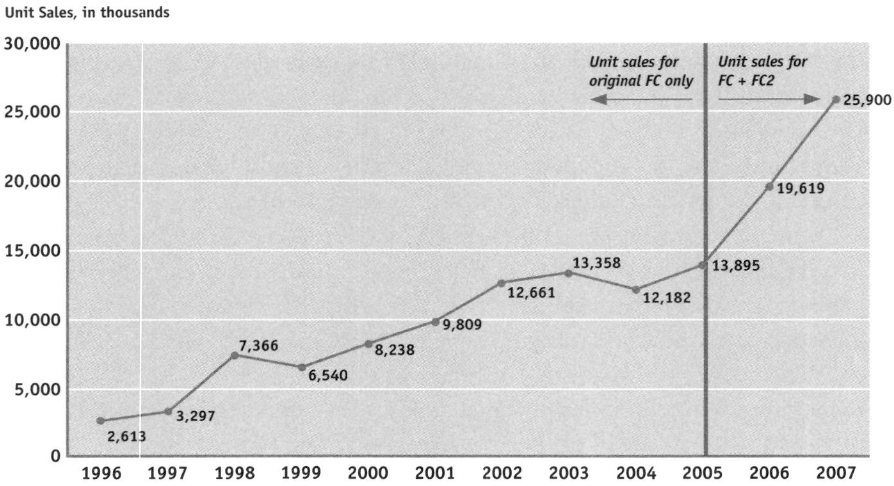

Unit Sales, in thousands

Note. All unit sales prior to 2005 refer to sales of the original female condom product (FC). In 2005, the company introduced a second product, known as the FC2. All unit sales in 2005 and the following years are of both the FC and FC2 products. Data from *Female Health Company Annual Reports*, available at http://www.femalehealth.com (retrieved March 22, 2008).

between 2002 and 2005, and neither did the proportion of female to male condoms sold.[67]

To remain viable, both the company and the technology required strategic change. Various product advocates and donors who sought to promote the female condom technology pursued three strategies: (1) new product development, (2) training and promotion, and (3) building architecture. These strategies represent efforts by the product champions and key stakeholders to improve consultation, cooperation, and consensus in order to reduce the barriers to access. The strategies seek to address continuing problems in affordability, provider and end-user adoption, and global architecture.

New Product Development

One way to reduce the high price of the female condom is to develop cheaper designs than the original polyurethane-based condom. As PATH vice president Michael Free remarked in a 1997 AIDSCAP meeting, "The only way to get the production price down is to break the technology barrier to create a much less expensive material."[68] New product designs could also allow new manufacturers to enter the female condom market. This could create competition in what was a monopoly market. In addition, new product designs could raise end-user adoption by improving the original product's lack of appeal to women.

The ideal female condom product, according to PATH, should have the following features: (1) be highly protective, (2) be stable and secure, (3) cost less than $0.10, (4) be extremely easy to use, (5) provide great sensation, and (6) allow for environmentally safe disposal.[69] To narrow the gap between the existing female condom and this ideal product, several alternative designs to the FC Female Condom are now under development (see Table 8.1 for a list of these products). The new designs differ according to their material (synthetic latex or polyurethane) and design features (for example, length, shape of outer ring, lubricated/nonlubricated, with/without anchoring sponge, separate from/built into underpants), and can be manufactured with or without a spermicide.

The first new product is the Female Health Company's FC2, which uses a nitrile polymer synthetic latex alternative to the FC Female Condom. Nitrile polymer (the material used in manufacturing surgical gloves) is cheaper than polyurethane and involves an improved, more efficient production process whereby condoms are dipped onto a mold, as opposed to welded together down a seam as was the case with the original polyurethane model. In 2005, the Female Health Company further cut costs for the FC2 by switching manufacturing operations from the Chartex facility in London to a factory in Kuala Lumpur, Malaysia. Initially, operations in Malaysia consisted of a borrowed line in a surgical glove factory, but by 2007, public-sector FC2 sales were doing well enough for the Female Health Company to increase its manufacturing capacity by opening its own factory.[70] Recently, the Female Health Company established a partnership with its FC distributor in India, the government parastatal Hindustan Latex Limited (HLL). HLL previously collaborated in social marketing for the original FC to high risk populations in six states across India, as well as private-sector distribution to the general population in two additional states. In 2008, HLL will begin production of the FC2 in India for the Indian governments' National AIDS Control Organization. The government, in partnership with NGOs, will sell the FC2 through social marketing in selected Indian states at heavily subsidized prices to end-users (approximately $0.13 per female condom compared with $1.00 per unit cost of production).[71]

In 2007, WHO gave the FC2 a positive technical review prior to the 2006 Toronto AIDS meeting. The Female Health Company and UNAIDS then negotiated a reduced price agreement that enabled the sale of the FC2 to the global

Table 8.1 | **Manufacturers of female condom products, as of 2008**

Manufacturer	Country	Product	Registration	Brand Names
Female Health Company	United Kingdom	FC Female Condom®	U.S. FDA CE plus 11 other countries	FC FC Female Condom Reality Femidom Dominique Femy MyFemy Protectiv´ Care FC2
Mediteam	Belgium	The Belgian Female Condom		
Silk Parasol Corporation	United States	Silk Parasol		Panty Condom
PATH	United States	Women's Condom		WC Woman's Condom
Natural Sensation Company (Acme Condoms)	Colombia	Panty Condom Female Condom	CE INVIMA (Bolivia) undergoing review in Brazil, Argentina, Australia, USA	Panty Condom
Medtech	India	VA Female Condom	CE Indian MOH undergoing review in China, Brazil, South Africa, Russia	VA Female Condom Reddy Female Condom V-Amour

public sector via UN agencies at a price of $0.74–0.87 per unit.[72] The FC2 also received a CE (European Conformity) mark from the European Economic Area for use by European public-sector agencies.[73] However, as of March 2008, the FC2 was still under review by the U.S. FDA. This means that while UN agencies and European donors have integrated the FC2 into their AIDS prevention programs, U.S. purchasers—including USAID (with whom the Female Health Company has one of its largest contracts), the City of New York, and Planned Parenthood—can only purchase the original FC. Consequently, though the

Female Health Company would prefer to discontinue the original FC and transfer all of its manufacturing operations to Malaysia, the London Chartex plant has to stay open to produce the original FC for U.S. purchasers.[74] The inability to discontinue production of the original FC also means that in countries in which both the UN and USAID supply female condoms to the public sector, whether a woman obtains either the original FC or the FC2 is determined entirely by which donor funds the supplier to her particular clinic, program, or region and not by consumer choice or market mechanisms.

The next two products, the VA Female Condom (also known as the Reddy Female Condom or V-Amour) and the Natural Sensation Panty Condom, are marketed in limited quantities outside the United States, but do not have U.S. FDA approval and are not currently purchased by major donors.[75] Three other new products are also in development. The furthest in development is a polyurethane prototype developed by PATH in partnership with CONRAD, the Andrew W. Mellon Foundation, the Bill & Melinda Gates Foundation, and a number of private donors. This product, called the PATH Woman's Condom, seeks to be more user-friendly and cost-effective than both the FC and the FC2. PATH's innovations include the addition of a dissolving insertion capsule, made of polyvinyl alcohol, which allows easy proper placement, a soft outer ring that sits snugly against a woman's body, and four small dots of foam on the condom's surface to ensure that the condom lines the vagina without twists, bunches, or movement.[76] In 2008, the PATH Woman's Condom was ready to begin the combined Phase II/III effectiveness trials required by the U.S. FDA pending funding.[77] PATH currently expects a public-sector price for the product of $0.30–0.40, but with scale-up and material and process innovations, the organization hopes to reduce this amount by half.[78] Early acceptability studies conducted in South Africa, Thailand, and Mexico have indicated a positive response from users, most notably ease of insertion and correct use from the first attempt.[79] Two additional products, the Silk Parasol and the Belgian Female Condom, are also in development. Regulatory approval is contingent on the companies' ability to find funding for clinical trials and regulatory applications.[80] Some female condom advocates argue for amending the clinical trial requirements and streamlining the regulatory approval process for female condoms in the United States in order to bring these new products to market more quickly.[81]

Even with new product designs and more competitive markets, the female condom will probably always cost more than a male condom because it is larger, more complex, and has increased performance demands.[82] The manufacturing process is simply more costly for female condoms, even at large numbers. Additional manufacturers and more competition will help lower prices, ensure steady product supply, and offer more choice to women, but it will take some time before the new products complete development and enter the market to compete with Female Health Company products. Until this occurs, affordability of the female condom for donors and national governments will depend on (1) the negotiation of reduced price agreements with the Female Health Company as a monopoly supplier and (2) a significant increase in demand for the FC2 to give the company economies of scale. A recent PATH and UNFPA document presents the Female Health Company's FC2 pricing strategy and challenges:

FHC hopes to develop a coalition of regional buyers to enable cost savings through bulk regional procurement. Nonetheless, to achieve even a 50 percent price reduction ($0.31), global sales and bulk purchasing will have to increase to 200 million units— more than 14 times the total 2005 sales of the FC Female Condom (14 million units). This will require a substantial increase in global demand.[83]

Increasing demand for the product around the world remains a persistent challenge for female condom advocates.

Training and Promotion

By the mid-2000s, acceptability studies among women showed that the design of the female condom—most notably its bulkiness, difficulty of insertion, and noise—constituted major barriers to ongoing use, as was the perception that male partners do not like the technology. Similarly, providers had serious doubts about donors' ability to maintain a consistent supply of female condoms. Providers also questioned the technology's usefulness when a cheap, effective, and available alternative existed—the male condom. Providers perceived a lack of demand for the product among women and their male partners. They also wondered about the effectiveness of the female condom in the absence of counseling and monitoring. Without training in sexual negotiation skills and lacking power in sexual relations, women seem as unlikely to propose a female condom to their male partner as they would a male condom.[84] To address these barriers to end-user and provider adoption, female condom advocates developed a number of training and promotion strategies. These include counseling and support for women and their male partners, provider training, the creation of user-friendly instructional materials, and the identification of nontraditional channels (such as taxi stations) through which to promote and distribute the condom.

Well-designed and implemented training programs and materials can significantly increase adoption. For instance, prior to the launch of its public-sector female condom program, the South African government organized a Training of Trainers program to prepare providers for the new technology.[85] The program created a network of trained health care workers to promote the method, train other providers, and give support to end-users. The training shifted providers' family planning and STI counseling from a "provider-centered" approach to a "client-centered" one in which clients choose technologies most appropriate to their personal needs and desires.[86] The training also encouraged providers to use the female condom themselves in order to gain firsthand experience and greater understanding of potential problems. A recent study in Brazil showed that extended provider counseling can overcome negative first impressions and can raise adoption and long-term use by some women.[87]

Some recent reports suggest that the involvement of male partners in female condom promotion can be effective in cultures where women have limited power and status.[88] In South Africa, for example, the Female Health Foundation has targeted male police officers in special workshops, and in Zambia, the Society for Family Health (the local PSI affiliate) distributes the product to men in barbershops. Program staff in both countries report high levels of interest by men who enjoyed the feeling of sex without a male condom and appreciated sharing the responsibility of protection and contraception with their partners.[89]

Building Architecture

A major barrier to female condom access has been the absence of an effective global architecture and champion. Beginning in the mid-2000s, a new architecture of female condom access began to emerge. Global agencies, particularly UNFPA, began to take a stronger advocacy role. In 2005, UNFPA launched the Global Female Condom Initiative to promote the device as a dual protection method. UNFPA thus became one of the Female Health Foundation's most enthusiastic partners. The UN agency aims to scale up female condoms in 22 countries through its global campaign for the technology.[90]

Female condom advocates also began to collaborate to expand access to the technology. In September 2005, a partnership among PATH, UNFPA, the Bill & Melinda Gates Foundation, USAID, the U.K. Department for International Development, and other advocates sponsored the Global Consultation on the Female Condom in Baltimore, Maryland. Experts from around the world attended this meeting to review evidence about the female condom's effectiveness and program experiences. To avoid repeating past mistakes, organizers set up a working group to ensure that commitments would be implemented. Participants also decided to identify and prioritize the next steps for scaling up into a strategic access plan.

The meeting agreed on four steps for action: (1) develop greater political and social support for the female condom at local, national, and international levels, (2) increase public and private-sector investment in female condoms, (3) move beyond the pilot stage to scale up the use of female condoms and to monitor and evaluate impact, and (4) conduct research to improve programming, including operational research to identify behavior change strategies and evaluations of long-term impacts.[91] UNFPA's female condom initiative and the Global Consultation, together with the launch of the FC2, marked a turning point in efforts to expand access to the female condom and produced a measurable rise in sales, although total sales are tiny compared to global sales of male condoms. One important result of this meeting was the abandonment of pilot projects in favor of national distribution strategies. UNFPA now only introduces female condoms within the context of national scale-up, and the Female Health Foundation actively distances itself from pilot projects.

Strategies for adoption of the female condom have also shifted to stress HIV/AIDS prevention and control. The Female Health Company rarely mentions contraception or family planning in its current literature, instead marketing the FC and FC2 as integral to the battle against HIV/AIDS. The disagreements between the AIDS and family planning policy communities are thus disappearing, as the AIDS context comes to dominate advocacy of the female condom.

Activists recently launched a new global campaign called Prevention Now! to push for universal access to female condoms (led by the nonprofit Center for Health and Gender Equity in Takoma Park, Maryland). While the campaign's advocacy literature briefly mentions the goal of reducing unintended pregnancies, its dominant message calls for accelerated prevention of HIV and other STIs through expanded use of female condoms. It remains to be seen what impact Prevention Now! will have on global adoption of the female condom, but the campaign does represent a large and diverse coalition of private and public partners and operates without a specific link to the Female Health Company. This independence may lend its efforts a credibility that the Female Health Foundation has lacked due to its ties to the main manufacturer.[92]

Advocates of different female-initiated methods are also moving toward more collaboration.[93] In late 2004, the Global Campaign for Microbicides organized a meeting in London to address barriers and opportunities for increasing access to the female condom. This meeting represented a major change from prior positions promoting microbicides as the better female-initiated barrier method.[94] PATH and UNFPA have come to believe that "strong introduction programs [for the female condom] can also help pave the way for the introduction of other new protection methods, such as cervical barriers and microbicides, which will become available in the next decade."[95]

Conclusions

In 1993, the report for an AIDSCAP meeting on the female condom came to the following conclusion:

Without concrete steps by the public sector and sustained interest on the part of both family planning and AIDS professionals, it is safe to predict that the female condom will not be available to women in low income countries, and one potential weapon in the fight against STDs/HIV in developing countries will be lost.[96]

This statement proved to be prescient. The story of female condom access has been one of disappointingly low uptake. Many advocates continue to hope that the product will eventually be more widely used, and they continue to work to make the female condom more available, affordable, and acceptable to women and their partners, as well as to national governments and donor agencies. As Latka notes, the female condom faces similar challenges to those of the tampon when first introduced in the United States in the early 1930s.[97] The example of the tampon shows that controversial products can become mainstream. Over time, the female condom may become more widely adopted throughout the world, but only if concerted efforts are made to overcome major barriers. In this review of female condom access, we have shown that such efforts are presently seeking to address blockages at multiple levels, including technology design, global architecture, product price, distribution, and adoption at all levels (see Table 8.2 for a summary of access barriers).

This chapter has emphasized that new technologies like the female condom face many access barriers at the local level. Providers have lacked capacity, training, and support to promote the female condom and counsel end-users. Many providers remain unconvinced about the acceptability of the female condom for their clients. Design problems and product price, as well as the necessity of having to practice the technology in order to use it effectively, have discouraged end-users, providers, and governments from adopting the female condom. Sociocultural issues have also played a role, such as a woman's inability to negotiate with male partners for contraceptive choice and the strong association of the female condom with commercial sex workers. As of March 2008, a few implementation studies have begun to emerge (for example, among sex workers in Madagascar).[98] These studies provide guidance on ways to address provider and end-user factors to enhance female condom access.

This chapter shows the importance of building global consensus and coordination for technology access. The failure to develop an effective global architecture and access plan to promote the female condom between 1992 and 2005 slowed progress on many fronts. Differences in donor requirements for product approval have meant that donors are providing two different Female Health Company products, sometimes within the same national context.

The lack of information and research—particularly field trials—has hampered efforts to guide scale-up. The absence of information and research on supply, demand, acceptability, and cost-effective implementation methods has proven to be a major problem for national governments and donors seeking to integrate the female condom into existing reproductive health policy. Governments also lack the assurance from large-scale epidemiological studies that the female condom is an effective and appropriate national-level intervention against HIV/AIDS and other STIs. This dearth of large-scale research represents a major barrier to national and global adoption of the female condom and is a direct result of long-term weaknesses in female condom architecture.

Recently, however, advocates for the female condom have begun to guide access forward. The Female Health Foundation, UNFPA, and other partners are working with national governments to move the female condom beyond pilot projects. Through new production processes and negotiated pricing agreements, public-sector prices have been reduced to make the technology more affordable to governments and donors. A variety of new designs are awaiting approval, with the innovative PATH Women's Condom likely to enter the marketplace in the next three to five years. The new products and manufacturers will introduce competition into what essentially has been a monopoly market. Program successes in countries such as South Africa, Zimbabwe, India, and Brazil have provided a positive blueprint for integrating the female condom into reproductive health initiatives. Governments, donors, and providers are learning from these experiences to manage the main national and local level challenges of the female condom: public-sector stock-outs, poor demand forecasting, lack of consumer choice, and advocacy for the product directed to male partners.

The access barriers for the female condom are numerous and exist at multiple levels. Presently, the most challenging problem for advocates is that many people do not believe that the female condom is an effective and cost-effective strategy for the control of STIs and the prevention of pregnancy. Expanding access to this technology may require substantial donor subsidies, intensive counseling and support mechanisms, new product designs, and a consistent supply of female condoms. A dedicated partnership of advocates for the female condom may be able to reshape this perception and the logistical realities that underpin it. But only a deep commitment to the female condom is likely to create wider access to this technology in the near future.

Table 8.2 | Female condoms access table

	BARRIER	STRATEGY	SPECIFIC ACTION
ARCHITECTURE	Lack of global architecture and global champion for female condoms	Identify effective leadership and design partnerships for the technology	UNFPA has taken on a global advocacy and promotion role for the female condom and launched a comprehensive initiative in 22 countries
			Advocates established the Prevention Now! campaign to promote universal access to female condoms within an integrated STI and pregnancy control program
	No strategic plan for female condom access	Create strategy for technology access	1997 AIDSCAP meeting identified 40 steps for scaling up the female condom, but these steps were never prioritized or written into a strategic plan
			UNFPA, PATH, the Bill & Melinda Gates Foundation, USAID, DFID, and other advocates sponsored the 2005 Global Consultation on the Female Condom and identified steps to boost support, increase investment, generate data, and scale up
ADOPTION	Lack of global consensus and global/national adoption	Produce acceptance of the technology at the global and national levels	Increasing numbers of field trials conducted on acceptability and effectiveness though large-scale epidemiological studies have yet to be carried out
	Lack of adoption by providers due to limited training and infrastructure, as well as provider preferences	Develop and implement provider training programs	Some countries launched provider training programs (such as Training of Trainers) to create networks for promotion, training, and counseling of providers
			The Female Health Foundation updated training manuals for providers so that infrastructure such as female pelvic models are no longer necessary
	Low adoption by end-users due to technical, cultural, and gender factors	Develop counseling services for end-users, programs that address stigma, and new product designs; identify nontraditional channels for distribution	Some programs developed extended counseling services to train and support end-users to use female condoms and build sexual negotiation skills

Table 8.2 | Female condoms access table (continued)

	BARRIER	STRATEGY	SPECIFIC ACTION
ADOPTION			Some programs identified nontraditional channels for female condom promotion and distribution including police officers, taxi stations, and barbershops
			Some programs implemented social marketing projects aimed at destigmatizing female condoms
			NGOs, companies, and donors formed partnerships to develop new products that address design problems
AFFORDABILITY	High product price (affecting government, donor, and end-user affordability)	Find ways to lower prices through subsidy programs, public-sector pricing, promotion of reuse, and competition.	Donors provided subsidies to distribute female condoms free of charge or at low prices; high product prices limit the scope of these programs
			UNAIDS negotiated a public-sector pricing agreement with the Female Health Company for the FC and FC2
			Advocates sought global consensus for female condom reuse but these efforts were unsuccessful
			NGOs, companies, and donors formed partnerships to develop new products with cheaper materials; once approved, these products will provide competition in the marketplace
			The Female Health Company, UNFPA, and other donors have begun negotiations for FC2 bulk purchasing to take advantage of economies of scale; success of this strategy depends on a major increase in global product demand
AVAILABILITY	Inconsistent supply of female condoms	Assure adequate quality and quantity of production; seek to develop multiple producers	Partnerships were formed to develop, bring to trial, and eventually scale up the new FC2 latex condom and PATH female condom

----

Endnotes

1   UNAIDS, *AIDS Epidemic Update 2006* (Geneva: UNAIDS, 2006), http://www.unaids.org/en/HIV_data/epi2006/ (retrieved March 5, 2007); and UNFPA, UNAIDS, and UNIFEM, *Women and AIDS: Confronting the Crisis* (Geneva: UNAIDS, 2004), http://www.unfpa.org/hiv/women (retrieved March 5, 2007).

2   UNAIDS.

3   For a review of these methods, see: Robin Shattock and Suniti Solomon, "Commentary: Microbicides––Aids to Safer Sex," *The Lancet* 363 (2004): 1002–1003; and Joanne E. Mantell, Shari L. Dworkin, Theresa M. Exner, Susie Hoffman, Jenni A. Smit, and Ida Susser, "The Promises and Limitations of Female-Initiated Methods of HIV/STI Protection," *Social Science and Medicine* 63 (2006): 1998–2009.

4   Arnaud Fontanet, Joseph Saba, Verapol Chandelying, Chuanchom Sakondhavat, Praphas Bhiraleus, Sungwal Rugpao, Chompilas Chongsomchai, Orawan Kiriwat, Sodsai Tovanabutra, Leonard Dally, Joep M. Lange, and Wiwat Rojanapithayakorn, "Protection Against Sexually Transmitted Diseases by Granting Sex Workers in Thailand the Choice of Using the Male or Female Condom: Results from a Randomized Controlled Trial," *AIDS* 12 (1998): 1851–1859; Paul J. Feldblum, Maureen A. Kuyoh, Job J. Bwayo, Mohamed Omari, Emelita L.Wong, Kathryn G. Tweedy, and Michael J. Welsh, "Female Condom Introduction and Sexually Transmitted Infection Prevalence: Results of a Community Trial in Kenya," *AIDS* 15 (2001): 1037–1044; and P. P. French, Mary Latka, Erica L. Gollub, C. Rogers, D. R. Hoover, and Zena A. Stein, "Use-Effectiveness of the Female Versus Male Condom in Preventing Sexually Transmitted Disease in Women," *Sexually Transmitted Diseases* 30 (2003): 433–439.

5   Elizabeth Powell and Gerry Yemen, *The Female Health Company (A)* (Charlottesville, VA: The University of Virginia Darden School Foundation, 2003, UVA-BC-0146), http://papers.ssrn.com/sol3/papers.cfm?abstract_id=907748 (retrieved March 22, 2008).

6   Cynthia A. Pearson, "National Women's Health Network and the US FDA: Two Decades of Activism," *Reproductive Health Matters* 3 (1995): 132–141.

7   Powell and Yemen.

8   Warren E. Leary, "Female Condom Approved for Market," *New York Times*, May 11, 1993, p. C5.

9   Leary, C5.

10 W. L. Drew, M. Blair, R. C. Miner, and M. Conant, "Evaluation of the Virus Permeability of a New Condom for Women," *Sexually Transmitted Diseases* 17 (1990): 110–112; and B. Voeller, S. Coulter, and K. Mayhan, "Gas, Dye, and Viral Transport Through Polyurethane Condoms," *Journal of the American Medical Association* 266 (1991): 2986–2987.

11 Robert A. Hatcher, James Trussel, Felicia H. Stewart, Anita L. Nelson, Willard Cates, Jr., Felicia Guest, and Deborah Kowal, *Contraceptive Technology,* 18th rev. ed. (New York: Ardent Media, 2004).

12 Bidia Deperthes and Theresa Hatzell Hoke, "Effectiveness of Female Condoms in the Prevention of Pregnancy and Sexually Transmitted Infections" (PowerPoint presentation to

the Global Consultation on the Female Condom, September 26–29, 2005), http://www.path. org/projects/womans_condom.gcfc2005.php/THERESA_BIDIAFCGS_effectiveness_sept_ 22_THH.pdf (retrieved March 5, 2007).

13 Feldblum; Fontanet; and French.

14 PATH and UNFPA, *Female Condom: A Powerful Tool for Protection* (Seattle, WA: PATH, 2006).

15 AMFAR, *The Effectiveness of Condoms in Preventing HIV Transmission* (Issue Brief 1, January, 2005).

16 Amy Kaler, "'It's Some Kind of Women's Empowerment': The Ambiguity of the Female Condom as a Marker of Female Empowerment," *Social Science and Medicine* 52 (2001): 783.

17 "Zimbabwe Women Petition State on Female Condom," *AIDS Weekly Plus,* December 23–30, 1996, p. 10.

18 Dominique Meekers and Kerry Richter, "Factors Associated with Use of the Female Condom in Zimbabwe," *International Family Planning Perspectives* 31 (2005): 30–37.

19 Susie Hoffman, Joanne Mantell, Theresa Exner, and Zena Stein, "The Future of the Female Condom," *International Family Planning Perspectives* 30 (2004): 140.

20 This meeting was attended by 45 participants and funded by USAID. A majority of the participants were from U.S. agencies. Others included representatives from WHO and the International Planned Parenthood Federation. See: Patrick Friel, "Review of Past Action Plans and Their Implementation" (Presentation to the Global Consultation on the Female Condom, September 26–29, 2005), http://www.path.org/projects/womans_condom.gcfc2005.php/ Female_Condom_Baltimore_9-2005.pdf (retrieved March 5, 2007).

21 AIDSCAP Women's Initiative, *The Female Condom: From Research to the Marketplace* (Arlington, VA: Family Health International/AIDSCAP, 1997).

22 World Health Organization, *WHO Information Update: Considerations Regarding Reuse of the Female Condom*, July 2002, http://www.who.int/reproductive-health/ stis/docs/reuse_FC2. pdf (retrieved March 5, 2007).

23 World Health Organization, *WHO/UNAIDS Information Update: Considerations on Reuse of the Female Condom,* July 2000, http://www.who.int/repro-health/ rtis/consultation_on_ reuse_of%20female_condom_Durban.en.html (retrieved March 5, 2007); and World Health Organization, *WHO Information Update.*

24 Gowri Vijaykumar, Zonke Mabude, Jenni Smit, Mags Beksinska, and Mark Lurie, "A Review of Female-Condom Effectiveness: Patterns of Use and Impact of Unprotected Sex Acts and STI Incidence," *International Journal of STD and AIDS* 17 (2006): 652–659.

25 Alice Welbourn, "Sex, Life and the Female Condom: Some Views of HIV Positive Women," *Reproductive Health Matters* 14 (2006): 32–40; Sarah C. Thomsen, Wilkister Ombidi, Cathy Toroitich-Ruto, Emily L. Wong, Heidi O. Tucker, Rick Homan, Nzioki Kingola, and Stanley Luchters, "A Prospective Study Assessing the Effects of Introducing the Female Condom in a Sex Worker Population in Mombasa, Kenya," *Sexually Transmitted Infections* 82 (2006): 397– 402; Lucy Mung'ala, Nduku Kilonzo, Patrick Angala, Sally Theobald, and Miriam Taegt- meyer, "Promoting Female Condoms in HIV Voluntary Counselling and Testing Centers in

Kenya," *Reproductive Health Matters* 14 (2006): 99–103; and Vibeke Rasch, Fortunata Yambesi, and Rose Kipingili, "Acceptance and Use of the Female Condom among Women with Incomplete Abortion in Rural Tanzania," *Contraception* 75 (2007): 66–70.

26 Friel, 8.

27 Paulo R. Telles Dias, Katia Souto, and Kimberly Page-Shafer, "Long-Term Female Condom Use among Vulnerable Populations in Brazil," *AIDS Behavior* 10, suppl. (2006): S67–S75.

28 AIDSCAP; Telles Dias; Welbourn; Rasch; Mireille Munyana, "Promoting the Female Condom in Burundi," *Exchange on HIV/AIDS, Sexuality and Gender* 2006-2, http://www.kit.nl/exchange/html/2006-2_promoting_the_female_condom (retrieved October 25, 2006); and M. Okunlola, I. Morhason-Bello, K. Owonikoko, and A. Adekunle, "Female Condom Awareness, Use and Concerns among Nigerian Female Undergraduates," *Journal of Obstetrics and Gynaecology* 26 (2006): 353–356.

29 Thamban Valappil, Joseph Kelaghan, Maurizio Macaluso, Lynn Artz, Harland Austin, Michael E. Fleenor, Lawrence Robey, and Edward W. Hook, III, "Female Condom and Male Condom Failure among Women at High Risk of Sexually Transmitted Diseases," *Sexually Transmitted Diseases* 32 (2005): 35–43; Susan S. Witte, Nabila El-Bassel, Louisa Gilbert, Elwin Wu, Mingway Chang, and Jennifer Hill, "Promoting Female Condom Use to Heterosexual Couples: Findings from a Randomized Clinical Trial," *Perspectives on Sexual and Reproductive Health* 38 (2006): 148–154; and Maurizio Macaluso, Richard Blackwell, Denise J. Jamieson, Andrzej Kulczycki, Michael P. Chen, Rachel Akers, Dhong-jin Kim, and Ann Duerr, "Efficacy of the Male Latex Condom and of the Female Polyurethane Condom as Barriers to Semen During Intercourse: A Randomized Clinical Trial," *American Journal of Epidemiology* 166 (2007): 88–96.

30 Macaluso.

31 Welbourn.

32 Mitchell Warren, "I've Read the News Today, Oh Boy: Global Politics of Condom Promotion" (PowerPoint presentation to the Global Consultation on the Female Condom, 2005, September 26–29), http://www.path.org/ projects/womans_condom.gcfc2005.php/FC_consultation.pdf (retrieved March 5, 2007); Jacqueline Papo, "Promoting the Female Condom to Refugees," *Forced Migration Review* 25 (2006): 65–66; and Welbourn.

33 Papo.

34 Munyana.

35 Thomsen.

36 S. Newmann, P. Sarin, N. Kumarasamy, E. Amalraj, M. Rogers, P. Madhivanan, T. Flanigan, S. Cu-Uvin, S. McGarvey, K. Mayer, and S. Solomon, "Marriage, Monogamy and HIV: A Profile of HIV-Infected Women in South India," *International Journal of STD and AIDS* 11 (2000): 250–253.

37 Steve Vickers, "Zimbabweans Make Condom Bangles," *BBC News,* February 10, 2005, http://news.bbc.co.uk/2/hi/africa/4250789.stm (retrieved March 5, 2007).

38 Mung'ala; Witte; and Thomsen.

[39] AIDSCAP; and Mung'ala.

[40] Deperthes and Hoke.

[41] Rasch.

[42] Hoffman; Witte; Thomsen; and Mantell, "The Promises and Limitations."

[43] Mantell, "The Promises and Limitations"; and Rasch.

[44] Warren; Hoffman; and Thomsen.

[45] Vastha Kibirige, "The Female Condom: Uganda Experience" (PowerPoint presentation to the Global Consultation on the Female Condom, September 26–29, 2005), http://www.path. org/projects/womans_condom.gcfc2005.php/UGANDA.pdf (retrieved March 5, 2007); Mark Rilling, "Overview: USAID's Procurement of Female Condoms" (PowerPoint presentation to the Global Consultation on the Female Condom, September 26–29, 2005), http://www.path.org/projects/womans_condom.gcfc2005.php/MARK_female_condom.pdf (retrieved March 5, 2007); and UNFPA, "Intensified FC Initiative—Global Overview: Ethiopia" (PowerPoint presentation to the Global Consultation on the Female Condom, September 26-29, 2005), http://www.path.org/projects/womans_condom. gcfc2005.php/ UNFPA_Female_Condom_presentation.pdf (retrieved March 5, 2007).

[46] Rilling; UNFPA; Mung'ala; and Welbourn.

[47] Thomsen; Mung'ala; and Rasch.

[48] Amy Kaler, "The Future of Female-Controlled Barrier Methods for HIV Prevention: Female Condoms and Lessons Learned," *Culture, Health & Sexuality* 6 (2004): 501–516; and David W. Dowdy, Michael D. Sweat, and David R. Holtgrave, "Country-Wide Distribution of the Nitrile Female Condom (FC2) in Brazil and South Africa: A Cost-Effectiveness Analysis," *AIDS* 20 (2006): 2091–2098.

[49] Kaler, "The Future."

[50] Friel, p. 4.

[51] Hoffman.

[52] Kaler, "The Future." Kaler notes that an exception is the work of women-and-AIDS groups located in Africa, particularly SWAA (Society for Women and AIDS) in Ghana and WASN (Women and AIDS Support Network) in Zimbabwe.

[53] Kaler, "The Future."

[54] Shattock and Solomon.

[55] Mantell, "The Promises and Limitations."

[56] Hoffman.

[57] Kaler, "The Future"; and Vijaykumar.

[58] Erica L. Gollub, "The Female Condom: Tool for Women's Empowerment," *American Journal of Public Health* 90 (2000): 1377–1381.

[59] Vijaykumar.

[60] Interview by author (Beth Anne Pratt) with anonymous officials, February 13, 2008.

[61] AIDSCAP.

[62] Friel, 5.

[63] Karen King, "FC Female Condom: Key Learnings, Key Challenges" (PowerPoint presentation to the Global Consultation on the Female Condom, September 26–29, 2005), http://www.path.org/projects/womans_condom.gcfc2005.php/KAREN_FHC_PATH%20MTG_SEPT_2005.pdf (retrieved March 5, 2007).

[64] Friel.

[65] The Female Health Company, *Hitting Our Stride: The Female Health Company 2002 Annual Report* (Chicago: The Female Health Company, 2002), http://www.femalehealth.com/InvestorRelations/investor_annualreports/FHC_AR_2002.pdf (retrieved March 12, 2008).

[66] The Female Health Company, *No More Excuses: The Female Health Company 2005 Annual Report* (Chicago: The Female Health Company, 2005), http://www.femalehealth.com/InvestorRelations/investor_annualreports/FHC_AR_2005.pdf (retrieved March 12, 2008); and King.

[67] The Female Health Company, *No More Excuses.*

[68] AIDSCAP, 15.

[69] Glenn Austin, "Presentation to the Global Consultation on the Female Condom" (PowerPoint presentation to the Global Consultation on the Female Condom September 26–29, 2005), http://www.path.org/projects/womans_condom.gcfc2005.php/GAustinPresentSpeakernotes-GCFC10-16-05.pdf (retrieved March 5, 2007).

[70] Interview with anonymous officials.

[71] The Female Health Company, *The Distance Traveled: The Female Health Company 2006 Annual Report* (Chicago: The Female Health Company, 2006), http://www.femalehealth.com/InvestorRelations/investor_annualreports/FHC_AR_2006.pdf (retrieved March 12, 2008); and Kounteya Sinha, "Female Condom for Rs 5 in India," *The Times of India*, March 6, 2008, http://timesofindia.indiatimes.com/Female_condom_for_Rs_5_in_India/articleshow/2841558.cms (retrieved April 7, 2008).

[72] The Female Health Company, *The Distance Traveled.*

[73] The Female Health Company, *The Distance Traveled.*

[74] Interview with anonymous officials.

[75] PATH and UNFPA.

[76] Austin.

[77] PATH, "Women's Condom: Building Protection against Unintended Pregnancy and HIV," http://www.path.org/projects/womans_condom.php (retrieved March 22, 2008); and PATH, *Technology Solutions for Global Health: Women's Condom* (Seattle, WA: PATH, 2008), http://www.path.org/files/TS_update_womans_condom.pdf (retrieved March 22, 2008).

78 Austin.

79 Patricia S. Coffey, Maggie Kilbourne-Brook, Glenn Austin, Yancy Seamans, and Jessica Cohen, "Short-term Acceptability of the PATH Woman's Condom among Couples at Three Sites," *Contraception* 73 (2006): 588–593.

80 PATH and UNFPA.

81 PATH and UNFPA.

82 Austin.

83 PATH and UNFPA, 27.

84 Mantell, "The Promises and Limitations."

85 Joanne E. Mantell, E. Scheepers, and Q. Abdool Karim, "Introducing the Female Condom Through the Public Health Sector: Experiences from South Africa," *AIDS Care* 12 (2000): 589–601.

86 Mantell, "Introducing the Female Condom."

87 Thomsen; Mung'ala; and Telles Dias.

88 Mantell, "The Promises and Limitations."

89 Interview with anonymous officials.

90 Garry Canille and Luka Monoja, "Intensified FC Initiative: Global Overview of UNFPA FC Situation Assessment Nigeria and Ethiopia" (PowerPoint presentation to the Global Consultation on the Female Condom, September 26–29, 2005), http://www.path.org/projects/womans_condom. gcfc2005.php (retrieved March 5, 2007).

91 PATH and UNFPA.

92 Interview with anonymous officials.

93 Friel.

94 Global Campaign for Microbicides and the UNAIDS Global Coalition on Women and AIDS, *Observations and Outcomes from the Experts' Meeting on Female Condoms* December 10, 2004, (retrieved March 5, 2007).

95 PATH & UNFPA, 7.

96 Quoted in Friel, 4.

97 Mary Latka, "Female-Initiated Barrier Methods for the Prevention of STI/HIV: Where Are We Now? Where Should We Go?" *Journal of Urban Health: Bulletin of the New York Academy of Medicine* 78 (2001): 571–580.

98 See: Theresa Hatzel Hoke, Paul Feldblum, Kathleen Van Damme, Marlina Nasution, Thomas Grey, Emelita Wong, Louisette Ralimamonjy, Leonardine Raharimalala, and Andry Rasamindrakotroka, "Randomized Controlled Trial of Alternative Male and Female Condom Promotion Strategies Targeting Sex Workers in Madagascar," *Sexually Transmitted Infections* 83 (2007): 448–453.

CHAPTER 9

SYNTHESIS:

No Success without Access

THE CASE STUDIES IN THIS BOOK DEMONSTRATE THE COMPLEXITY OF CREATING ACCESS for health technologies in developing countries. Bottlenecks to access occur at many points along the pathways to the end-user. Our analysis of these bottlenecks has identified barrier points and facilitating factors, both of which are shaped by social, economic, political, and cultural processes. Health technologies thus appear as "traveling technologies" that acquire different meanings as they travel from factory gate to end-user.[1] The case studies show that successful access requires the capacity to understand and shape these diverse meanings as well as to implement strategies for availability, affordability, and adoption, all organized by a supporting architecture.

Each technology in this book has its own access story. Many challenges to scaling-up access are specific to the technology, the related health condition, the key actors involved, and the context in which the technology is introduced. But some recurring themes do emerge that provide important lessons about access, despite the uniqueness of each product. In this chapter, we present our findings— cross-cutting themes that add to knowledge about access to health technology in poor countries. In consolidating our findings into six lessons, we inevitably lose some of the nuance and detail found in each access story. We believe, however, that the lessons presented here can help product developers and champions in designing practical steps to improve access for health technologies. While one cannot anticipate every obstacle and opportunity, careful assessment based on historical experience can improve the chances of access to health technologies for poor people in poor countries.

Finding #1: Developing a safe and efficacious technology is necessary but not sufficient for ensuring technology access and health improvement. Products do not fly off the shelf on their own.

When a research and development project demonstrates that a new technology is safe and efficacious in clinical trials, the results are cause for celebration. Working through the regulatory affairs process to license the new technology also represents a significant achievement. These measures (safety, efficacy, and licensing), however, are not final endpoints. *We have argued in this book that the outputs of safety, efficacy, and licensing are midway successes in a complicated access process.* Getting a technology ready for regulation is only part of the process of creating access. This argument is supported by each of the access stories in this book. Take the example of Norplant. Scientific evidence showed it to be one of the safest products in clinical testing, with a high contraceptive efficacy, yet its use in the field faced many hurdles. Creating access requires a broader view of what needs to be done for these products that are not market-driven; that view needs to encompass everything up to and including how the end-user will actually use the technology. Otherwise, the technology's potential benefits will remain unfulfilled.

This lesson challenges the commonly held view that "if we make a good product that addresses an important health problem in developing countries, it will be used." Good health technologies need to be persistently promoted and actively guided through the access process, with careful attention to architecture, availability, affordability, and adoption in order to overcome the numerous obstacles to reaching the end-user. Products do not fly off the shelf on their own—especially for technologies aimed at improving health conditions in poor countries.

Finding #2: Creating access depends on effective product advocacy. Our case studies show that product advocacy has three important components: a product champion, a coordinating architecture, and an access plan with strategies.

Advocacy and Product Champions

Our stories of product access demonstrate that an essential component of the architecture for access is the product champion. *Product champions in global health are people or organizations that believe in new technologies and take a special interest in ensuring that the products are developed and made widely available in poor countries. The champions are committed, dedicated, even obsessed with the technology and its potential.* In his landmark study of agenda setting for public policy, Kingdon refers to champions of specific new public policies as "policy entrepreneurs" whose defining characteristic is "their willingness to invest their resources—time, energy, reputation, and sometimes money—in the hope of a future return. That return might come to them in the form of policies of which they approve, satisfaction from participation, or even personal aggrandizement in the form of job security or career promotion."[2] Product champions for global health technologies similarly invest their resources in seeking to expand access to the product they believe can have a significant impact on health improvement.

Product champions appear in many types of organizations working in global health. In the case of vaccine vial monitors (VVMs), PATH staff collaborated closely with WHO staff to ensure the introduction and scale-up of VVMs on all EPI vaccines. For Norplant, Population Council staff developed the product, introduced it, and acted as product champion for this new contraceptive delivery system. The main product champion for the female condom has been the manufacturer, the Female Health Company, and its foundation. In our case studies, the product champions are affiliated with international technical agencies for health, nonprofit organizations, academic institutions, or manufacturers. Funding was key to their effectiveness. Product champions sought external funding from foundations and bilateral donors or drew from existing resources within their organizations. Other characteristics of the champions, such as time, energy, reputation, and passion, were equally important for fulfilling their goals.

The product champion's role depends on the individual or organization, the product, and other circumstances. It ranges from stimulating awareness of the technology among specific groups to taking strategic actions to overcome development or access barriers. An example of this latter role is PATH's work with Temptime Corporation, the developer of vaccine vial monitors. At a critical point, when Temptime had decided to "give up" on the project, representatives from PATH visited the company, explained the global significance of VVMs, and convinced Temptime to continue its work (without additional funding). PATH staff members continued to promote VVMs in the introduction and scaling-up periods, and provided crucial support to WHO staff through mentoring and other activities.

While product champions are essential for ensuring access, the case studies show that *champions also need to be cautioned against having blind faith in their technology.* In a study of why new business initiatives can gain momentum even when it is clear they are doomed, Royer investigates the "dark side" of deep-rooted beliefs among managers in the inevitability of their product's success.[3] Such faith can blind champions to negative feedback about a product, whether from developers, partners, or end-users. Some analysts of the Norplant case study, for example, have argued that the Population Council's role as product champion in Indonesia led its staff to underestimate the problems with implant removal and counseling.

Royer suggests ways to avoid the pitfalls of blind faith. One way is to create an early warning system that includes control procedures and criteria for assessing project feasibility at each stage of development and access. Another is to include doubters along with believers on project teams. Promoting research by people with different perspectives can balance the views of enthusiasts with those of critics. These approaches can help safeguard against the blind faith that tends to thrive among product champions (and drive them). These kinds of measures could have been useful in the Norplant case, for example, since Indonesia lacked strong "watchdog" groups to monitor contraceptive services and counter the views of Norplant enthusiasts.[4] On the other hand, product champions may see these safeguards as unnecessary obstacles and slowing down uptake.

Advocacy and Coordinating Architecture

Ensuring widespread access to a health technology requires an organizational architecture and coordinating organization to steer and connect the availability, affordability, and adoption activities. The female condom case study shows that access efforts falter when product advocates do not create an architecture for access. The organizational structure in the other case studies varied in form and roles, depending on the specific product, partners, and circumstances. In all but the female condom case, one organization held the central coordinating role, linking with key partners. In one case, a new organization was established to conduct access activities (the Schistosomiasis Control Initiative), while for the other products, the staffs of existing organizations (the World Health Organization and the Population Council) fulfilled the coordinating role. In all cases, one or more dedicated staff members within an organization created an architecture and managed the technology's adoption and availability activities.

Three different models of organizational structure exist in our case studies. The first model involves WHO as the primary coordinating body. For vaccine vial monitors, WHO's Vaccines and Biologicals Division provided a structure for the initial introduction of the technology and was loosely affiliated with the other partners (PATH, UNICEF, Temptime, and vaccine producers). One WHO staff member, Ümit Kartoglu, was given primary responsibility for VVM scale-up. The role of Kartoglu and others in managing and implementing product access activities decreased once the technology became widely available and the need for a coordinating mechanism declined. A similar organizational model was employed for malaria rapid diagnostic tests (RDTs). WHO's Western Pacific Regional Office (WPRO) took responsibility for the coordination of RDT availability and adoption activities. WHO was late in assuming this role; it was not until 2002, after RDTs had already been introduced in poor countries and expert consultations had recommended that WHO take on a greater role, that the agency hired David Bell in WPRO. He then became the "global focal point" for RDTs and for creating WHO policy on when and where the products should be used. Until that time, there was little coordination among producers, potential purchasers, and global actors, and considerable confusion about the accuracy and quality of the available commercial tests. These problems affected national and health worker adoption of

RDTs and inhibited widespread access. This experience suggests that establishing an appropriate architecture *before* a product launch makes a big difference to the tempo of access and the prospects for success.

A second organizational model is the creation of a new initiative to manage access activities for an existing product. The Schistosomiasis Control Initiative (SCI), started with a grant of $27.6 million from the Bill & Melinda Gates Foundation, is a new initiative housed in Imperial College, London, where its director, Alan Fenwick, established an academic base. SCI's partners are Imperial College, Harvard University, WHO, and the Gates Foundation. Together, these partners oversee the availability, affordability, and adoption activities undertaken by the SCI. A major issue for this university-based approach is the organization's future—and the implications for ongoing access to praziquantel—once the funding from the Gates Foundation ends. Similarly, a new initiative manages the global access activities for the hepatitis B vaccine. Worried that immunization rates had leveled off in some poor countries and declined in others, a consortium of national and global organizations—WHO, UNICEF, the World Bank, the Bill & Melinda Gates Foundation's Children's Vaccine Program, the Rockefeller Foundation, the International Federation of Pharmaceutical Manufacturers & Associations, and some national governments—established the GAVI Alliance. GAVI began with a Gates Foundation grant of $750 million and grants from the United States, Norway, the Netherlands, and the United Kingdom. Through the GAVI Fund, the initiative helps poor countries finance the procurement of new and underutilized vaccines, including hepatitis B vaccine. Ongoing access to the hepatitis B vaccine in the short and medium term depends on the sustainability of the GAVI model.

A third model, represented by the Norplant case, places the research and development of the product, along with all introduction activities, within a single non-governmental organization (the Population Council). The Population Council steered the development of Norplant and its introduction into the public sector in developing countries. The manufacturers assumed responsibility for introducing the product to the private sector in developing countries and to both public and private sectors in developed countries. Conducting both development and public-sector introduction activities within one organization allowed close collaboration between developers and access staff on early planning for introduction. One downside of this approach, however, is the challenge of controlling "blind faith" in the technology, as discussed above.

The operations of the coordinating organization in each case required external funds. In the case of RDTs, funding for WHO coordination activities (such as holding expert meetings and establishing a quality assurance mechanism) was limited until a 2006 grant from the Gates Foundation and funding from Australian AID and TDR. This problem is in stark contrast to the increased availability of external financing (through the Global Fund to Fight AIDS, TB and Malaria) for governments to purchase RDTs. With more funding for coordination, WHO could act more effectively to address unexpected technical issues in product development and challenges in the product's adoption by national governments and health workers.

Advocacy and Access Plans

An important lesson from the case studies is that *product champions and their partners need an access plan that frames their work activities and takes into account the diverse perspectives of actors involved in access.* The work of product champions involves navigating and shaping the complex terrain of access. This requires understanding both potential barriers and opportunities at the global, national, and local levels. The case studies show that product champions must work with diverse individuals and groups with differing views of a technology's value and use. Product champions need an access plan to frame their activities, map the position and power of these diverse actors, identify obstacles and opportunities, and prepare strategies to promote access.[5] The access plan should be a flexible tool, with champions reshaping their analysis and strategies as unexpected circumstances arise and the broader context evolves. The female condom case shows what can happen when there is no access plan. In the product introduction phase, individuals and organizations promoting the female condom identified "next steps" for access in global meetings. These next steps, however, were not prioritized or written into a plan; as a result, the next steps were never systematically implemented. This lack of plan meant that advocates had no clear guide for moving access efforts forward.

Finding #3: Access requires the creation and shaping of product adoption by four key groups: global experts, national policy makers, providers, and end-users.

Adoption of new health technologies depends on acceptance and demand-generation at the global, national, and local levels. Product champions and their partners need to create and shape product adoption with a focus on four key groups: global experts, national policy makers, health care providers, and end-users. Our case studies draw important lessons for product adoption by global experts and end-users, which are explained below. Additional research—through national-level case studies—is needed to investigate product adoption in developing countries, with a particular focus on the key individuals and organizations involved in national product adoption, their perceptions of new health technologies, the barriers to acceptance, and the factors that facilitate adoption at the national level.

Adoption and Creating Consensus

Our case studies highlight the importance of expert consensus, both within the directly involved international technical agencies and the broader international public health community. Other public health analysts emphasize the role of expert consensus as well.[6] Our cases demonstrate that global consensus is one of the first issues that product champions need to address. A lack of global consensus can spell failure for efforts to expand access to a product, as shown with the case of female condoms where global experts held widely divergent views on the need for the technology and its relationship to other family planning and HIV prevention technologies.

The key question is: *Whose* consensus needs to be gained at the global level? The case studies show that the answer differs by product because the specific actors vary. But in all our cases, approval by the relevant international technical agency—whether WHO, UNAIDS, UNFPA, PAHO, or UNICEF—was required to move forward. Agencies signaled their adoption with official decisions about the technology and the related disease or health condition. For example, a resolution adopted at the World Health Assembly in May 2001 raised the profile of schistosomiasis and soil-transmitted helminths, and helped promote new efforts to make praziquantel more widely available in Africa. In the case of vaccine vial monitors, UNICEF's request that all prequalified vaccine producers include VVMs in their tender signaled that agency's adoption of the technology. These official decisions or resolutions on adoption by an international agency make a major difference in establishing an official acceptance of the technology.

The global consensus process depends on the participation of experts in global health policy communities: researchers, donors, program implementers, and champions. A policy community is a network of people and agencies in a given policy area.[7] Examples of policy areas in global health are family planning, malaria, AIDS, and vaccines. The access stories show that *creating* consensus among experts is particularly difficult for technologies that span policy communities. In the female condom case, for example, early champions sought consensus from experts in both family planning and AIDS policy communities. Because the female condom protects against unintended pregnancy at levels less than hormonal contraceptive methods, some family planning providers were reluctant to support the device, and donors of family planning products were hesitant to procure female condoms (particularly given the product price). Without an effective strategy to bring together family planning and AIDS prevention experts in favor of female condoms, access to the technology has faltered.

Achieving agreement among *all* technical agencies and experts was also a major challenge in our cases. For example, PAHO never adopted vaccine vial monitors. The highest leadership levels in PAHO believed that VVMs were not necessary in the region. So while adoption of the technology was required by at least one procurement agency (UNICEF) to move forward, full consensus among PATH, WHO, UNICEF, and PAHO was not attained. While PAHO's resistance to VVMs did not create an insurmountable barrier, it adds complexity to the production processes for manufacturers that sell vaccines to both UNICEF's Supply Division and PAHO's Revolving Fund. These producers need two different types of labels to make both VVM-labeled and nonlabeled vaccines. Lacking consensus among all global actors is not an overwhelming problem, but it can have consequences for access. As part of access planning, therefore, product champions need to conduct a stakeholder analysis of the key players involved and design political strategies for managing the stakeholders and producing an effective consensus to support their technology. In sum, this lesson from the case studies is that *product champions need to create consensus about their health technology among experts in international technical agencies and global health policy communities, including shared perceptions about the technology's place in health programs.*

Adoption and End-User Acceptance

In all the case studies, whether the end-user of the technology was a patient, consumer, or provider, acceptance and demand generation by the end-user were vital to ensuring access. End-user adoption was influenced by the particular health problem and characteristics of the technology, and these were in turn influenced by the specific social, political, and historical contexts. The Norplant case shows that for some women, Norplant acceptance was influenced by the health issue that the technology addresses—that is, preventing pregnancy in healthy women. Many users of Norplant were less likely to accept the side effects of the product (heavy bleeding) than if these had occurred for a product to treat a life-threatening disease. On the other hand, the implant characteristics of the technology made it appealing to Islamic women in Indonesia who viewed the contraceptive as an acceptable alternative to sterilization, which is forbidden by Islam. In the case of female condoms, characteristics of the technology made acceptance difficult for end-users in some contexts. Research shows that it takes many women an average of four separate attempts to use the technology effectively and with comfort. Some women were unwilling to endure an extended period of awkward and embarrassing "practice sessions" in order to get the female condom right, no matter how empowering the technology might be in the long run. New female condom designs that are in development are seeking to address these negative technology characteristics and make female condoms more user friendly. To promote the adoption of these new female condoms, however, will still require well designed and financed social marketing campaigns.

Society's perception of the technology and its purposes also influenced end-user adoption. In the United States, the introduction of Norplant to low-income women led to concerns and public debate about social coercion. Some researchers argue that the public debate about Norplant was a "double-edged sword": on the one hand, it may have reduced social coercion by providing increased vigilance, but on the other hand it served to stigmatize Norplant among American women.[8] The problem of stigmatization, combined with litigation about implant removals, negative media coverage, and negative word of mouth among users all contributed to Norplant's downfall in the United States.

Many examples of the influence of social perceptions of technology can be found outside the cases examined in this book, with both negative and positive effects. For instance, social perceptions played a critical role in the boycott of polio vaccinations in northern Nigeria in 2004, where rumors spread about contamination.[9] Rumors about vaccines as infertility agents have arisen in other developing countries,[10] and have led to the cancellation of vaccination campaigns. The Global Polio Eradication Initiative and others have learned that ensuring national ownership of campaigns and involving political, traditional, and religious leaders within communities can help confront rumors and negative perceptions of technologies. One example of a strategy to ensure community ownership is the community-directed treatment with ivermectin for onchocerciasis (or river blindness), an approach used by the African Programme for Onchocerciasis Control.[11] This approach uses community volunteers, often drawn from kinship groups, to deliver ivermectin within the local context. This strategy works for ivermectin in part because the medicine is safe and easy to administer. The example also illustrates the importance of local as well as national ownership for implementing disease control programs.

Because a technology's characteristics influence end-user adoption, paying attention to these issues should begin early in the life of a new technology. Thinking about end-users should begin in the product development phase (first access phase), when the technical characteristics of a new technology are under consideration. A focus on end-users should continue in both the introduction and scaling-up stages (second and third access phases), when managing the perceptions of end-users and community leaders become central to access activities. Paying attention to end-user adoption requires an understanding of end-user preferences and concerns, and the sociocultural context in which end-users interpret new technologies. The values and symbolic environments of end-users matter in how they perceive technologies. Strategies to help deepen the understanding of product developers include early research on end-user perceptions, applying research findings to product development and program design, involving experts in the product development phase who understand operational realities in poor country contexts, and creating strategies for national and local ownership in program implementation. Overall, our case studies show that *end-user adoption of the technology is an essential but often overlooked component of the access process. Attention to the perspectives of the end-user needs to begin in the development stage and continue through introduction and scaling-up activities.*

Finding #4: The cost of health technologies is a key barrier to access. Strategies to expand access must address affordability.

Affordability and Lowering Prices

Much of the literature on access to health technology emphasizes cost to governments and individuals as a major obstacle. Our findings support this observation. The praziquantel case study demonstrates that patents influence prices, a finding that has been well documented for a number of new health technologies. Even though the price of praziquantel is now more affordable (as low as $0.174–$0.072 per tablet) because the original product and process patents have expired, SCI continues to try to lower the drug's price. SCI has expanded competition by assisting a South Korean manufacturer, Shin Poong, with the registration process for praziquantel in some African countries. This has increased competition in government tenders and contributed to lower purchase prices for several governments. SCI has also sought to stimulate formulation in Africa by working with African companies and helping them purchase the active ingredient from reputable manufacturers in China and India, so that the African companies can formulate and sell the drug to their own governments and then register and market the product in neighboring countries. Finally, SCI has used a bulk purchasing approach to lower product prices. Since 2004, SCI has procured large quantities of praziquantel on the global market for the six African countries it works with. Indeed, SCI became the single largest purchaser of praziquantel on the global market (and an oligopsonist), buying more than 90% of global trade of the drug. This bulk purchasing approach has broader applications for improving access to other medicines, and has been used, for example, in purchasing treatments for tuberculosis by the Global Drug Facility for TB.[12]

The hepatitis B vaccine story also shows that a technology's affordability affects uptake. The vaccine's price was unaffordable for developing countries so demand outside of industrialized countries was low. With low demand, manufacturers were unwilling to increase production capacity for the vaccine, keeping prices high and supply low. To make the vaccine more affordable to developing country governments, the International Task Force on Hepatitis B Immunization and the GAVI Alliance sought product price reductions by fostering competition and showing companies that a market for the vaccine exists in developing countries. Key factors that facilitated these strategies included the creation of collaborative public-private relationships, the establishment of a procurement fund (the GAVI Fund), patent expiration, and the improvement of national drug regulation and clinical testing capacities in vaccine-producing countries (such as Korea).

Other approaches to pushing down prices also exist. For example, the Population Council, in seeking an affordable price for Norplant, looked for a company that would manufacture, register, and distribute Norplant at the lowest possible price to the public sector. They created a tiered pricing system, with a lower price ($23 per implant kit) for public-sector family planning programs in developing countries compared to $350 per implant kit in the United States. Female condom advocates used a different approach—the development of new female condom designs—to decrease product price. Some of the designs under development will be cheaper to produce than the current female condom product. The new products and manufacturers will also introduce competition into what has been a monopoly market. Another strategy for pushing down prices is to threaten compulsory licensing of the product. This approach has been used successfully by Brazil to renegotiate the government's purchase price of several antiretroviral products for HIV/AIDS.[13]

But driving down prices can have unanticipated consequences. The findings from the RDT case study caution against pushing prices too low. In that instance, low prices created a disincentive for some producers to make needed quality improvements to their technologies. While public-sector purchasers depend on low prices due to their limited budgets, private-sector producers need higher prices to justify investments in product quality and to achieve their profit objectives.

The cases thus demonstrate a range of strategies that have succeeded in decreasing product costs for governments. In all our case studies, the cost of procurement was a key factor that influenced access. As the praziquantel case shows, however, making a technology more affordable is rarely sufficient on its own to make the product more accessible. *Strategies to lower product prices for governments and individuals represent a necessary but not sufficient effort for expanding access.* Availability constraints as well as factors related to adoption and architecture all need to be considered.

Affordability and Financial Support

A major problem for many developing countries is the lack of government funds for purchasing health products. One strategy to address this persistent problem is to push down the product's price as discussed above. Another is to seek external funding for governments. Most poor governments purchase malaria RDTs, for example, with Global Fund financing. SCI is supported by the Bill & Melinda Gates Foundation to finance praziquantel purchases for the six African countries it works with. For hepatitis B vaccine, eligible countries apply to the GAVI Fund for procurement financing. (UNICEF Supply Division procures the vaccine, using bulk purchasing and a competitive bidding process.)

The biggest problem with external financing is the question of sustainability over the long term (or even the medium term), given that donors persistently seek to limit the timeframe of their funding commitments. Experts on malaria and diagnostics fear that widespread use of RDT products is unlikely to continue in the future without sustained external assistance. Recipients seek *sustained* assistance systems, while donors seek *sustainable* health systems. In its first phase of operation, the GAVI Alliance sought sustainability by agreeing to help a country procure new or underutilized vaccines such as hepatitis B for free for five years. During this time, GAVI hoped, vaccine prices would decrease, and then developing country governments and bilateral and other donors would take on the financing of procurement. Vaccine prices, however, did not decrease, countries could not afford procurement, and other donors did not step in to help. GAVI has reworked its business model and now asks developing countries to "co-pay" for vaccine procurement from the beginning to promote sustainability. It is too early to know whether this model will increase sustainability or become a barrier to hepatitis B vaccine access in poor countries. In sum, a key lesson about affordability is that *it can be constrained by a lack of government financing for product procurement.* Our cases show that *innovative means of providing adequate financial support from external resources are often essential to assure affordability.*

Finding #5: Supply-side strategies that assure the availability of a technology are needed to help expand access for health technologies in developing countries.

Availability and Information Failures

Availability of health technologies in developing countries is often limited by information failures. Producers sometimes are not aware of market opportunities in developing countries, and government procurement agencies in poor countries often do not know about available products and suppliers. *Reducing these information asymmetries can increase availability.*

Suppliers often lack good information about product demand in developing countries. These information problems affect supply since manufacturers may underestimate the potential market in a poor country or region and may not take the necessary steps to enter the market (such as registering the product with the government). SCI has addressed this problem by disseminating information to manufacturers (outside of Africa) about demand for praziquantel and by assisting companies in the government's product registration procedures so that the technology can be sold within the country. This activity can introduce the product into a new market, or it can raise competition among suppliers, resulting in price reductions (as discussed earlier).

Another information barrier is that government procurement agencies in poor countries often have incomplete information about available products and suppliers for a particular health technology. For example, although many government procurement agencies have financing from the Global Fund to procure malaria RDTs, the purchasing officials confront a rapidly changing range of available products and producers, making the selection of diagnostics extremely difficult. The WHO has addressed this problem by giving countries regularly updated information about RDT products and producers on their RDT website (www.wpro.who.int/rdt) and in a "Sources and Prices" document for malaria products.[14] The Schistosomiasis Control Initiative has used a similar approach in providing information directly to African government procurement agencies about specific praziquantel suppliers as well as the safety, efficacy, and price of the drug. The strategy of providing potential purchasers with information about prices and quality of products from different manufacturers helps reduce some of the asymmetry of information between sellers and buyers (a classic market failure) of these health technologies in developing countries. This information strategy could be applied for many other health technologies relevant for poor countries, as illustrated by its use for antiretroviral drugs and other AIDS-related medicines.[15]

Availability and Competent Manufacturers

The access stories of vaccine vial monitors and malaria rapid diagnostic tests point to the difficulties of identifying commercial partners willing to develop and/or manufacture a technology for use in poor countries, particularly for lower profit technologies (relative to, for instance, drugs and vaccines for sale in rich countries). For such technologies, potential commercial partners worry about whether a market exists, how big it is, and who actually chooses and purchases the technology.[16]

When PATH and WHO set out to find companies that could develop time temperature technologies for vaccines, a number of firms expressed interest and attended international meetings on the topic, and several received funding from PATH through its USAID HealthTech project. But only Temptime, a midsized company in Morristown, New Jersey, succeeded in developing a product at a low price that met the performance requirements of WHO and UNICEF. Temptime's success may be related to the core technologies used by other companies, as well as the lower overhead of Temptime compared to its competitors. Temptime remains the sole supplier of VVMs. Although Temptime has not had supply shortfalls with its product, some vaccine producers and UNICEF identified the lack of multiple suppliers as a reason why they were initially reluctant to adopt the technology. They disliked the reliance on a single producer and the supply risks of such arrangements.

Similarly, it took many years for the U.S. Walter Reed Army Institute to find a suitable commercial partner to manufacture a rapid diagnostic test for malaria. The diagnostic would be used for American soldiers so Walter Reed needed to identify a company that would take the product to the U.S. FDA for regulatory approval. After years of searching, they found an appropriate partner in Binax, Inc.—like Temptime, a midsized company. In looking for a commercial partner, Walter Reed learned that most diagnostic companies are small "mom-and-pop" businesses that do not possess the resources, know-how, experience, or willingness to navigate the U.S. FDA process. They also discovered that the large companies with these features were not interested in partnering because the technologies were not considered profitable enough for them.

These examples show that suitable commercial partners for lower profit technologies may sometimes be found in midsized companies (that is, 50–100 employees) that have existing commercial products, are already generating revenues from these products, and have experience in working with regulatory authorities (such as the FDA). In their search to find a commercial partner, Walter Reed staff learned to develop business skills and perspective. Having staff with these skills from the beginning would have advanced the development and production schedules for their product. In sum, *finding a competent manufacturing partner to ensure a sustainable, high-quality supply can be a challenge, especially for lower profit technologies. There is a need, therefore, to explore small and midsized companies willing to take on niche products and also high-quality manufacturing firms in emerging markets (such as China and India).*

Finding #6: Limited health infrastructure in many developing countries impedes technology access. Efforts to scale up access to technologies need to invest in health system strengthening to ensure sustained access.

Strategies to make the market work better are important for ensuring product availability, but so are downstream actions aimed at improving a country's health system. The successful delivery of technologies to patients and consumers depends in large part on the capacity of the health sector's human resources, the financing of both public and private providers, and the availability of functioning equipment—in short, how the health system performs on a daily basis.[17]

Our case studies show that introducing new technologies requires new learning and education for health care providers. Norplant, for example, as a new contraceptive implant technology, required both insertion and removal by a trained provider. In the rapid scale-up of Norplant in countries like Indonesia and the United States, many providers received training (particularly on insertion techniques) but the instruction was not deep or comprehensive enough. As a result, many health professionals were not well trained on removal techniques, and these training shortfalls led to later difficulties with implant removals. In the United States, removal problems led to lawsuits and negative media coverage, contributing to the product's withdrawal from the market. Problems with removal were also experienced in Indonesia because few practitioners were trained in removal techniques. Successful training programs in the Norplant case were those in which practitioners had to prove competency in both insertions and removals, something that the training programs did not always require. Other health system problems that emerged globally with Norplant included the lack of sufficient information and counseling about the method for end-users and concerns about informed choice, particularly whether uneducated, poor women were targeted for Norplant or steered to that method over other contraceptives.

Issues of provider training and delivery are particularly important for provider-dependent technologies like Norplant. But infrastructure problems can also create access barriers for products that are designed for use in areas at the periphery of the health system, where facilities often lack functioning equipment. Malaria rapid diagnostic tests, for example, are designed for use in remote clinics. But to ensure accuracy of some of these diagnostic tests, health workers need a timer or clock to know when to read the test. They need sufficient training on how to use the tests, including how much blood is required. To address these inadequacies in basic health infrastructure, a few RDT producers have improved the technical characteristics of their products. But for many producers, there is no incentive to make such technical improvements. In another example, researchers have shown that female condom uptake requires providers to provide sufficient instruction, counseling, and follow-up to their clients. But many providers lack the basic tools required for client instruction, such as female pelvic models to demonstrate how to use the female condom.

A critical question is *how* to invest in health systems to assure sustained access to new health technologies in poor countries—how to strengthen health systems in poor countries effectively. Our case studies show that successful strategies are product-specific and context-specific. In the Norplant case, product champions and national-level actors recognized the need for provider training of health professionals. Yet in those countries where the government and end-users were excited about the new product, scale-up occurred quickly and before sufficient provider training had been implemented. In this example, a sufficient investment in health systems—through provider training—required financing for the training as well as adequate *time* to complete these tasks.

The hepatitis B case study provides an example where different strategies for investing in health systems have been attempted. When it was first established, the GAVI Alliance (through the GAVI Fund) provided eligible countries with financing for hepatitis B vaccine procurement, as well as performance-based financial incentives for improving immunization infrastructure. GAVI has since decided that focusing on immunization infrastructure was too narrow because it did not address broader health-system barriers. Today, GAVI allocates half of its resources to eligible governments for health system strengthening, such as improving the frequency of supervisory visits.

Conclusions

The case studies in this book show different degrees of success in creating access to health technologies for poor people in poor countries. The individual chapters with the access stories provide rich contextual descriptions of what happened with each technology—how the various systemic failures were addressed or not addressed in specific cases. The individual chapters also provide explanations for the different degrees of success in creating access. In this concluding chapter, we have distilled those narratives into six broad findings about creating access to health technologies. The over-arching lesson is clear: there is no success without access.

The stories in this book demonstrate that access to health technologies in poor countries can be achieved. In that sense, we are optimistic about the potential for good health technologies to improve the lives of disadvantaged people. But creating access requires that individuals and organizations devote time, passion, and resources to a new technology—for its development, introduction, and scaling up—and carefully craft strategies for resolving the multiple barriers along the pathways to access. We believe that our analysis of these six technologies and the six lessons presented in this concluding chapter hold important operational implications—things that can be done by product developers, product champions, the donors, and others involved in inventing new health technologies aimed at developing countries. It is our hope that these lessons from history can help advance the process of creating access and help assure that new, safe, and effective health technologies reach the hands of people in poor countries who most need them and can use them to produce tangible health benefits.

Endnotes

[1] Amy Kaler, "'It's Some Kind of Women's Empowerment': The Ambiguity of the Female Condom as a Marker of Female Empowerment," *Social Science and Medicine*, 52 (2001): 783.

[2] John W. Kingdon, *Agendas, Alternatives and Public Policies* (Boston: Little, Brown, 1984), 129.

[3] Isabelle Royer, "Why Bad Projects Are So Hard to Kill," *Harvard Business Review* 81 (2003): 48–56.

[4] Jayanti Tuladhar, Peter J. Donaldson, and Jeanne Noble, "The Introduction and Use of Norplant Implants in Indonesia," *Studies in Family Planning* 29 (1998): 291–299.

[5] One approach for doing this kind of applied political analysis is provided by: Michael R. Reich and David M. Cooper, *PolicyMaker: Computer-Assisted Political Analysis, Software and Manual* (Brookline, MA: PoliMap, 1996–98).

[6] Ruth Levine, *Millions Saved: Proven Successes in Global Health* (Washington, DC: Center for Global Development, 2004).

[7] Kingdon.

[8] Andrew R. Davidson and Debra Kalmuss, "Topics for Our Times: Norplant Coercion—An Overstated Threat," *American Journal of Public Health* 87 (1997): 551.

[9] Ebrahim Samba, Francis Nkrumah, and Rose Leke, "Getting Polio Eradication Back on Track in Nigeria," *New England Journal of Medicine* 350 (2004): 645–646.

[10] Pamela Feldman-Savelsberg, Flavien T. Ndonko, and Bergis Schmidt-Ehry, "Sterilizing Vaccines or the Politics of the Womb: Retrospective Study of a Rumor in Cameroon," *Medical Anthropology Quarterly* 14, no. 2 (2000): 159–179.

[11] Uche V. Amazigo, William R. Brieger, Moses N. Katabarwa, O. Akogun, M. Ntep, B. Boatin, J. N'Doyo, M. Noma, and Azodoga Seketeli, "The Challenges of Community-Directed Treatment with Ivermectin (CDTI) within the African Programme for Onchocerciasis Control (APOC)," *Annals of Tropical Medicine and Parasitology* 96, supplement 1 (2002): 41–58.

[12] Jacob Kumaresan, Ian Smith, Virginia Arnold, and Peter Evans, "The Global TB Drug Facility: Innovative Global Procurement," *International Journal of Tuberculosis & Lung Disease* 8 (2004): 130–138.

[13] Michael R. Reich and Priya Bery, "Expanding Global Access to ARVs: The Challenges of Prices and Patents," in *The AIDS Pandemic: Impact on Science and Society*, eds. Kenneth H. Mayer & Hank F. Pizer (San Diego, CA: Elsevier Academic Press, 2005).

[14] World Health Organization, *Sources and Prices of Selected Products for the Prevention, Diagnosis and Treatment of Malaria* (Geneva: WHO, 2004).

[15] World Health Organization, UNICEF, UNAIDS, and MSF, *Sources and Prices of Selected Medicines and Diagnostics for People Living with HIV/AIDS* (Geneva: WHO, 2005).

[16] Michael J. Free, "Achieving Appropriate Design and Widespread Use of Health Care Technologies in the Developing World: Overcoming Obstacles that Impede the Adaptation and Diffusion of Priority Technologies for Primary Health Care," *International Journal of Gynecology & Obstetrics* 85, supplement 1 (2004): S3–S13.

[17] Marc J. Roberts, William Hsiao, Peter Berman, and Michael R. Reich, *Getting Health Reform Right: A Guide to Improving Performance and Equity* (New York: Oxford University Press, 2004).

GLOSSARY

This glossary provides definitions for key terms related to access, plus certain public health concepts and diseases and health conditions mentioned in the book.

access: An end-user's ability to consistently obtain and appropriately use good quality health technologies when they are needed.

access activities: The events that determine whether a health technology successfully reaches the end-user and achieves its intended health benefits.

access plan: A set of strategies for overcoming obstacles to access to a health technology and for ensuring successful delivery and use of the technology, including an analysis of the actors involved and an assessment of the opportunities and threats to access. An access plan should be considered a flexible tool, regularly revised over the course of a technology's development, introduction, and scaling up.

active ingredient: The element of a medicine or other pharmaceutical product that produces the technology's intended pharmacological effect. Active ingredients typically require combination with excipients—inactive ingredients—in the production of a consumable pharmaceutical product. *See* **excipient**.

activity stream: The actions that must be considered under architecture, availability, affordability, and adoption, when seeking to create access for a health technology.

adoption: The acceptance, demand, and appropriate use of health technologies across multiple levels, including global, national, provider, and end-user.

affordability: The degree to which cost influences the ability and/or willingness to purchase a health technology for international organizations, national governments, health-care providers, and health consumers.

anemia: A shortage of red blood cells and/or hemoglobin marked by pallor of skin, weakness, fatigue, problems with concentration, shortness of breath, and, if severe, heart palpitations and/or failure. Anemia is often a symptom of other health problems; therefore, treatment and prevention are largely dependent on its cause.

antibody: An immunoglobulin molecule produced by white blood cells as part of the body's adaptive immune system. Antibodies target and bind to specific amino acid sequences (or antigens) present on foreign microorganisms, either by blocking them from binding to and entering healthy cells or by stimulating and activating other immune system cells to respond to infection.

antigen: A sequence of proteins specific to a particular foreign microorganism that triggers the body's immune system to respond by producing antibodies.

appropriate use: The degree to which an end-user puts a technology to effective and safe use in the manner intended to produce health benefits.

architecture: Organizational structures and relationships established with the purpose of coordinating and steering the various activities necessary to ensure access to a health technology. Architecture involves a well-defined division of labor and roles, as well as effective channels of communication, decision-making, accountability, monitoring, and evaluation.

availability: Factors influencing the consistency of supply of a health technology at the global, national, regional, and local levels, especially those activities and logistics involved in producing, ordering, shipping, storing, distributing, and delivering the technology to the end-user.

barriers to access: Environmental, political, economic, sociocultural, biological, and technological factors that limit the abilities of end-users to successfully obtain and appropriately use a health technology. These can include lack of political commitment by international organizations or national governments, poor health system capability, end-user mistrust, high product costs, faulty and ineffective technologies, and changing disease characteristics.

bulk purchase: An agreement among multiple buyers to jointly purchase large quantities of a health technology such as a vaccine or a drug, thereby reducing the price per unit.

cirrhosis: A chronic and often deadly condition marked by the replacement of healthy liver tissue with fibroids and nodules that, in turn, lead to a number of life-threatening complications, most notably liver failure. Cirrhosis is typically a symptom of other serious health problems, such as alcoholism or infection with hepatitis B or C viruses.

cold chain: A supply chain requiring that a health product be kept within a specific temperature-controlled environment from its point of manufacture until it reaches its destination. If the cold chain is broken, the product loses its effectiveness. The cold chain involves specialized equipment and information systems to track a product's packaging, shipping, storage, and delivery in order to ensure that the required temperature range has been maintained and the product has not been damaged.

cool chain: Similar to cold chain, a cool chain requires the maintenance of a temperature-controlled environment from a technology's point of manufacture to its point of delivery. A cool chain differs from a cold chain in that there is a greater range of temperature within which a product can be kept, as well as both an upper and a lower limit to temperature fluctuation.

contraceptive: Any health technology that has as its primary purpose the prevention of pregnancy. Contraceptives can also include "dual technologies" such as condoms and microbicides, which are capable of preventing both pregnancy and sexually transmitted infections and which are primarily implemented within the context of HIV/AIDS prevention and control.

cost-effectiveness: A measure that compares the overall cost of a technology to the quantity of outcome produced. For health technologies, the measure is usually presented as a ratio of cost of resources invested in delivering the technology to units of health outcomes achieved (cases averted, deaths averted, healthy years of life saved, quality-adjusted life years, etc.).

delivery: The point in the supply chain at which the technology is physically transferred to its intended end-user by private or public channels, including pharmacies, hospitals, health clinics, shops, and mass distribution campaigns.

development: The initial stage of creating a health technology that involves key decisions about its purpose, efficacy, safety, and overall design. These decisions often play a major role in determining end-user access.

diagnostic: An instrument that aids in assessing the presence or absence of a particular disease or health state, used for the clinical diagnosis of an individual patient and for population surveys of disease prevalence. Diagnostics involve many different technologies, from clinical checklists to microscopy to pathogen cultures to serological identification of pathogen-specific antigens and/or antibodies. New rapid diagnostic tests increasingly use immunochromatographic technology.

diphtheria: A life-threatening disease of the upper respiratory tract caused by toxins produced by *Corynebacterium diphtheria* bacteria. Diphtheria is characterized by fever, sore throat, and neck swelling. Its most notable clinical feature is a pseudomembrane of inflamed and necrotic epithelial cells in the nasopharyngeal area that seriously obstructs breathing. Diphtheria toxin can also enter the blood or lymphatic system and cause heart failure and paralysis. The best method of prevention is immunization with the diphtheria toxoid vaccine.

distribution: Part of the supply chain; the path by which health technologies are (1) ordered and dispatched from the manufacturer and/or supplier, (2) received, cleared, and inspected at port by public or private procurement agencies, and (3) transported, inventoried, and stored by private- or public-sector entities to the point at which they are available for delivery to the end-user.

eclampsia: A pregnancy-related condition characterized by high blood pressure, edema, and abnormal amounts of protein in the urine leading to convulsions and occasionally coma and/or death. Eclampsia can be treated with magnesium sulphate therapy.

effectiveness: The health impact of a technology under conditions of normal use, often measured in the reduction in new cases of a health condition following the introduction of a technology within the target population. Different from **efficacy**, which involves an assessment of impact within a controlled setting.

efficacy: The ability of a technology to achieve specific results within a controlled setting such as a clinical or field trial. Different from **effectiveness**, which involves an assessment of impact under conditions of normal use within a target population.

end-user: The consumer for whose use the health technology is intended. The end-user can refer to different kinds of consumers, from someone purchasing a female condom at a shop to a patient receiving a hepatitis B immunization at a birth clinic to a health-care provider conducting a malaria rapid diagnostic test at a district hospital.

epidemiology: The study of the determining factors, distribution, and frequency of health conditions in a given population.

Essential Drugs List: As defined by WHO, the medicines a health care system requires to meet a population's priority health care needs, selected according to criteria of disease prevalence, evidence on efficacy and safety, and comparative cost-effectiveness. The WHO model list is revised every other year to provide guidance for regulatory and procurement decisions by national ministries of health. Used interchangeably with essential medicines.

excipient: The inactive elements that are combined with the active ingredient of a pharmaceutical product or allow it to be produced in a form that enables consumption.

facilitating factors: Factors that promote the ability of end-users to successfully obtain and use a health technology. These factors can include increased involvement of product champions, political commitment on the part of international organizations or national governments, increased delivery capacity of health systems, end-user acceptability, reduced product costs, and changes in technology design.

formulation: Part of the secondary manufacturing process for medicines; the means by which different pharmaceutical substances—both active ingredients and excipients—are combined to make a pharmaceutical product capable of being consumed by the patient.

good manufacturing practice (GMP): A set of directives applied to the pharmaceutical industry specifying the regulation of pharmaceutical quality control. National governments and international organizations such as WHO issue GMP directives. These directives include the control and regulation of research design, data collection and dissemination, methods of traceability, manufacturing and packaging processes, and other factors to ensure that effective, safe, high-quality pharmaceutical products reach the market.

***Haemophilus influenzae* type b (Hib):** One of six opportunistic airborne strains of *Haemophilus influenzae* bacteria that under certain conditions can invade either the lower respiratory system, causing a pneumonia-like illness, or the central nervous system, causing meningitis. It can also cause cellulitis, arthritis, hearing loss, mental retardation and other complications. Hib can be treated with antibiotics; the main mode of prevention is through vaccination in early childhood.

hepatitis A: A *Hepatovirus* of the *Picornaviridae* family, hepatitis A is unrelated to other hepatitis viruses except in its targeting of liver cells. This acute illness is transmitted through the fecal-oral route, causing symptoms such as jaundice, dark-colored urine, extreme fatigue, vomiting, and fever. The infection often takes several months to recover from but rarely leaves lasting damage to the liver. Immunoglobulin injection is the established prophylaxis for hepatitis A exposure; however, there is no treatment if one falls ill. Control and prevention are through vaccination and improved sanitation and hygiene, especially during food preparation.

hepatitis B: A *Hepadnavirus,* so-called for its DNA genome and its targeted infection of liver cells, hepatitis B is usually cleared quickly by the body's immune system—sometimes following a period of malaise, nausea, jaundice, and abdominal pain. Many people recover completely from acute infection, but those who still have the virus in their blood for more than six months are diagnosed with the chronic infection. The body's immune response to this chronic infection, most notably the continual destruction and regeneration of liver cells, is a primary cause of cirrhosis and liver cancer in much of Africa and Southeast Asia. Hepatitis B can be transmitted sexually, vertically (from mother to fetus), and parenterally (through contaminated blood or blood products); however, throughout much of the world, the virus is transmitted during the neonatal period by the mother or via contaminated health care settings. Besides protective measures (such as barrier contraception and increased safety procedures when working with blood products and contaminated equipment), the primary method of prevention for those at risk is the hepatitis B vaccine, which is considered effective in 90% of healthy adults. Treatment is primarily through the antiviral medication lamivudine.

HIV: A virus that specifically targets CD4+ immune system cells, HIV (or human immunodeficiency virus) is a member of the *Retroviridae* family of viruses that uses the reverse transcriptase enzyme to integrate itself into host cell DNA. HIV is transmitted sexually, vertically (mother to child), and parenterally (through contaminated blood or blood products). It initially presents with a mononucleosis-like illness involving fever, malaise, and swollen lymph nodes. A short time later, HIV enters into a long latent period in which the virus continues to replicate, damaging existing immune system cells and eventually inhibiting the body's ability to respond to opportunistic and other infections. At this point, the individual can be said to have progressed to AIDS (acquired immune deficiency syndrome). Once a patient makes the clinical transition to AIDS, in the absence of any intervention, death is almost certain. There is no cure for HIV. Prevention is through health education, behavior change, the provision of condoms, and increased blood safety initiatives. Treatment is presently through a combination of three or four antiretroviral medications.

incidence: The number of *new* cases of a particular health condition arising in a specific population over a given period of time.

intellectual property rights (IPR): Patents and other legally binding, time-limited entitlements that protect an inventor's ability to retain ownership of a particular product and/or process and to prevent others from claiming rights or benefits without first acquiring a license.

introduction: The first phase of making a new technology available to a specific population in a field setting in order to test its accessibility, acceptability, and effectiveness in the general population, and refine plans for the scaling up of production, distribution, and delivery.

key actor: An individual or institution that plays a determining role in facilitating or obstructing access to technologies.

leprosy: Also known as Hansen's disease, a chronic infection caused by the mycobacterium *M. leprae* that invades peripheral nerves, upper respiratory mucosa, and skin. Clinically, leprosy infection can present in a number of different ways, from thickened numb patches on the skin that are vulnerable to injury and secondary infection (tuberculoid leprosy) to serious deterioration and collapse of skin, facial structures (especially the nasal septum), and other extremities (lepromatous leprosy). *M. leprae* is thought to be spread through direct contact with infected persons or through inhalation of airborne bacteria. Treatment of leprosy involves a multidrug therapy with rifampin, dapsone, and clofazimine, currently donated free of charge by Novartis.

licensing: The issuance of a document by the legal owner of rights to a particular form of intellectual property that grants permission for another party to make use of the property under conditions stipulated in the agreement.

lymphatic filariasis: A debilitating and disfiguring tropical disease caused by the invasion of the lymphatic tissues by the filiarial nematode worms, *Wuchereria bancrofti* and *Brugia malayi*. Following transmission by mosquito bite, larvae enter the lymphatic system and mature into adults. Adult worms grow very long and inflame and block lymphatic tissue, causing chronic inflammation, a build-up of fluid in the affected body cavities, and in some cases, excessive enlargement of limbs and other body parts (also known as elephantiasis). Prevention involves mosquito vector control. Current treatment regimes are less than satisfactory but can include diethylcarbamazine, ivermectin, albendazole, and certain antibiotics.

malaria: An infection transmitted by the bite of a female *Anopheline* mosquito and caused by one of four *Plasmodium* protozoa, the most virulent of which is *P.*

falciparum. Malaria is characterized by regular peaks of fever, the interval of which depends on the species of *Plasmodium*, as well as headache, vomiting, muscle pains, and shivering. Malaria can also lead to anemia, lactic acid build-up, low blood sugar, and other complications, the most serious of which is cerebral malaria, which can lead to convulsions, coma, and death if left untreated. Prevention and control of malaria are primarily through environmental and personal protection measures in the form of insecticide-treated bednets, indoor residual spraying of pyrethroid insecticides, and control of mosquito habitats. Depending on local drug resistance, treatment may involve any number of antimalarial medications, including quinine, chloroquine, and artemisin-based combination therapies.

measles: A highly contagious airborne *Paramyxovirus* infecting the upper and lower respiratory tract, lymphatic system, and blood, spreading on occasion to other parts of the body as well. Patients develop coldlike symptoms, followed by conjunctivitis and, eventually, the appearance of Koplik's spots on the inner cheek and the characteristic maculopapular rash across the body. In developed countries, measles is rarely serious; however, in developing countries there are high rates of fatality for young children who succumb to complications such as pneumonia, encephalitis, corneal lesions, and hemorrhagic rash. The measles vaccine and the combination measles, mumps, and rubella (MMR) vaccine are the primary methods of prevention and control. There is no treatment outside of palliative support and medications to treat complications.

medical device: Health technologies that support the application of and/or add value to other existing technologies, drugs, or interventions. Vaccines, drugs, contraceptives, and diagnostics are *not* considered devices, but rather those products that facilitate their delivery (vaccine vial monitors, Uniject syringes) or the delivery of other integrated programs for the treatment of critical health problems (insecticide-treated bednets, fumigant canisters). Devices are often developed and manufactured by industries outside the pharmaceutical sector.

monitoring: The systematic, ongoing assessment of how well an intervention is being carried out according to its original plan and the degree to which it is meeting its objectives and targets. Monitoring provides a feedback mechanism for assessing the implementation of interventions, allowing a flexible response to changing circumstances.

morbidity: The prevalence of a particular health problem or of the disability created by the health problem.

mortality rate: The rate of death in a particular population over a particular period of time, typically adjusted for age, sex, cause of death, and additional risk factors.

onchocerciasis: Also known as river blindness, an invasion of the skin and eye by the filiarial nematode *Onchocerca volvulus*, the larvae of which are transmitted to human hosts through the bite of the *Simulium* black flies. Larvae develop into adult worms that exist harmlessly in subcutaneous nodules. However, when adult worms reproduce, the females produce thousands of microfilariae offspring that accumulate under the skin, causing severe itching and discoloration. More seriously, microfilariae can migrate to the eyes, leading to inflammation of the cornea, uvea, and retina, atrophy of the optic nerve, and eventually blindness. Vector control and mass treatment with a single yearly dose of ivermectin are the primary means of prevention. The treatment for onchocerciasis is ivermectin, which is available through a drug donation program by Merck & Co., Inc.

patent: A set of exclusive rights and entitlements granted by the state for a particular period of time to the inventor of a product or a process of production. Patents regulate the ownership, manufacturing, selling, purchasing, and/or use of the product or process and prevent others from claiming benefit without first being granted a license.

perinatal: The period of time extending from five months prior to birth until one month after.

pertussis: Also known as whooping cough, a serious childhood illness caused by the airborne bacterium *Bordella pertussis*. Initially pertussis resembles the common cold but eventually results in a paroxysmal series of short mucous-producing coughs, followed by the characteristic "whoop" sound made by the patient gasping for breath. Complications include pneumonia and encephalitis. The best method of prevention is through immunization with the diphtheria-tetanus-pertussis (DTP) vaccine. Treatment typically involves a course of antibiotics.

policy community: A group of individuals who share in common a particular set of policy goals and who interact to advocate, formulate, and implement them.

poliomyelitis: A disease caused by one of three serological types of *Poliovirus*, a member of the *Picornaviridae* family of viruses. The virus is spread by the fecal-oral route and in 95% of the cases infects only the gastrointestinal tract, either asymptomatically or in a manner resembling stomach flu. In approximately 1%

of the cases, however, the virus enters the bloodstream and travels to the central nervous system, causing meningitis-like symptoms and sometimes the destruction of motor neurons, potential respiratory failure, paralysis, and weakening of the limbs leading to permanent disability. There is no treatment except for palliative care, respiratory support, and eventual physical therapy. Prevention is primarily through one of two polio vaccines—the Salk inactivated polio vaccine and the Sabin live attenuated vaccine, both of which have benefits and limitations. Vaccination also is considered the primary route for population-wide polio control and eradication, as polio is spread from person to person and the virus is unable to survive without a human host.

prevalence: The proportion of individuals within a specific population at a given point or over a given period of time who exhibit a particular health condition, calculated by the number of individuals afflicted divided by the total population at risk.

procurement: The purchasing of health products from either private or public suppliers, in order to ensure availability of a health technology. Decisions about procurement are influenced by the unit cost of the product, the quantities required, the quality of available goods, the potential for bulk purchase or minimal cost plus mark-up arrangements, the budget constraints and tendering procedures of institutional or government purchasing agencies, the availability of adequate data with which to forecast either demand or supply, and the accessibility of transparent information on suppliers, prices, and products.

public-private partnership: A formal collaboration between one or more public organizations and one or more private organizations that involves both a shared division of labor and a mutual appreciation of partner contribution.

quality assurance: Systematic and standardized mechanisms for ensuring the quality control of products, processes, and services.

registration: The listing and licensing of a particular health technology with the relevant national regulatory authority in order to ensure that it meets public standards of safety, quality, and effectiveness.

regulation: The monitoring and enforcement by a government or other institution with authority of laws, statutes, and codes as they pertain to a particular technology and its production, procurement, distribution, use, and sale in the market.

scaling up: A phase of technology access following product development and introduction that involves increasing (1) the production of a health technology, (2) its geographic availability, (3) the administrative and health system capacity to ensure its supply, and (4) the number of people to whom it is available and in demand.

schistosomiasis: Also known as bilharzia, one of three different fluke infections sharing in common a lifecycle requiring aquatic snails as intermediate hosts. Schistosomes attack the human liver, lungs, and, depending on the species, bowel or bladder. While the initial fluke infection causes fever, diarrhea, and enlarged lymph nodes, more serious problems occur later primarily due to the immune system's response to chronic infection, as polyps and inflammation on the walls of the bowel and/or bladder lead to eggs being returned to the liver, thereby causing liver disease, hemorrhaging, and possible death. Praziquantel is the drug of choice for treatment. Population-wide chemotherapy is the WHO-recommended control strategy, targeted at children and other at-risk groups.

sensitivity: A statistical measure that assesses the proportion of people with a disease who are accurately identified by a diagnostic test as diseased. A sensitivity calculation takes the number of true positives and divides by the number of true positives plus the number of false negatives. A sensitivity of 100% means that the test recognizes all diseased people as such (and there are no false-negative results). The measures of sensitivity and **specificity** are the two most widely used statistics to assess the performance of diagnostic tests.

social marketing: A social change technique borrowed from commercial advertising that seeks to promote a health technology by (1) comprehensively analyzing the targeted population, (2) identifying relevant consumer segments, and (3) designing interventions for these groups' needs, desires, and beliefs via audience-appropriate products, packaging, and messages.

specificity: A statistical measure that determines the proportion of healthy people who are accurately identified by a diagnostic test as healthy. A specificity calculation takes the number of true negatives and divides by the number of true negatives plus the number of false positives. A specificity of 100% means that the test recognizes all healthy people as such (and there are no false-positive results). The measures of **sensitivity** and specificity are the two most widely used statistics to assess the performance of diagnostic tests.

supply chain: All activities—from the manufacturing of a health technology to its procurement, distribution, and delivery—that, taken together, ensure the product's availability to its intended end-user.

syphilis: A sexually transmitted or congenital infection caused by the spirochete bacterium *Treponema pallidum*. If left untreated, syphilis often progresses through several stages, the first of which involves lesions at the point of infection and enlarged lymph nodes. Months later, rashes, fever, and a multitude of other symptoms occur, including a number of neurological problems. A small proportion of cases will go on, sometimes years later, to develop tertiary syphilis involving tumorlike growths throughout the body and gradual dementia and/or cardiac disease. Treatment includes antibiotics such as penicillin, tetracycline, and ceftriaxone. Control measures involve barrier contraceptives and screening of pregnant women.

technology transfer agreement: A legal agreement in which the patent holder for a particular technology consents to transfer in part or in full the development, manufacturing, retail, or use rights of the technology in question to another party.

tender process: The process by which suppliers of a product or service are invited to bid for a contract. The organization requesting bids either restricts applicants to vendors who already meet prequalification criteria (invited tender) or opens the tendering process up to anyone willing to submit a bid (open tender).

tetanus: A disease of the central nervous system resulting from a toxin (tetanospasmin) produced by the *Clostridium tetani* bacterium and typically acquired through wound contamination by bacterial spores. The toxin produces muscle spasms, lockjaw (trismus), neck stiffness, and other clinical symptoms that can result in respiratory failure and high rates of death, especially if contracted in infancy through postpartum contamination of the umbilical cord stump. Methods of control include an antitetanus immunoglobulin injection if infection is suspected, while preventative measures include tetanus toxoid immunization and better hygiene among health care workers, especially at birth clinics.

trachoma: A disease of the conjunctiva of the eye caused by *Chlamydia trachomatis* bacteria and transmitted by contact with contaminated fingers, washcloths, or flies. Repeated chronic infections of *C. trachomatis* cause inflammation and eyelash inversion (trichiasis), leading to corneal abrasion, ulceration, scarring, and eventual blindness. WHO recommends that trachoma control programs involve a four-part SAFE strategy of trichiasis surgery, a single oral dose of azithromycin antibiotic currently donated by Pfizer Inc., frequent face and hand washing, and environmental interventions providing clean water and sanitation.

trial: An experimental study involving a standardized, systematic, replicable, quantitative methodology. A trial uses a randomized sample of participants typically divided into groups, at least one of which receives the intervention or treatment in question, while the other serves as a "control."

TRIPS: The 2001 Agreement on Trade-Related Aspects of Intellectual Property Rights, established to protect product and process patent holders. TRIPS requires World Trade Organization member states to enact intellectual property legislation protecting patents by certain dates, depending on the country's development status. In response to protests by AIDS activists and other health advocates over the affordability of antiretroviral therapy, clarifications and amendments were made to TRIPS regarding provisions for compulsory licensing of patented technologies under conditions of public health emergencies.

tuberculosis (TB): A disease caused by one of the many *Mycobacteria*, specifically *M. tuberculosis*, a slow-growing, intracellular bacterium that spreads via airborne droplets or unpasteurized milk. The bacterium causes both respiratory and disseminated illness in both humans and animals. Predominantly a disease of the poor and a key opportunistic infection in AIDS patients, tuberculosis is named for the tubercules that develop on the lungs of those infected. Control methods include upgrading housing and standards of living, vaccination with the BCG vaccine, isoniazid prophylaxis, and pasteurization of milk. Presently, the best treatment is combination therapy with isoniazid, ethambutol, rifampicin, and/or pyrazinamide administered through a short course of directly observed therapy (DOTS).

vaccine: An inactivated, altered, or cloned antigen, or fraction of an antigen, toxin, or other substance, that, when inoculated into a human or other animal, artificially activates the recipient's immunological memory through the production of B cell and T cell lymphocytes so that the immune system's response to future encounters with the particular pathogen is efficient, quick, and effective.

visceral leishmaniasis: Also known as kala-azar or black fever, a condition affecting the spleen and liver that is marked by fever, weight loss, and, if left untreated, eventual spleen and liver failure and death. It is caused by one of three different species of *Leishmania* protozoa present in Africa, India, the Mediterranean, and

South America, all of which are transmitted via a sandfly vector. The best method of control is vector control via bednets and the elimination of sandfly hosts. The best treatment is currently antimonial drugs or pentamidine, although new medicines are under development.

yellow fever: A member of the *Flaviviridae* family of viruses, transmitted by the Aedes mosquito and present in tropical zones of Africa and Central and South America. Clinically, yellow fever patients initially present with a sudden fever, headache, malaise, and other symptoms. A significant proportion of cases end up with liver hemorrhage, not infrequently leading to death. The best methods of prevention are via vector control (such as bednets and insecticide spraying) and vaccination. There is no treatment except for palliative support.

INDEX

PHOTO CREDITS

CHAPTER 1
Photo by Rob Huibers/Panos Pictures; Sierra Leone. Used with permission.

CHAPTER 2
Photo by Michael Goroff; Dhaka, Bangladesh, 2008. Used with permission.

CHAPTER 3
Photo by Albis Gabrielli, Schistosomiasis Control Initiative.
Used with permission.

CHAPTER 4
Photo by Philippe Blanc/Angalia-Photo; Cambodia, 2004.
Used with Permission.

CHAPTER 5
Photo by Mary Coll-Black/World Health Organization, RITM.
Used with permission.

CHAPTER 6
Photo by Suzie Elliott/Population Council. Used with permission.

CHAPTER 7
Photo by Ümit Kartoglu/World Health Organization. Used with permission.

CHAPTER 8
Photo from The Female Health Foundation. Used with permission

CHAPTER 9
Photo by Alfredo D'Amato/Panos Pictures; Mozambique.
Used with permission.

ABOUT THE AUTHORS AND CONTRIBUTORS

AUTHORS:

Laura Frost is a consultant in global health and Partner at Global Health Insights, LLC, based in New Jersey.

Michael R. Reich is Taro Takemi Professor of International Health Policy at the Harvard School of Public Health.

CONTRIBUTORS:

Alan Fenwick is Professor of Tropical Parasitology in the Department of Infectious Disease Epidemiology, Faculty of Medicine, Imperial College London.

Beth Anne Pratt is a Zambia-based anthropologist and Partner at Global Health Insights, LLC.

Howard Thompson was the Program Manager of the Schistosomiasis Control Initiative from 2002 until 2008.